drawnandquarterly.com

978-1-77046-341-7
First edition: March 2019
Printed in China
10 9 8 7 6 5 4 3 2 1

Cataloguing data available from Library and Archives Canada.

Published in the USA by Drawn & Quarterly, a client publisher of
Farrar, Straus and Giroux. Orders: 888.330.8477

Published in Canada by Drawn & Quarterly, a client publisher of
Raincoast Books. Orders: 800.663.5714

Published in the United Kingdom by Drawn & Quarterly, a client publisher of
Publishers Group UK. Orders: info@pguk.co.uk

Credo

The ROSE WILDER LANE Story

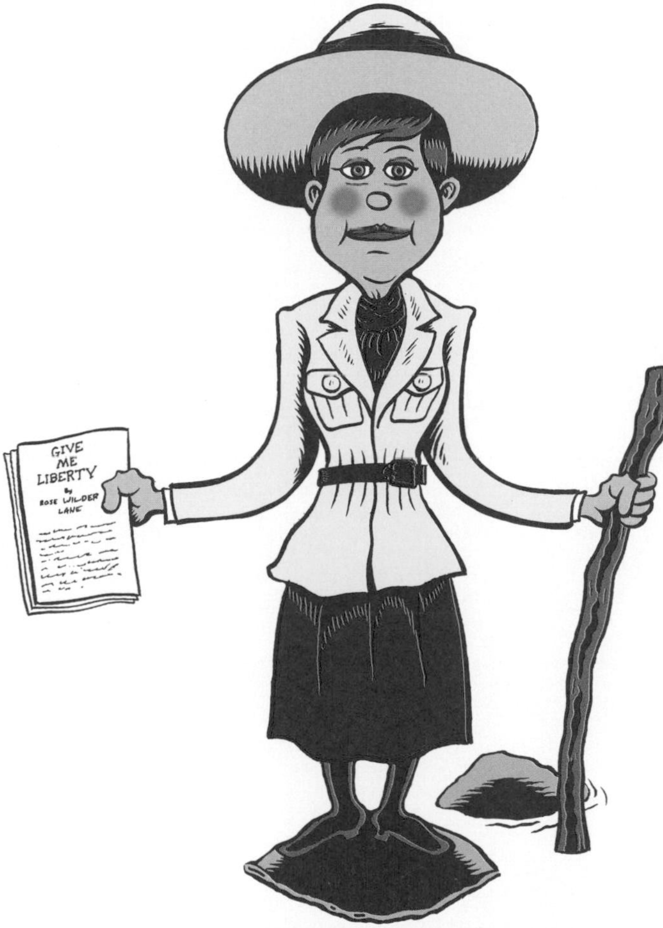
GIVE ME LIBERTY
By ROSE WILDER LANE

PETER BAGGE
COLORING BY JOANNE BAGGE

DRAWN + QUARTERLY

WHY LANE?

Rose Wilder Lane first came to my attention about ten years ago, while reading *Radicals for Capitalism*, an all-encompassing history of the modern American libertarian movement. Lane stuck out from the rest of the players in the book not only for her pointed views on the subject, but for her willingness to "walk the walk," so to speak. While others were writing papers and debating colleagues, Lane (by then in her late fifties) was protesting government food rationing by literally growing all of her own food! She also refused to pay into (or accept) social security (which she accurately labeled a "Ponzi scheme"); deliberately maintained a poverty-line income to avoid paying income taxes; and, after being questioned by a state trooper about her political views, wrote an explosive editorial accusing the government of "Gestapo tactics," which was then picked up by the national press. And this was all during World War II, when the rest of the country was in its most patriotic and unquestioning mindset. So I, like the rest of her countrymen did at the time, couldn't help but wonder: "Who is this crazy lady?"

And let there be no doubt: Rose Wilder Lane could be pretty crazy. She was, at turns, a drama queen, a fabulist, and a conspiracy theorist embarrassingly prone to hyperbole. All of this extreme behavior could be directly contributed to the fact that she suffered from a clear case of what is now labeled bipolar disorder, though during her lifetime underwent many ever-changing euphemisms, including—if the sufferer happened to be female—"hysteria" (though Lane herself didn't rule out a hormonal imbalance as the culprit for her woes). This also contributed to a lifetime of suicidal tendencies (including at least one serious attempt) and undiagnosable physical maladies.

Lane was painfully aware of her condition, however, and was determined from an early age to address it. (She herself once wrote of how she always despised women who were prone to fainting spells and uncontrollable crying jags, and thus was mortified by the knowledge that she herself was *one* of those women!) After early attempts at self-medicating with alcohol and patent medicines, she instead developed a lifetime of habits that helped, or at least helped her remain productive— habits that essentially boiled down to working on her own writing when in high spirits and confident in her own talents, and editing or ghost-writing for others when she was down in the dumps and convinced she was the worst writer in the world. As prolific as she was, everything about her life and work was a *struggle*—

starting with her struggle to understand herself, which then lead to a lifelong, never-ending philosophical struggle to understand the world around her.

But Lane was an excellent writer: self-taught yet highly skilled and always engaging. She also lived off her writing from her early twenties, working (in order of first attempts) as a copywriter, reporter, columnist, biographer, novelist, travel writer, needlework expert, and eventually, a polemicist—and there was (and remains) much debate and controversy surrounding most of what she wrote throughout these various phases (refer to the rest of this book for the details). She also worked as a ghostwriter and/or editor throughout her career, and several of these wound up ironically being the most successful books she's ever had a hand in—the most famous (and controversial) of all being her own mother's *Little House* children's book series.

Due to the enduring popularity of the *Little House* books, Rose Wilder Lane has, at least since the 1950s, been best known, if at all, as the daughter of Laura Ingalls Wilder, the sole credited writer of that series. Today there is no doubt that Lane collaborated with her mother on all of those books (even if people still debate the extent and nature of that collaboration). The evidence of their collaboration was as plain as day to anyone who bothered to look at the original manuscripts and correspondences that have long been available to the public at the Herbert Hoover Presidential Library, yet it wasn't until scholar William Holtz wrote the first ever biography about Lane—1993's *The Ghost in the Little House*—that this collaboration was made more widely known, and the wrath of the "Bonnet Heads" (as hardcore Wilder fans call themselves) was unleashed.

While one could argue (and many still do) that Holtz was overly sympathetic to Lane—while simultaneously sounding somewhat condescending towards her mother—many readers initially *refused* to believe that Wilder didn't write every word of her book, since this notion stood in stark contrast to the image they had of her: the honest, noble, independent-minded pioneer woman. Not that this image was a false one, and it is in fact an accurate (if incomplete) description of Laura Ingalls Wilder. Yet what her daughter did was *burnish* this image as a way of packaging it to make it more sellable and part of this marketing ploy (known to no one except these two women themselves during their lifetimes) was to credit the mother as the sole writer. When asked, Lane initially would simply downplay her involvement with the *Little House* books, though toward the end of her life she would angrily denounce *any* involvement, and even threatened to not cooperate with Wilder's first biographer, William Anderson, if he dared to suggest otherwise. So this wrath that Lane's biographer received three decades later was a monster of his own subject's creation!

An inherent pitfall that most biographers struggle with is a tendency to become overly sympathetic toward their main subject, which in turn leads to becoming overly critical of their main subject's adversaries. I'm as guilty of this as anyone, and as such I made a conscious effort—hey, I'm afraid of the Bonnet Heads, too!—to be as fair as possible in my portrayal of Laura Ingalls Wilder. Because more often than not, these two women were adversaries, and while I wouldn't describe theirs as a love/hate relationship, it certainly was a love/*resentment* one. On the surface, their issues were fairly typical of most mothers and daughters, yet with these two you have to factor in that both were not only highly intelligent, but extremely opinionated and mindbogglingly *stubborn*. The mere fact that they butted heads as often as they did was and is often viewed as a form of disrespect on the past of Lane when viewed from the perspective of Wilder's friends and admirers.

Another third rail I'm sure I'll fail to avoid hitting is the steadily increasing demonization of Lane's name and reputation as a result of twenty-first century partisan politics. The first salvos where a handful of widely read articles dealing primarily with Lane's mother (they're *always* "officially" about Wilder), with the authors trying to reconcile their lifelong love with the *Little House* books with their own modern day progressive views—views that Wilder's own opinions and values clearly fly in the face of. For anyone with a partisan agenda, the answer is to blame Wilder's "crazy" daughter for "poisoning" her mother's books with her extreme politics—which they then proceed to distort (it's hard to tell if these writers don't understand what Lane belived in or simply don't care), while also falsely insisting that Wilder either didn't share her daughter's views or was too country-folks to understand them. Always added to this is a strained game of guilt-by-association these writers indulge by linking Lane with billionaire political donors Charles and David Koch, who appear to be the real target for their ire.

As a result, when I now search for Lane's name on social media, it's often accompanied by descriptives like "a horror," "a monster," and most often—and as a perfect illustration of the maturity level of these newly minted Lane-haters—"a dick." It's all a carbon copy of what I experienced when I first started researching the subject of my first biography, Margaret Sanger, who had also recently been the subject of a handful of reality bending, reputation-destroying "biographies." The motive of these books was similar to the motives of Lane's recent biographers, i.e.: "To destroy the reputation of Planned Parenthood, we must first destroy the reputation of that organization's founder." And so the cascade of lies against Sanger began. And it worked. And it's still working, since almost everyone across the political spectrum is shamefully inclined to believe the worst about everyone else. The only difference between Sanger's assassins and Lane's is that none of the former hacks were ever awarded a Pulitzer Prize.

As I touched on earlier (and discuss further in this book), Lane herself had a casual relationship with facts, though in her case it was never to destroy somebody, or willfully misrepresent their words and opinions. Instead, she simply would get caught up in her narrative, at which point the facts be damned. It was a constant point of contention between her and her mother while collaborating on the *Little House* series, with Lane constantly arguing in favor of "the Greater Truth" (though this was hardly the only issue these two continually wrestled over in their collaborations).

I love Lane's greater truths. She was all about freedom and individuality, along with universal kindness and mutual cooperation. All my favorite things! She also was against wars and borders, which makes sense, since she was also completely opposed to any and all forms of government—the great dehumanizer, in her mind, which by default converts individuals into catagories and statistics. Though Lane is widely regarded as a "founding mother" of the modern libertarian movement, she was at heart an anarchist—or more specifically what is now referred to as a "minarchist," meaning someone who'd only tolerate a barebones form of government to protect people from force and fraud, since she was well-aware that humans haven't evolved to the point that would make anarchy workable.

Speaking of facts, I have a disclaimer to make: while I did my best to stick to the facts as closely as possible, Lane's life was such a whirlwind of ever-changing people, places, and events that this book would have been unworkable had I not altered actors and timelines to some degree (all of which will be pointed out and explained in the back notes of this book). And as with my pervious biographies, I often stumbled across conflicting "facts" in my research, and had to decide which facts to commit to. But like Lane herself, I believe I managed to remain faithful throughout to The Greater Truth!

Peter Bagge
Tacoma, WA, 2018

Credo

The ROSE WILDER LANE Story

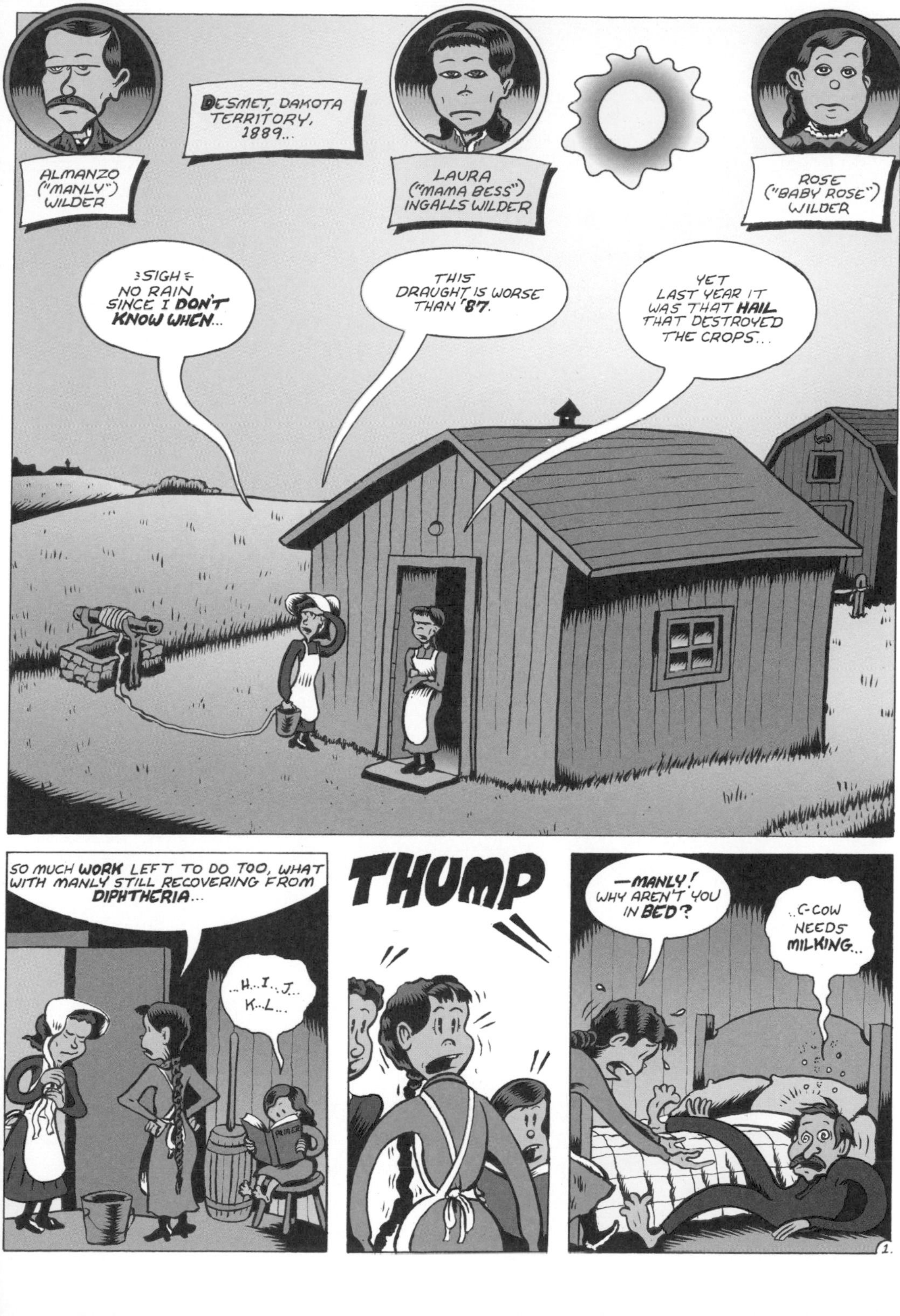

ALMANZO ("MANLY") WILDER
DESMET, DAKOTA TERRITORY, 1889...
LAURA ("MAMA BESS") INGALLS WILDER
ROSE ("BABY ROSE") WILDER
=SIGH= NO RAIN SINCE I DON'T KNOW WHEN...
THIS DRAUGHT IS WORSE THAN '87.
YET LAST YEAR IT WAS THAT HAIL THAT DESTROYED THE CROPS...
SO MUCH WORK LEFT TO DO TOO, WHAT WITH MANLY STILL RECOVERING FROM DIPHTHERIA...
..H...I...J... K...L...
THUMP
—MANLY! WHY AREN'T YOU IN BED?
..C-COW NEEDS MILKING...

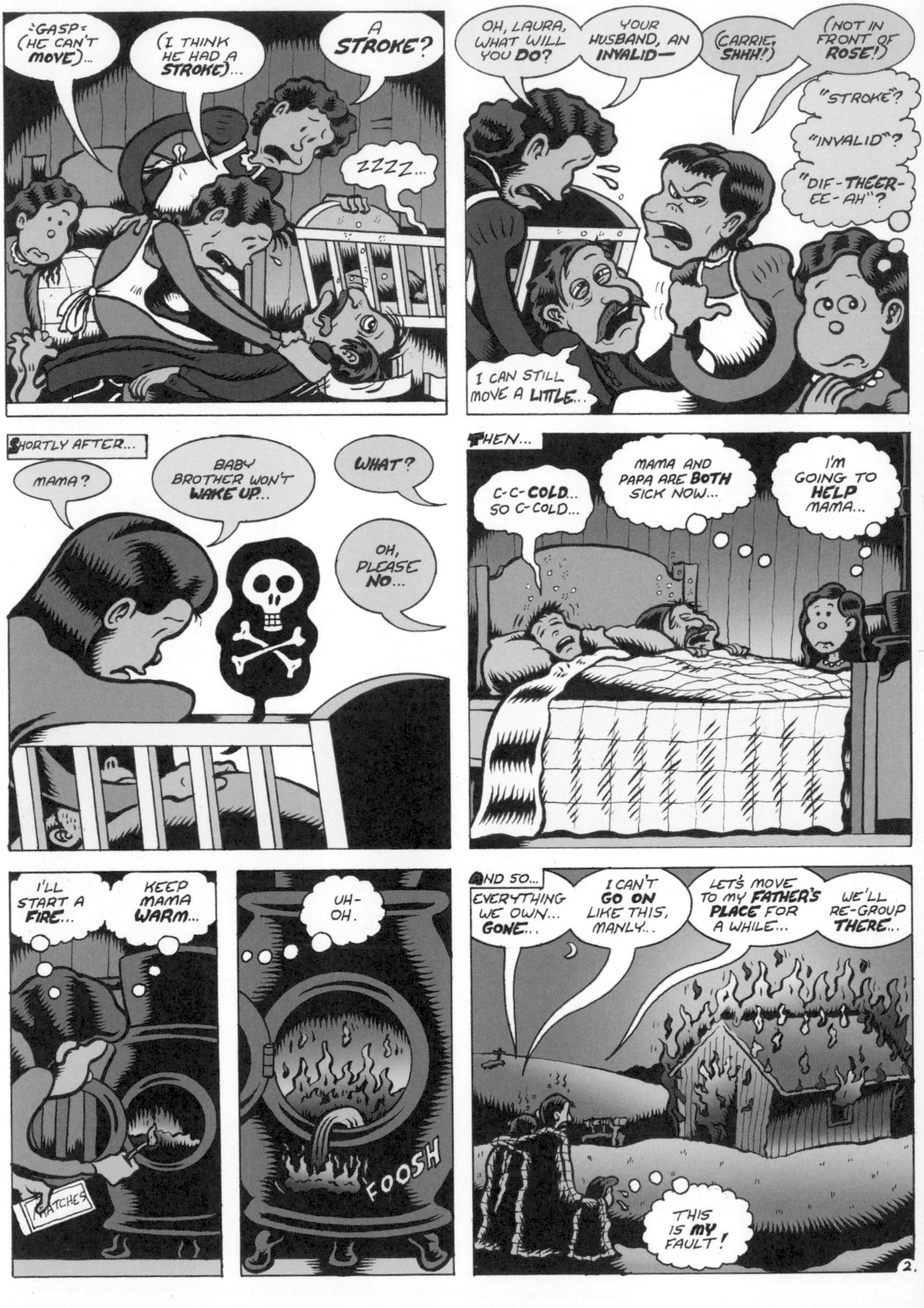

:GASP: (HE CAN'T MOVE)...
(I THINK HE HAD A STROKE)...
A STROKE?
ZZZZ...
OH, LAURA, WHAT WILL YOU DO?
YOUR HUSBAND, AN INVALID—
(CARRIE, SHHH!)
(NOT IN FRONT OF ROSE!)
"STROKE"?
"INVALID"?
"DIF-THEER-EE-AH"?
I CAN STILL MOVE A LITTLE...
SHORTLY AFTER...
MAMA?
BABY BROTHER WON'T WAKE UP...
WHAT?
OH, PLEASE NO...
THEN...
C-C-COLD... SO C-COLD...
MAMA AND PAPA ARE BOTH SICK NOW...
I'M GOING TO HELP MAMA...
I'LL START A FIRE...
KEEP MAMA WARM...
MATCHES
UH-OH.
FOOSH
AND SO...
EVERYTHING WE OWN... GONE...
I CAN'T GO ON LIKE THIS, MANLY...
LET'S MOVE TO MY FATHER'S PLACE FOR A WHILE...
WE'LL RE-GROUP THERE...
THIS IS MY FAULT!

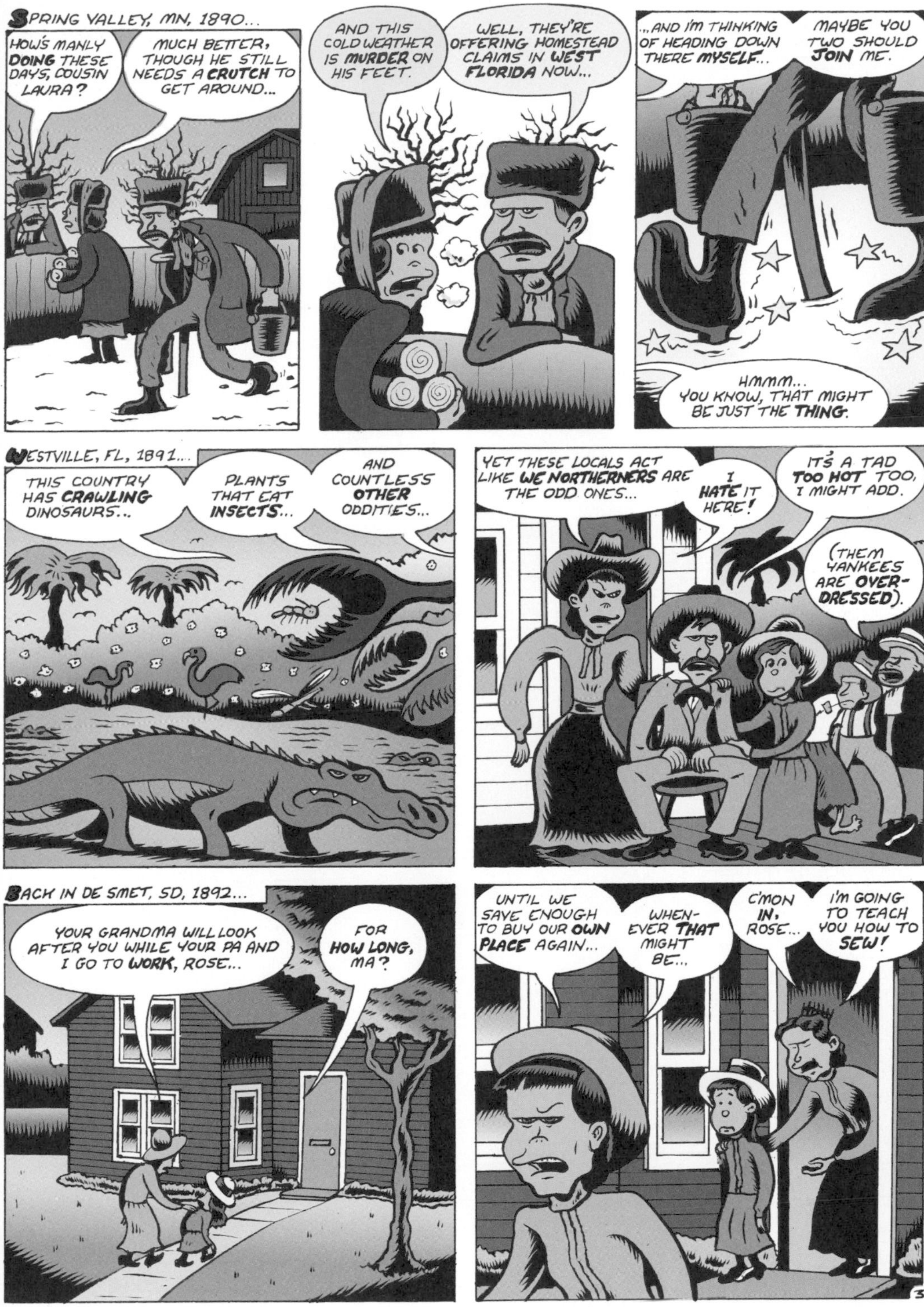

SPRING VALLEY, MN, 1890...
HOW'S MANLY DOING THESE DAYS, COUSIN LAURA?
MUCH BETTER, THOUGH HE STILL NEEDS A CRUTCH TO GET AROUND...
AND THIS COLD WEATHER IS MURDER ON HIS FEET.
WELL, THEY'RE OFFERING HOMESTEAD CLAIMS IN WEST FLORIDA NOW...
...AND I'M THINKING OF HEADING DOWN THERE MYSELF...
MAYBE YOU TWO SHOULD JOIN ME.
HMMM... YOU KNOW, THAT MIGHT BE JUST THE THING.
WESTVILLE, FL, 1891...
THIS COUNTRY HAS CRAWLING DINOSAURS...
PLANTS THAT EAT INSECTS...
AND COUNTLESS OTHER ODDITIES...
YET THESE LOCALS ACT LIKE WE NORTHERNERS ARE THE ODD ONES...
I HATE IT HERE!
IT'S A TAD TOO HOT TOO, I MIGHT ADD.
(THEM YANKEES ARE OVER-DRESSED).
BACK IN DE SMET, SD, 1892...
YOUR GRANDMA WILL LOOK AFTER YOU WHILE YOUR PA AND I GO TO WORK, ROSE...
FOR HOW LONG, MA?
UNTIL WE SAVE ENOUGH TO BUY OUR OWN PLACE AGAIN...
WHEN-EVER THAT MIGHT BE...
C'MON IN, ROSE...
I'M GOING TO TEACH YOU HOW TO SEW!

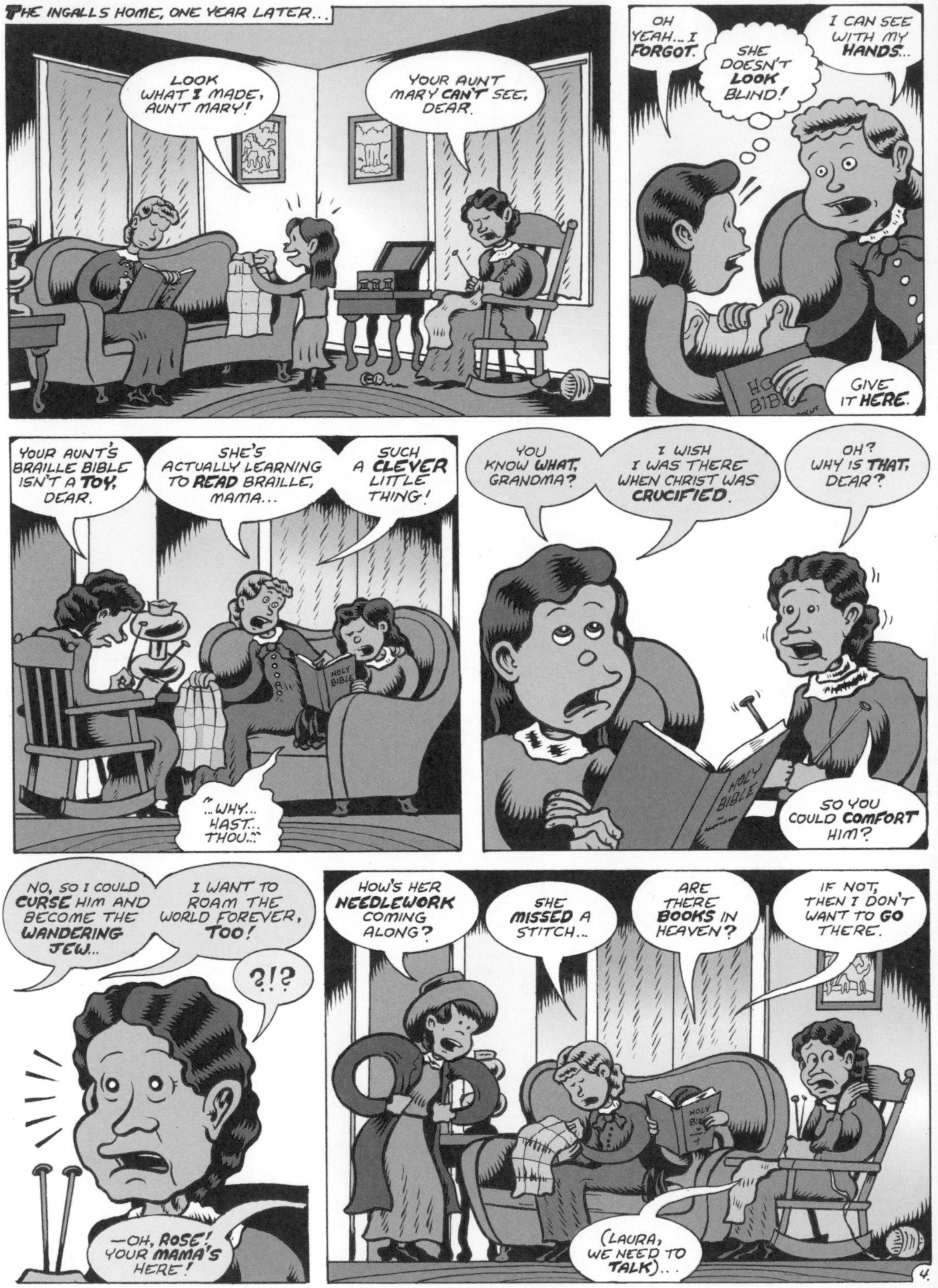
THE INGALLS HOME, ONE YEAR LATER...
LOOK WHAT I MADE, AUNT MARY!
YOUR AUNT MARY CAN'T SEE, DEAR.
OH YEAH... I FORGOT.
SHE DOESN'T LOOK BLIND!
I CAN SEE WITH MY HANDS...
GIVE IT HERE.
HOLY BIBLE
YOUR AUNT'S BRAILLE BIBLE ISN'T A TOY, DEAR.
SHE'S ACTUALLY LEARNING TO READ BRAILLE, MAMA...
SUCH A CLEVER LITTLE THING!
"...WHY... HAST... THOU..."
YOU KNOW WHAT, GRANDMA?
I WISH I WAS THERE WHEN CHRIST WAS CRUCIFIED.
OH? WHY IS THAT, DEAR?
SO YOU COULD COMFORT HIM?
NO, SO I COULD CURSE HIM AND BECOME THE WANDERING JEW...
I WANT TO ROAM THE WORLD FOREVER, TOO!
?!?
—OH, ROSE! YOUR MAMA'S HERE!
HOW'S HER NEEDLEWORK COMING ALONG?
SHE MISSED A STITCH...
ARE THERE BOOKS IN HEAVEN?
IF NOT, THEN I DON'T WANT TO GO THERE.
(LAURA, WE NEED TO TALK)...

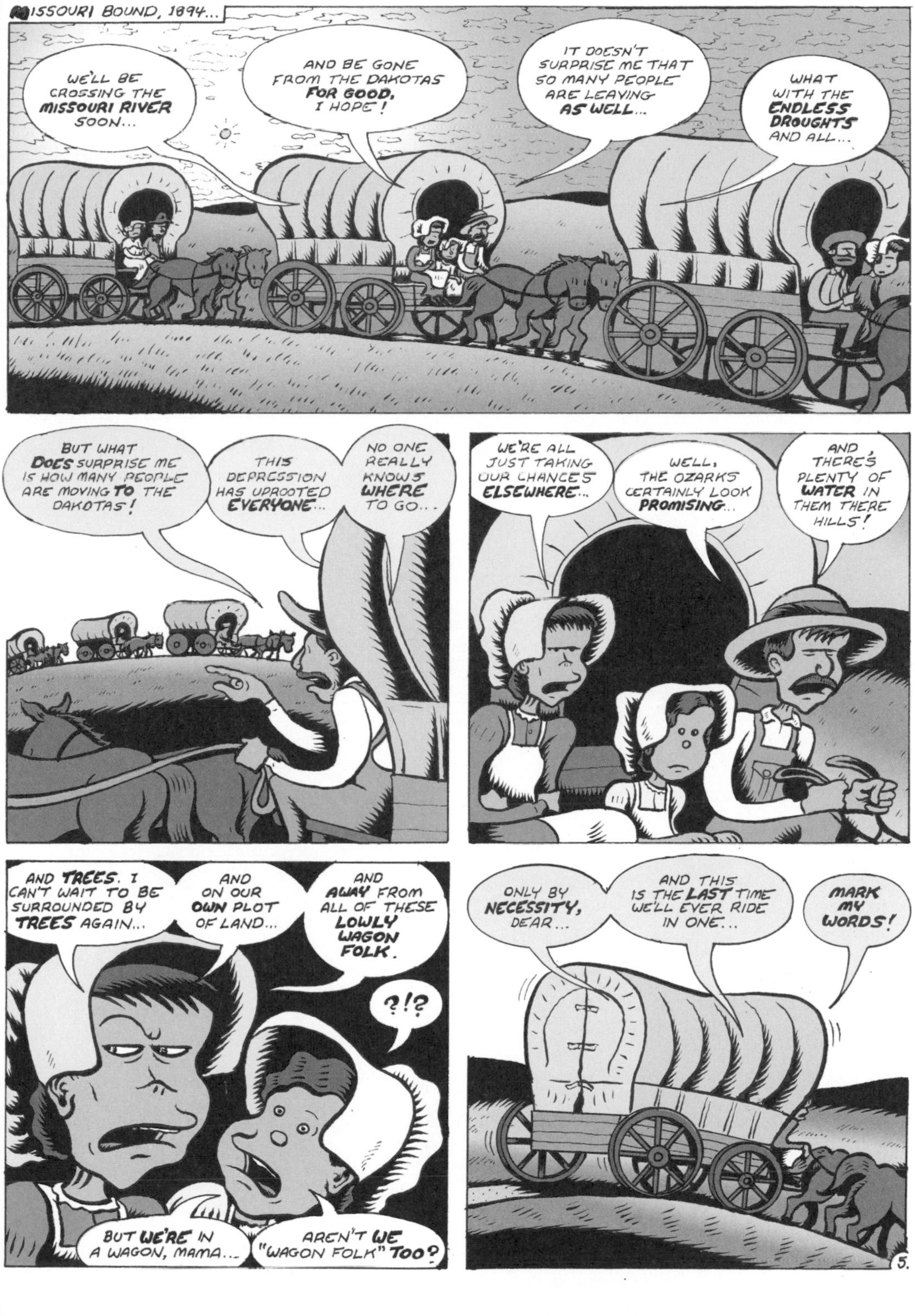
MISSOURI BOUND, 1894...
WE'LL BE CROSSING THE MISSOURI RIVER SOON...
AND BE GONE FROM THE DAKOTAS FOR GOOD, I HOPE!
IT DOESN'T SURPRISE ME THAT SO MANY PEOPLE ARE LEAVING AS WELL...
WHAT WITH THE ENDLESS DROUGHTS AND ALL...
BUT WHAT DOES SURPRISE ME IS HOW MANY PEOPLE ARE MOVING TO THE DAKOTAS!
THIS DEPRESSION HAS UPROOTED EVERYONE...
NO ONE REALLY KNOWS WHERE TO GO...
WE'RE ALL JUST TAKING OUR CHANCES ELSEWHERE...
WELL, THE OZARKS CERTAINLY LOOK PROMISING...
AND, THERE'S PLENTY OF WATER IN THEM THERE HILLS!
AND TREES. I CAN'T WAIT TO BE SURROUNDED BY TREES AGAIN...
AND ON OUR OWN PLOT OF LAND...
AND AWAY FROM ALL OF THESE LOWLY WAGON FOLK.
?!?
BUT WE'RE IN A WAGON, MAMA...
AREN'T WE "WAGON FOLK" TOO?
ONLY BY NECESSITY, DEAR...
AND THIS IS THE LAST TIME WE'LL EVER RIDE IN ONE...
MARK MY WORDS!

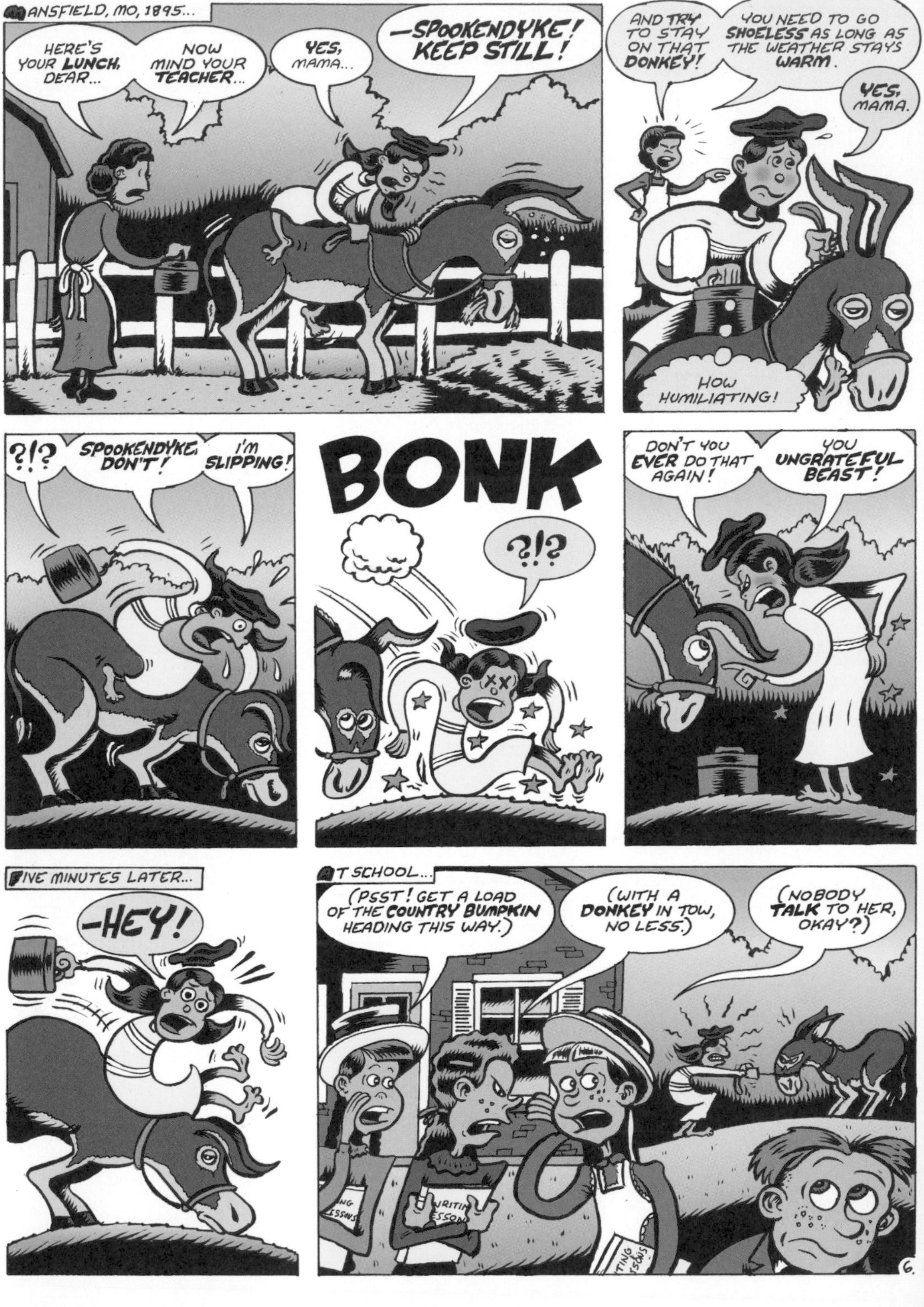
MANSFIELD, MO, 1895...
HERE'S YOUR LUNCH, DEAR...
NOW MIND YOUR TEACHER...
YES, MAMA...
—SPOOKENDYKE! KEEP STILL!
AND TRY TO STAY ON THAT DONKEY!
YOU NEED TO GO SHOELESS AS LONG AS THE WEATHER STAYS WARM.
YES, MAMA.
HOW HUMILIATING!
?!?
SPOOKENDYKE, DON'T!
I'M SLIPPING!
BONK
?!?
DON'T YOU EVER DO THAT AGAIN!
YOU UNGRATEFUL BEAST!
FIVE MINUTES LATER...
—HEY!
AT SCHOOL...
(PSST! GET A LOAD OF THE COUNTRY BUMPKIN HEADING THIS WAY.)
(WITH A DONKEY IN TOW, NO LESS.)
(NOBODY TALK TO HER, OKAY?)
6.

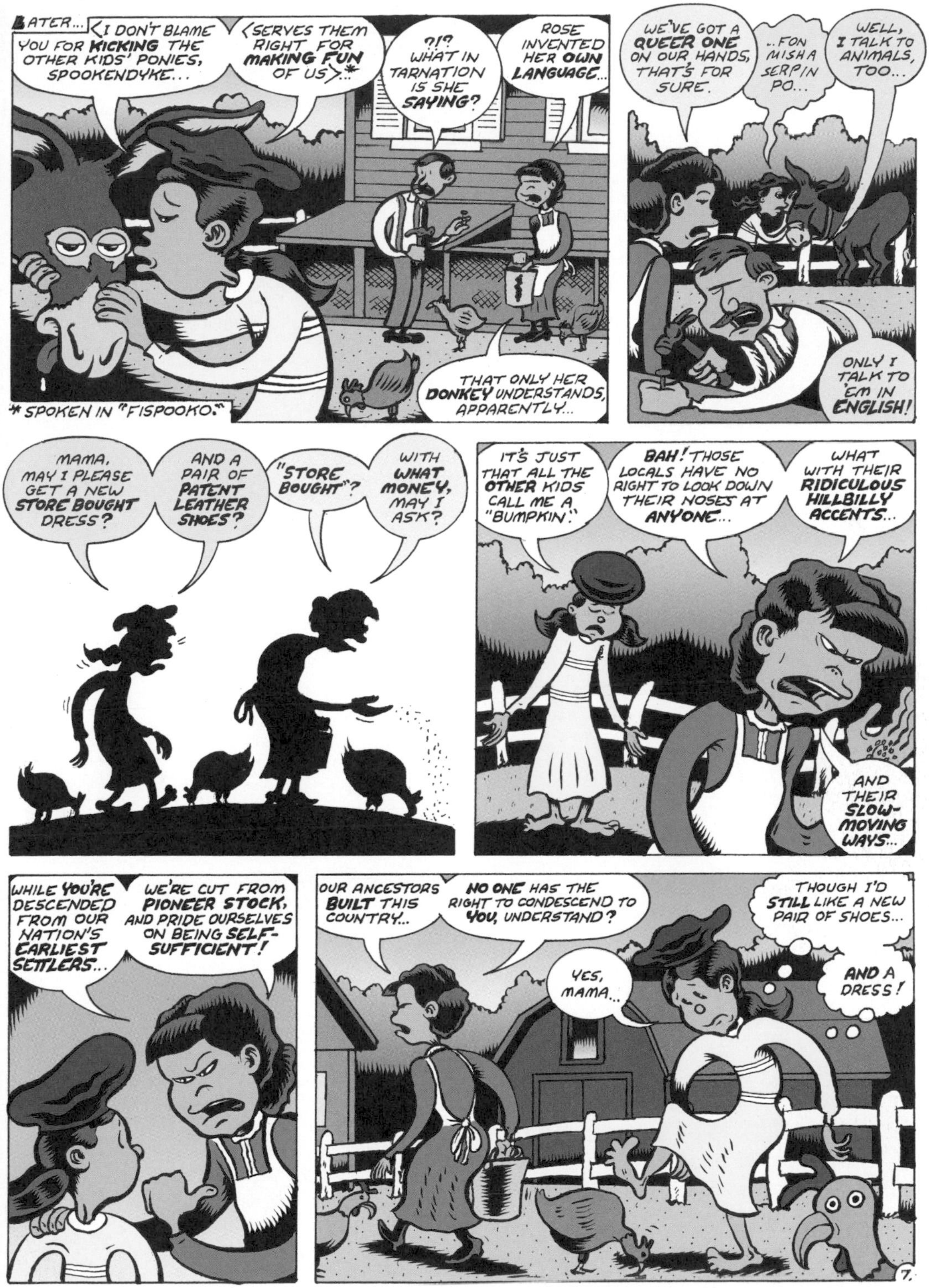
LATER...
<I DON'T BLAME YOU FOR KICKING THE OTHER KIDS' PONIES, SPOOKENDYKE...
<SERVES THEM RIGHT FOR MAKING FUN OF US>...*
?!? WHAT IN TARNATION IS SHE SAYING?
ROSE INVENTED HER OWN LANGUAGE...
THAT ONLY HER DONKEY UNDERSTANDS, APPARENTLY...
* SPOKEN IN "FISPOOKO."
WE'VE GOT A QUEER ONE ON OUR HANDS, THAT'S FOR SURE.
..FON MISHA SERPIN PO...
WELL, I TALK TO ANIMALS, TOO...
ONLY I TALK TO 'EM IN ENGLISH!
MAMA, MAY I PLEASE GET A NEW STORE BOUGHT DRESS?
AND A PAIR OF PATENT LEATHER SHOES?
"STORE BOUGHT"?
WITH WHAT MONEY, MAY I ASK?
IT'S JUST THAT ALL THE OTHER KIDS CALL ME A "BUMPKIN."
BAH! THOSE LOCALS HAVE NO RIGHT TO LOOK DOWN THEIR NOSES AT ANYONE...
WHAT WITH THEIR RIDICULOUS HILLBILLY ACCENTS...
AND THEIR SLOW-MOVING WAYS...
WHILE YOU'RE DESCENDED FROM OUR NATION'S EARLIEST SETTLERS...
WE'RE CUT FROM PIONEER STOCK, AND PRIDE OURSELVES ON BEING SELF-SUFFICIENT!
OUR ANCESTORS BUILT THIS COUNTRY...
NO ONE HAS THE RIGHT TO CONDESCEND TO YOU, UNDERSTAND?
YES, MAMA...
THOUGH I'D STILL LIKE A NEW PAIR OF SHOES...
AND A DRESS!

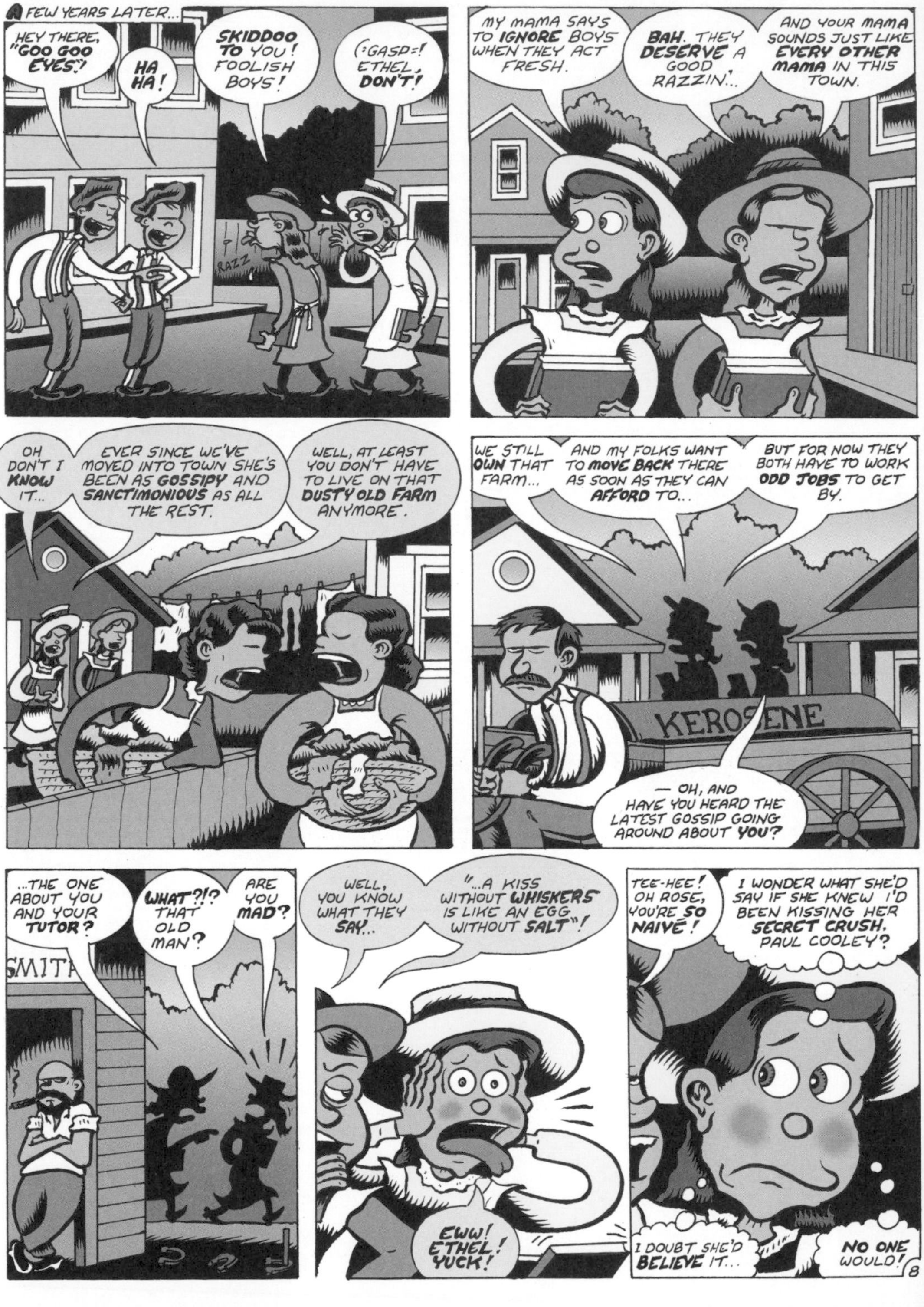
A FEW YEARS LATER...
HEY THERE, "GOO GOO EYES"!
HA HA!
SKIDDOO TO YOU! FOOLISH BOYS!
RAZZ
(=GASP=)! ETHEL, DON'T!
MY MAMA SAYS TO IGNORE BOYS WHEN THEY ACT FRESH.
BAH. THEY DESERVE A GOOD RAZZIN'...
AND YOUR MAMA SOUNDS JUST LIKE EVERY OTHER MAMA IN THIS TOWN.
OH DON'T I KNOW IT...
EVER SINCE WE'VE MOVED INTO TOWN SHE'S BEEN AS GOSSIPY AND SANCTIMONIOUS AS ALL THE REST.
WELL, AT LEAST YOU DON'T HAVE TO LIVE ON THAT DUSTY OLD FARM ANYMORE.
WE STILL OWN THAT FARM...
AND MY FOLKS WANT TO MOVE BACK THERE AS SOON AS THEY CAN AFFORD TO...
BUT FOR NOW THEY BOTH HAVE TO WORK ODD JOBS TO GET BY.
KEROSENE
— OH, AND HAVE YOU HEARD THE LATEST GOSSIP GOING AROUND ABOUT YOU?
...THE ONE ABOUT YOU AND YOUR TUTOR?
WHAT?!? THAT OLD MAN?
ARE YOU MAD?
SMITH
WELL, YOU KNOW WHAT THEY SAY...
"...A KISS WITHOUT WHISKERS IS LIKE AN EGG WITHOUT SALT"!
EWW! ETHEL! YUCK!
TEE-HEE! OH ROSE, YOU'RE SO NAIVÉ!
I WONDER WHAT SHE'D SAY IF SHE KNEW I'D BEEN KISSING HER SECRET CRUSH, PAUL COOLEY?
I DOUBT SHE'D BELIEVE IT...
NO ONE WOULD!

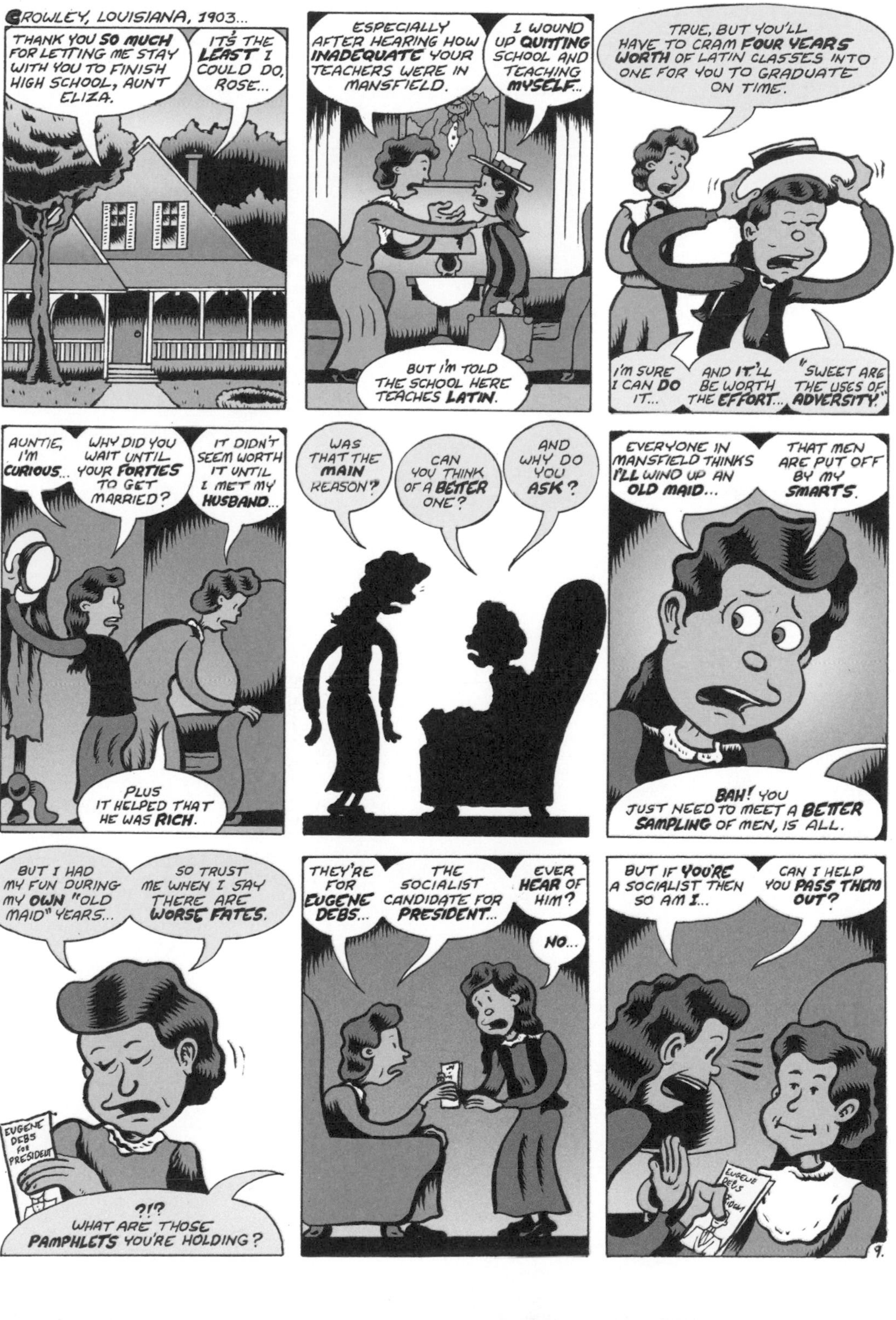
CROWLEY, LOUISIANA, 1903...
THANK YOU SO MUCH FOR LETTING ME STAY WITH YOU TO FINISH HIGH SCHOOL, AUNT ELIZA.
IT'S THE LEAST I COULD DO, ROSE...
ESPECIALLY AFTER HEARING HOW INADEQUATE YOUR TEACHERS WERE IN MANSFIELD.
I WOUND UP QUITTING SCHOOL AND TEACHING MYSELF...
BUT I'M TOLD THE SCHOOL HERE TEACHES LATIN.
TRUE, BUT YOU'LL HAVE TO CRAM FOUR YEARS WORTH OF LATIN CLASSES INTO ONE FOR YOU TO GRADUATE ON TIME.
I'M SURE I CAN DO IT...
AND IT'LL BE WORTH THE EFFORT...
"SWEET ARE THE USES OF ADVERSITY."
AUNTIE, I'M CURIOUS...
WHY DID YOU WAIT UNTIL YOUR FORTIES TO GET MARRIED?
IT DIDN'T SEEM WORTH IT UNTIL I MET MY HUSBAND...
PLUS IT HELPED THAT HE WAS RICH.
WAS THAT THE MAIN REASON?
CAN YOU THINK OF A BETTER ONE?
AND WHY DO YOU ASK?
EVERYONE IN MANSFIELD THINKS I'LL WIND UP AN OLD MAID...
THAT MEN ARE PUT OFF BY MY SMARTS.
BAH! YOU JUST NEED TO MEET A BETTER SAMPLING OF MEN, IS ALL.
BUT I HAD MY FUN DURING MY OWN "OLD MAID" YEARS...
SO TRUST ME WHEN I SAY THERE ARE WORSE FATES.
EUGENE DEBS FOR PRESIDENT
?!? WHAT ARE THOSE PAMPHLETS YOU'RE HOLDING?
THEY'RE FOR EUGENE DEBS...
THE SOCIALIST CANDIDATE FOR PRESIDENT...
EVER HEAR OF HIM?
NO...
BUT IF YOU'RE A SOCIALIST THEN SO AM I...
CAN I HELP YOU PASS THEM OUT?
EUGENE DEBS

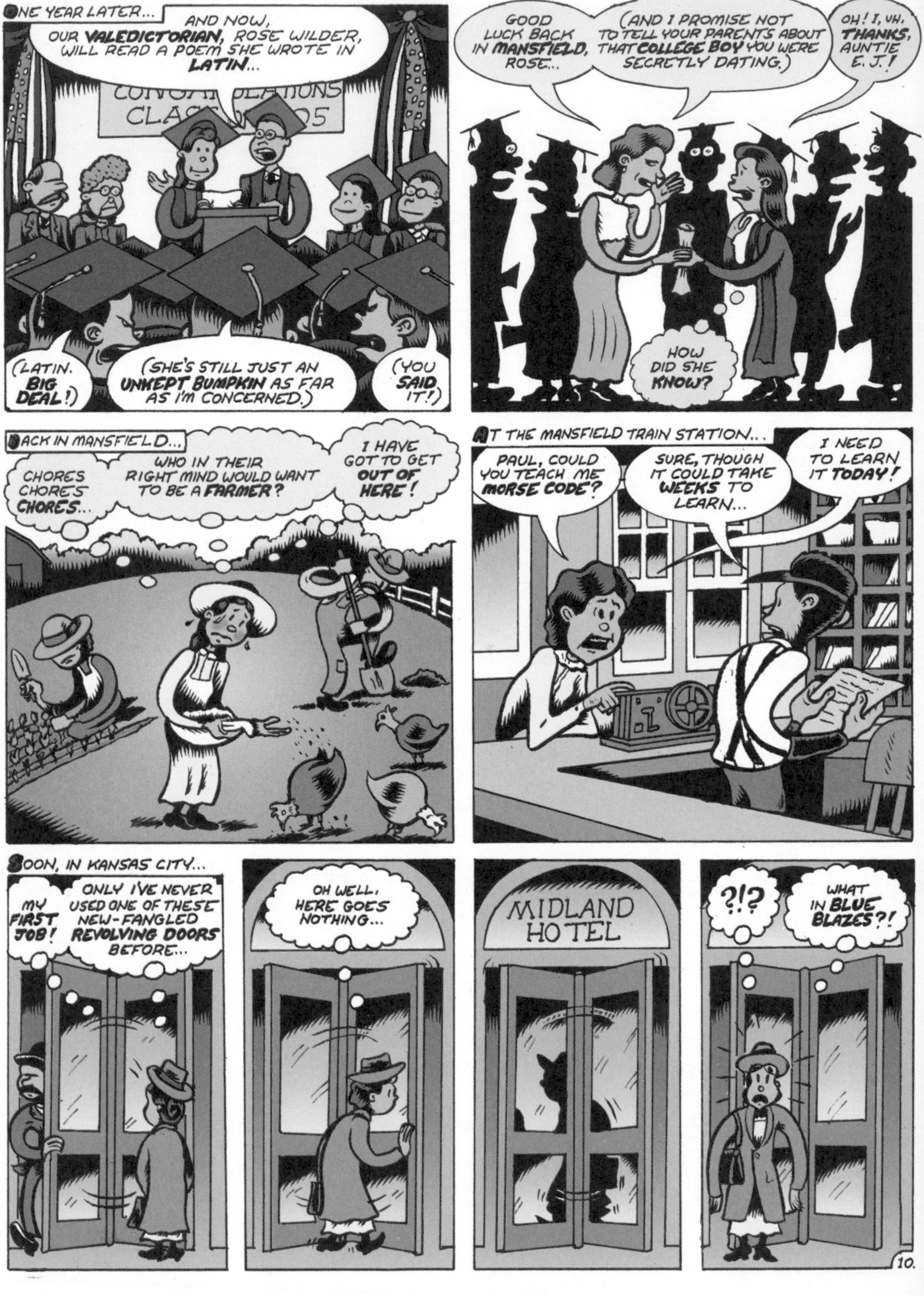
ONE YEAR LATER...
AND NOW, OUR VALEDICTORIAN, ROSE WILDER, WILL READ A POEM SHE WROTE IN LATIN...
(LATIN. BIG DEAL!)
(SHE'S STILL JUST AN UNKEPT BUMPKIN AS FAR AS I'M CONCERNED.)
(YOU SAID IT!)
GOOD LUCK BACK IN MANSFIELD, ROSE...
(AND I PROMISE NOT TO TELL YOUR PARENTS ABOUT THAT COLLEGE BOY YOU WERE SECRETLY DATING.)
OH! I, UH, THANKS, AUNTIE E. J.!
HOW DID SHE KNOW?
BACK IN MANSFIELD...
CHORES CHORES CHORES...
WHO IN THEIR RIGHT MIND WOULD WANT TO BE A FARMER?
I HAVE GOT TO GET OUT OF HERE!
AT THE MANSFIELD TRAIN STATION...
PAUL, COULD YOU TEACH ME MORSE CODE?
SURE, THOUGH IT COULD TAKE WEEKS TO LEARN...
I NEED TO LEARN IT TODAY!
SOON, IN KANSAS CITY...
MY FIRST JOB!
ONLY I'VE NEVER USED ONE OF THESE NEW-FANGLED REVOLVING DOORS BEFORE...
OH WELL, HERE GOES NOTHING...
MIDLAND HOTEL
?!?
WHAT IN BLUE BLAZES?!

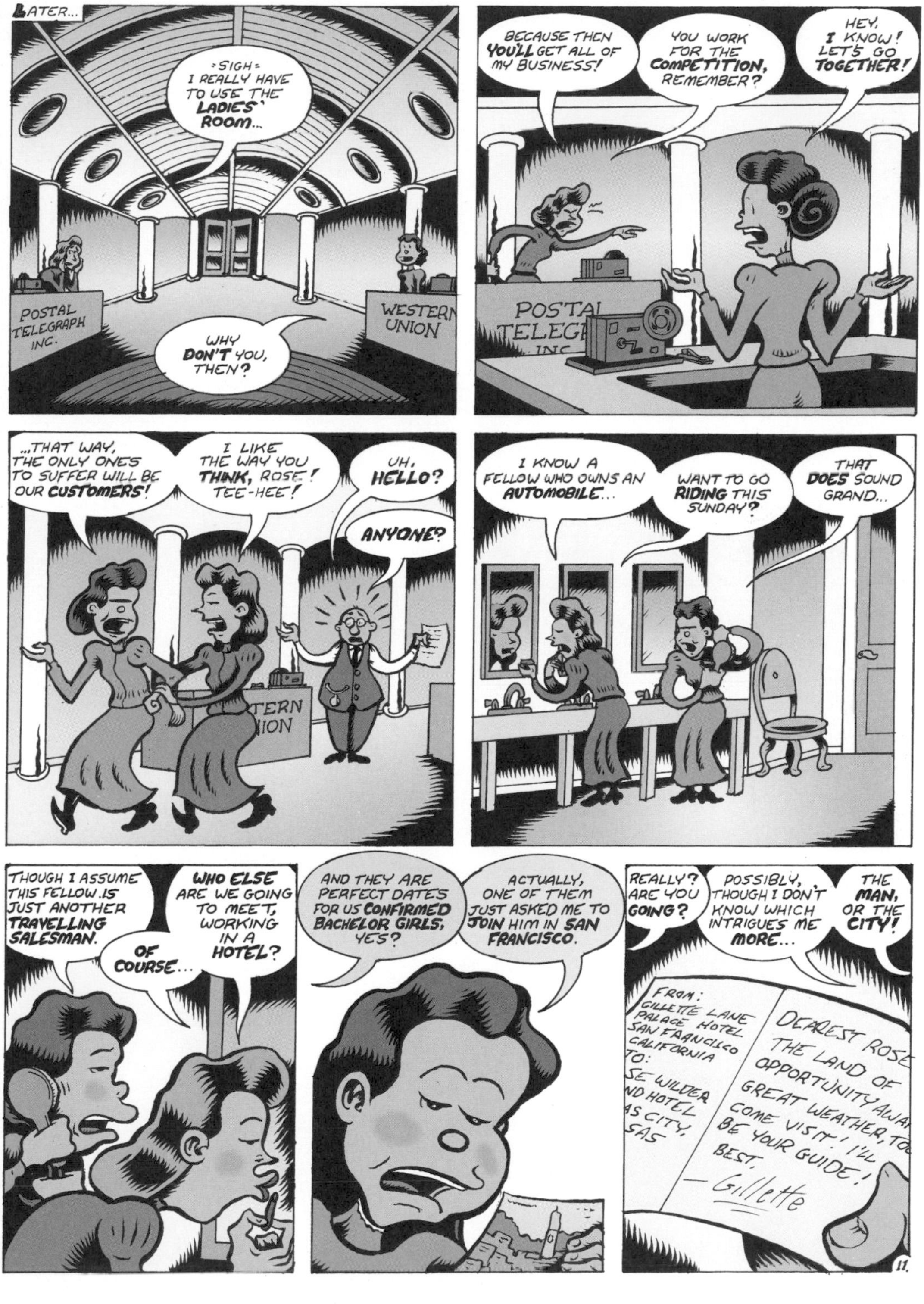
LATER...
=SIGH= I REALLY HAVE TO USE THE LADIES' ROOM...
WHY DON'T YOU, THEN?
BECAUSE THEN YOU'LL GET ALL OF MY BUSINESS!
YOU WORK FOR THE COMPETITION, REMEMBER?
HEY, I KNOW! LET'S GO TOGETHER!
POSTAL TELEGRAPH INC.
WESTERN UNION
...THAT WAY, THE ONLY ONES TO SUFFER WILL BE OUR CUSTOMERS!
I LIKE THE WAY YOU THINK, ROSE! TEE-HEE!
UH, HELLO?
ANYONE?
I KNOW A FELLOW WHO OWNS AN AUTOMOBILE...
WANT TO GO RIDING THIS SUNDAY?
THAT DOES SOUND GRAND...
THOUGH I ASSUME THIS FELLOW IS JUST ANOTHER TRAVELLING SALESMAN.
OF COURSE...
WHO ELSE ARE WE GOING TO MEET, WORKING IN A HOTEL?
AND THEY ARE PERFECT DATES FOR US CONFIRMED BACHELOR GIRLS, YES?
ACTUALLY, ONE OF THEM JUST ASKED ME TO JOIN HIM IN SAN FRANCISCO.
REALLY? ARE YOU GOING?
POSSIBLY, THOUGH I DON'T KNOW WHICH INTRIGUES ME MORE...
THE MAN, OR THE CITY!
FROM: GILLETTE LANE PALACE HOTEL SAN FRANCISCO CALIFORNIA
TO:
DEAREST ROSE THE LAND OF OPPORTUNITY AWA GREAT WEATHER, TO COME VISIT! I'LL BE YOUR GUIDE! BEST, —Gillette

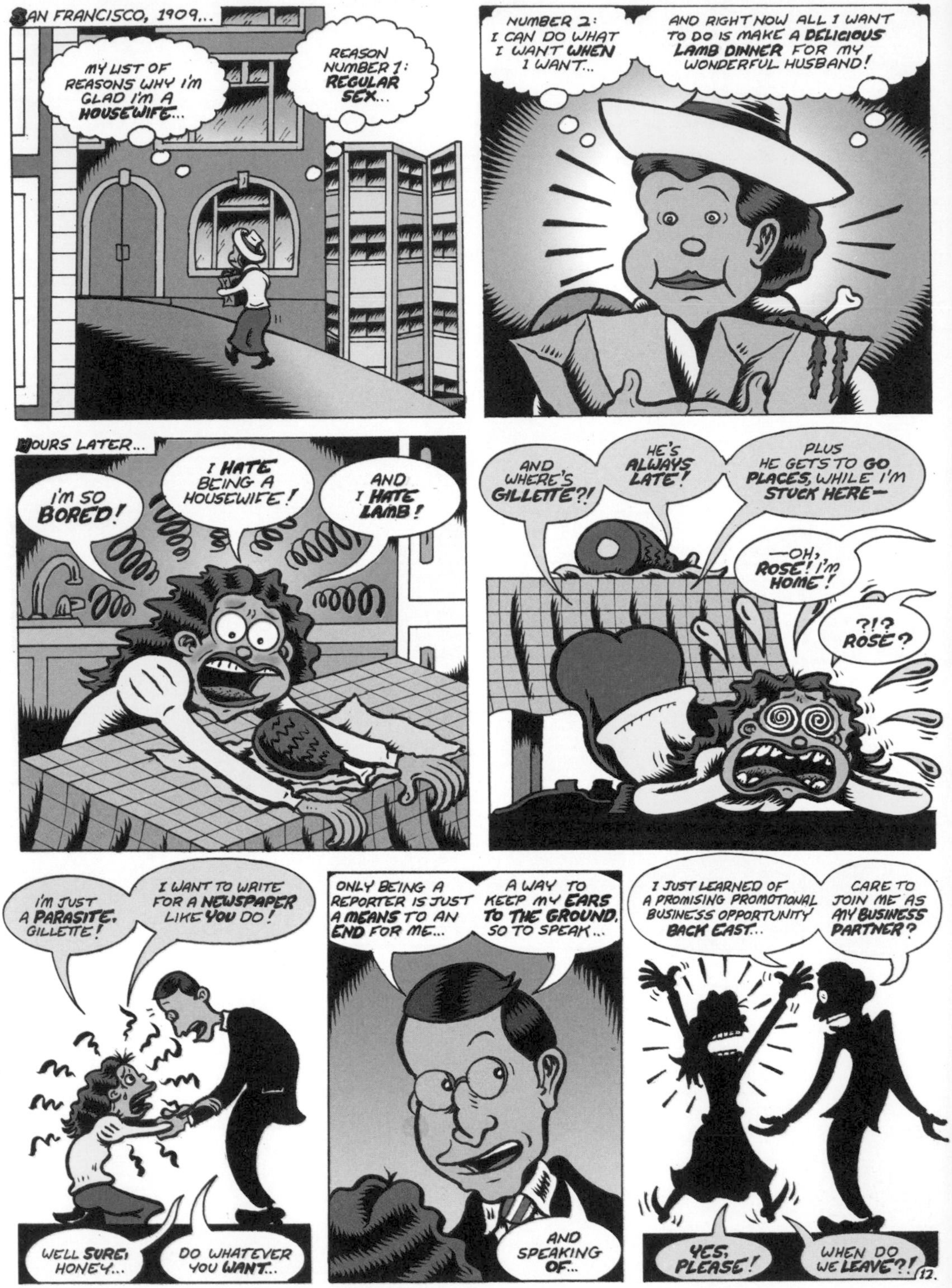
SAN FRANCISCO, 1909...
MY LIST OF REASONS WHY I'M GLAD I'M A HOUSEWIFE...
REASON NUMBER 1: REGULAR SEX...
NUMBER 2: I CAN DO WHAT I WANT WHEN I WANT...
AND RIGHT NOW ALL I WANT TO DO IS MAKE A DELICIOUS LAMB DINNER FOR MY WONDERFUL HUSBAND!
HOURS LATER...
I'M SO BORED!
I HATE BEING A HOUSEWIFE!
AND I HATE LAMB!
AND WHERE'S GILLETTE?!
HE'S ALWAYS LATE!
PLUS HE GETS TO GO PLACES, WHILE I'M STUCK HERE—
—OH, ROSE! I'M HOME!
?!? ROSE?
I'M JUST A PARASITE, GILLETTE!
I WANT TO WRITE FOR A NEWSPAPER LIKE YOU DO!
WELL SURE, HONEY...
DO WHATEVER YOU WANT...
ONLY BEING A REPORTER IS JUST A MEANS TO AN END FOR ME...
A WAY TO KEEP MY EARS TO THE GROUND, SO TO SPEAK...
AND SPEAKING OF...
I JUST LEARNED OF A PROMISING PROMOTIONAL BUSINESS OPPORTUNITY BACK EAST...
CARE TO JOIN ME AS MY BUSINESS PARTNER?
YES, PLEASE!
WHEN DO WE LEAVE?!

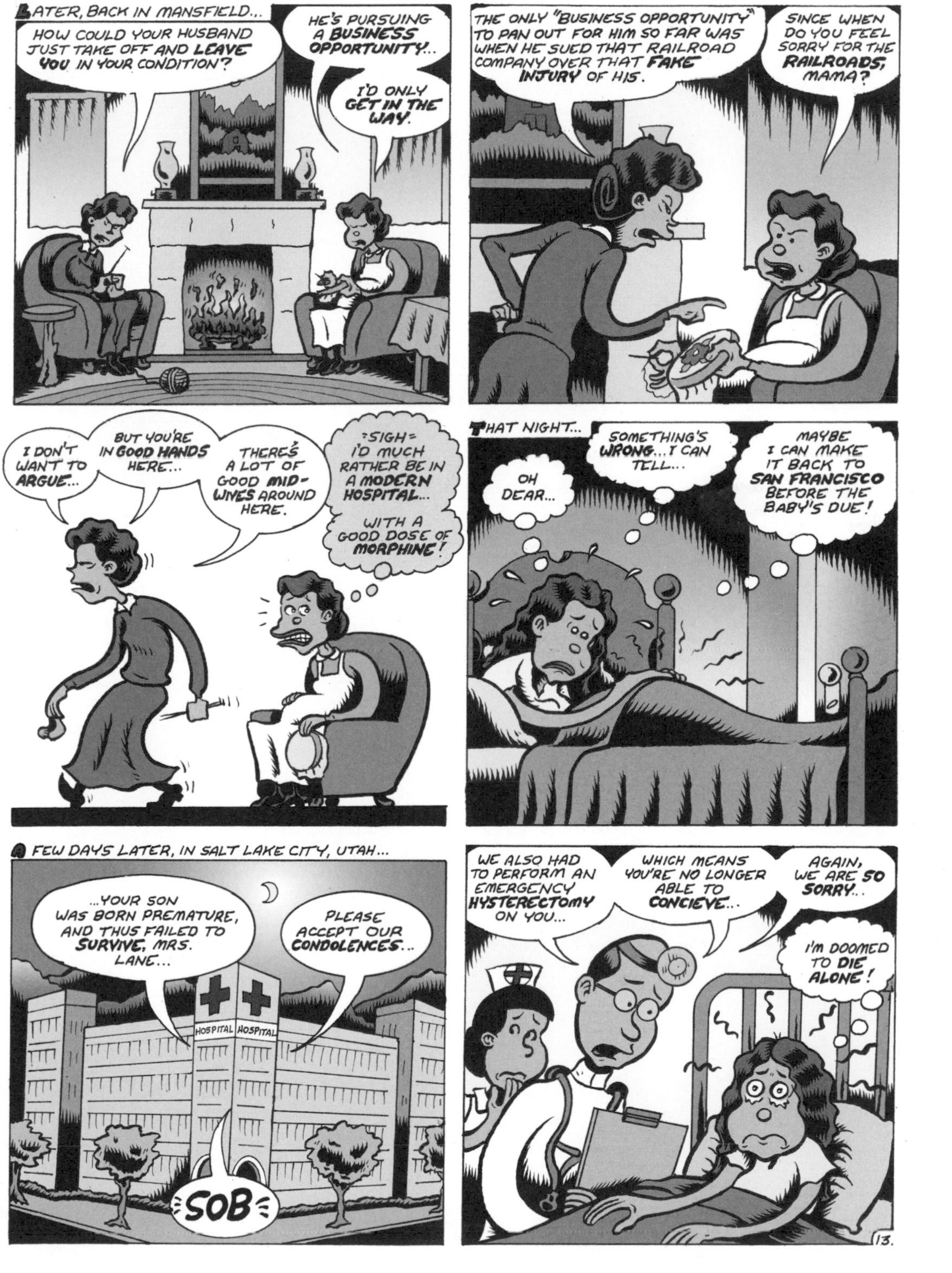
LATER, BACK IN MANSFIELD...
HOW COULD YOUR HUSBAND JUST TAKE OFF AND LEAVE YOU IN YOUR CONDITION?
HE'S PURSUING A BUSINESS OPPORTUNITY...
I'D ONLY GET IN THE WAY.
THE ONLY "BUSINESS OPPORTUNITY" TO PAN OUT FOR HIM SO FAR WAS WHEN HE SUED THAT RAILROAD COMPANY OVER THAT FAKE INJURY OF HIS.
SINCE WHEN DO YOU FEEL SORRY FOR THE RAILROADS, MAMA?
I DON'T WANT TO ARGUE...
BUT YOU'RE IN GOOD HANDS HERE...
THERE'S A LOT OF GOOD MID-WIVES AROUND HERE.
=SIGH= I'D MUCH RATHER BE IN A MODERN HOSPITAL...
WITH A GOOD DOSE OF MORPHINE!
THAT NIGHT...
OH DEAR...
SOMETHING'S WRONG... I CAN TELL...
MAYBE I CAN MAKE IT BACK TO SAN FRANCISCO BEFORE THE BABY'S DUE!
A FEW DAYS LATER, IN SALT LAKE CITY, UTAH...
...YOUR SON WAS BORN PREMATURE, AND THUS FAILED TO SURVIVE, MRS. LANE...
PLEASE ACCEPT OUR CONDOLENCES...
HOSPITAL HOSPITAL
SOB
WE ALSO HAD TO PERFORM AN EMERGENCY HYSTERECTOMY ON YOU...
WHICH MEANS YOU'RE NO LONGER ABLE TO CONCIEVE...
AGAIN, WE ARE SO SORRY...
I'M DOOMED TO DIE ALONE!

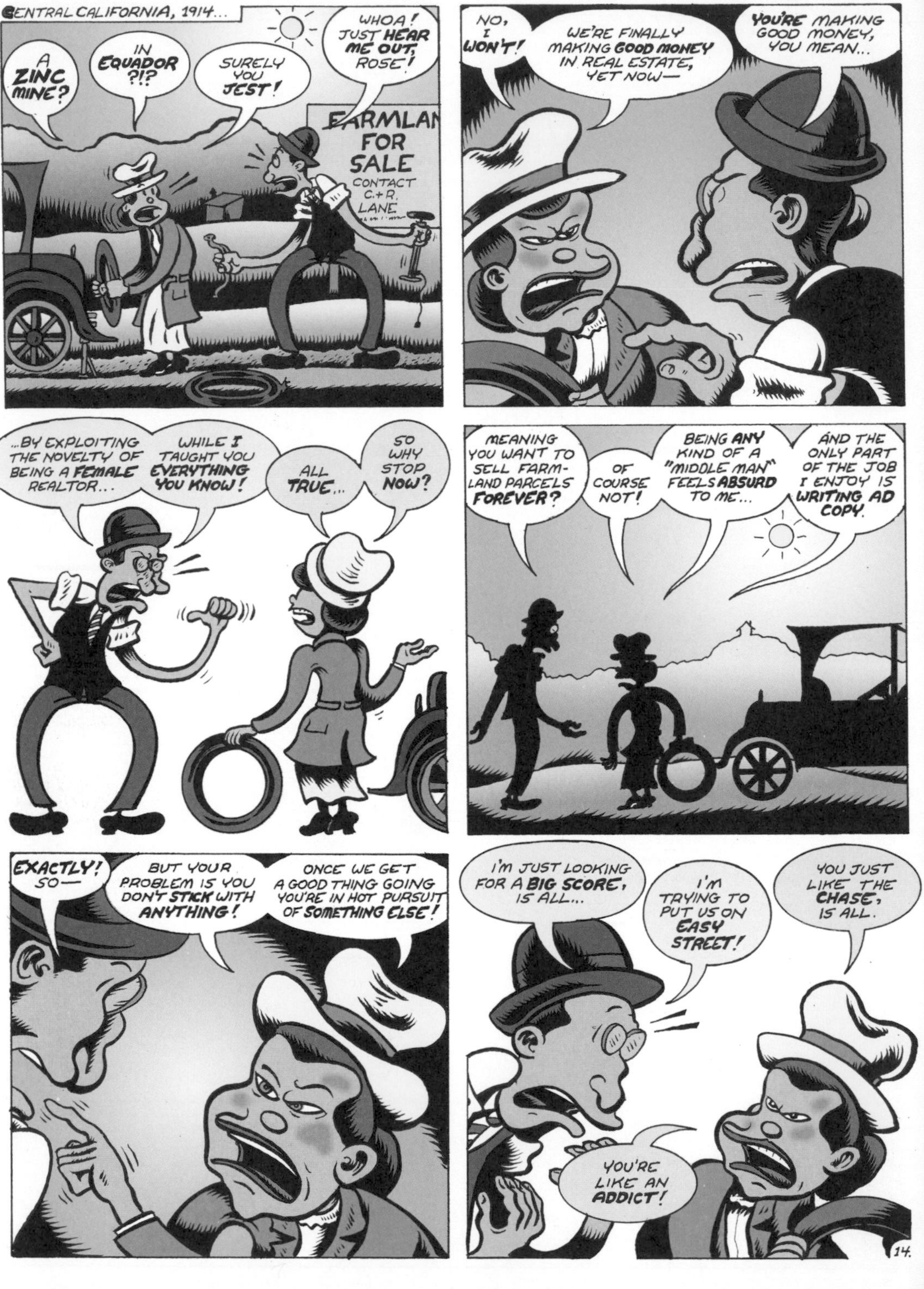
CENTRAL CALIFORNIA, 1914...
A ZINC MINE?
IN EQUADOR ?!?
SURELY YOU JEST!
WHOA! JUST HEAR ME OUT, ROSE!
FARMLAN FOR SALE CONTACT C.+R. LANE
NO, I WON'T!
WE'RE FINALLY MAKING GOOD MONEY IN REAL ESTATE, YET NOW—
YOU'RE MAKING GOOD MONEY, YOU MEAN...
...BY EXPLOITING THE NOVELTY OF BEING A FEMALE REALTOR...
WHILE I TAUGHT YOU EVERYTHING YOU KNOW!
ALL TRUE...
SO WHY STOP NOW?
MEANING YOU WANT TO SELL FARM-LAND PARCELS FOREVER?
OF COURSE NOT!
BEING ANY KIND OF A "MIDDLE MAN" FEELS ABSURD TO ME...
AND THE ONLY PART OF THE JOB I ENJOY IS WRITING AD COPY.
EXACTLY! SO—
BUT YOUR PROBLEM IS YOU DON'T STICK WITH ANYTHING!
ONCE WE GET A GOOD THING GOING YOU'RE IN HOT PURSUIT OF SOMETHING ELSE!
I'M JUST LOOKING FOR A BIG SCORE, IS ALL...
I'M TRYING TO PUT US ON EASY STREET!
YOU JUST LIKE THE CHASE, IS ALL.
YOU'RE LIKE AN ADDICT!

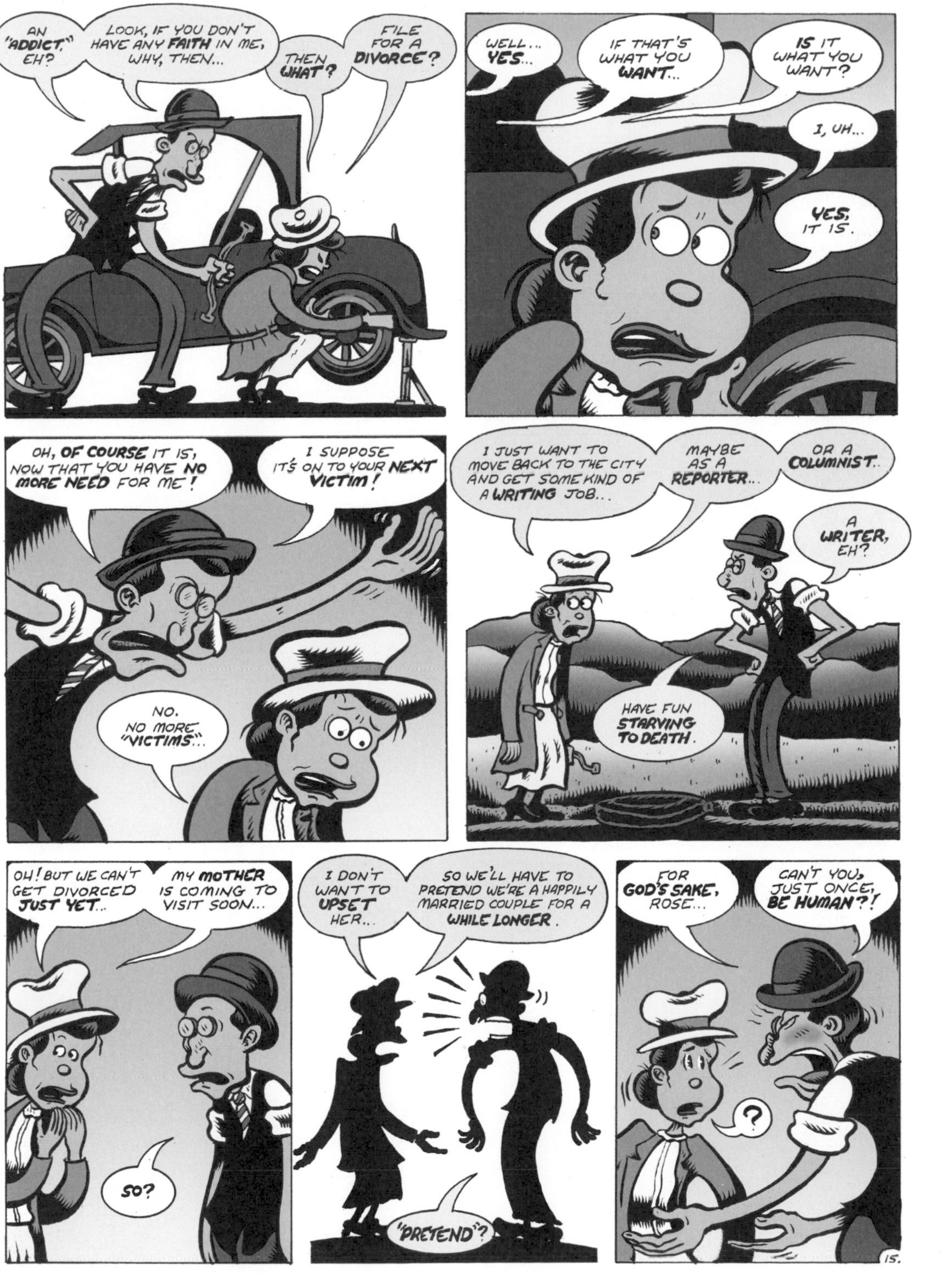
AN "ADDICT," EH?
LOOK, IF YOU DON'T HAVE ANY FAITH IN ME, WHY, THEN...
THEN WHAT?
FILE FOR A DIVORCE?
WELL... YES...
IF THAT'S WHAT YOU WANT...
IS IT WHAT YOU WANT?
I, UH...
YES, IT IS.
OH, OF COURSE IT IS, NOW THAT YOU HAVE NO MORE NEED FOR ME!
I SUPPOSE IT'S ON TO YOUR NEXT VICTIM!
NO. NO MORE "VICTIMS"...
I JUST WANT TO MOVE BACK TO THE CITY AND GET SOME KIND OF A WRITING JOB...
MAYBE AS A REPORTER...
OR A COLUMNIST...
A WRITER, EH?
HAVE FUN STARVING TO DEATH.
OH! BUT WE CAN'T GET DIVORCED JUST YET...
MY MOTHER IS COMING TO VISIT SOON...
SO?
I DON'T WANT TO UPSET HER...
SO WE'LL HAVE TO PRETEND WE'RE A HAPPILY MARRIED COUPLE FOR A WHILE LONGER.
"PRETEND"?
FOR GOD'S SAKE, ROSE...
CAN'T YOU, JUST ONCE, BE HUMAN?!
?

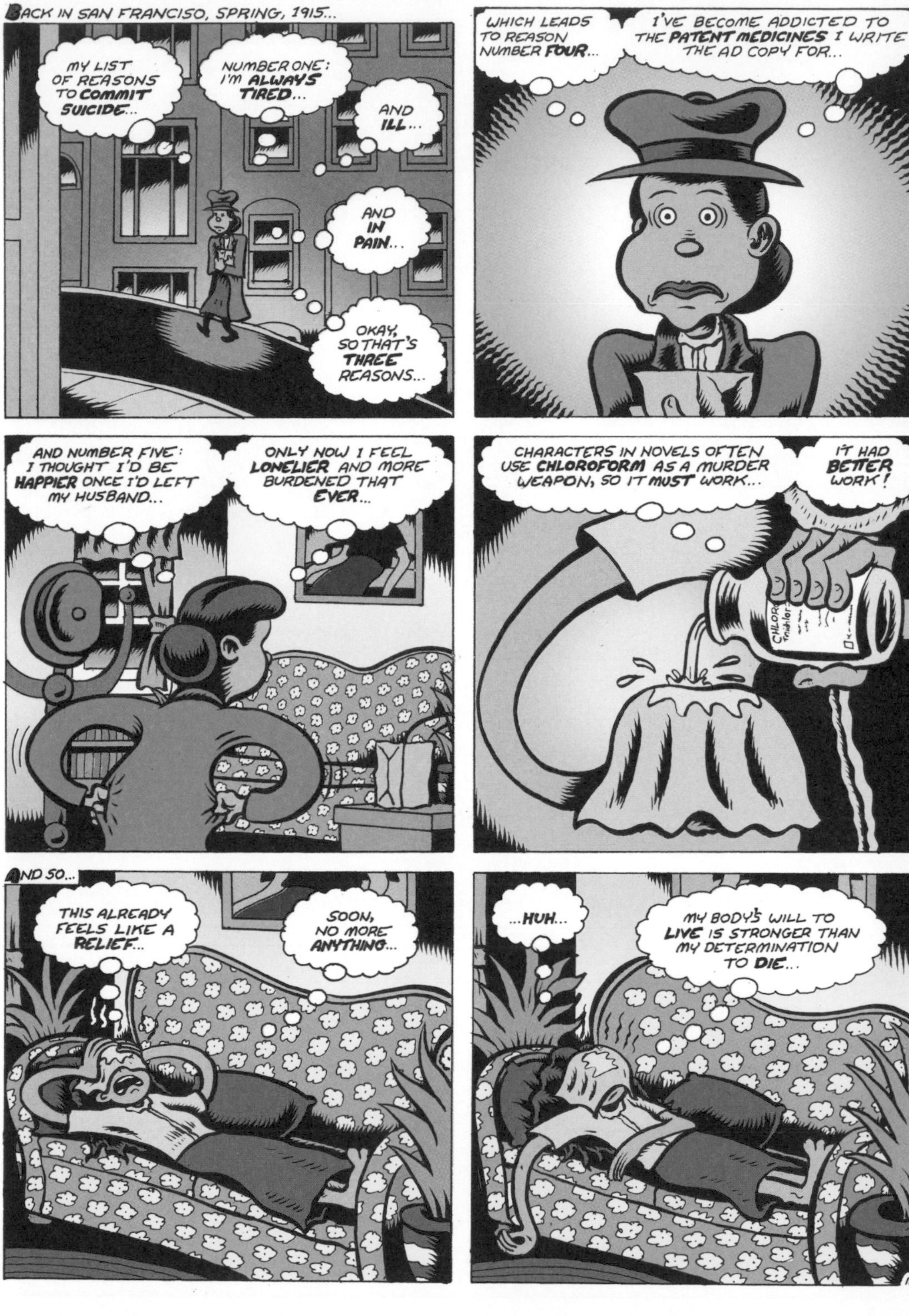
BACK IN SAN FRANCISO, SPRING, 1915...
MY LIST OF REASONS TO COMMIT SUICIDE...
NUMBER ONE: I'M ALWAYS TIRED...
AND ILL...
AND IN PAIN...
OKAY, SO THAT'S THREE REASONS...
WHICH LEADS TO REASON NUMBER FOUR...
I'VE BECOME ADDICTED TO THE PATENT MEDICINES I WRITE THE AD COPY FOR...
AND NUMBER FIVE: I THOUGHT I'D BE HAPPIER ONCE I'D LEFT MY HUSBAND...
ONLY NOW I FEEL LONELIER AND MORE BURDENED THAT EVER...
CHARACTERS IN NOVELS OFTEN USE CHLOROFORM AS A MURDER WEAPON, SO IT MUST WORK...
IT HAD BETTER WORK!
AND SO...
THIS ALREADY FEELS LIKE A RELIEF...
SOON, NO MORE ANYTHING...
...HUH...
MY BODY'S WILL TO LIVE IS STRONGER THAN MY DETERMINATION TO DIE...

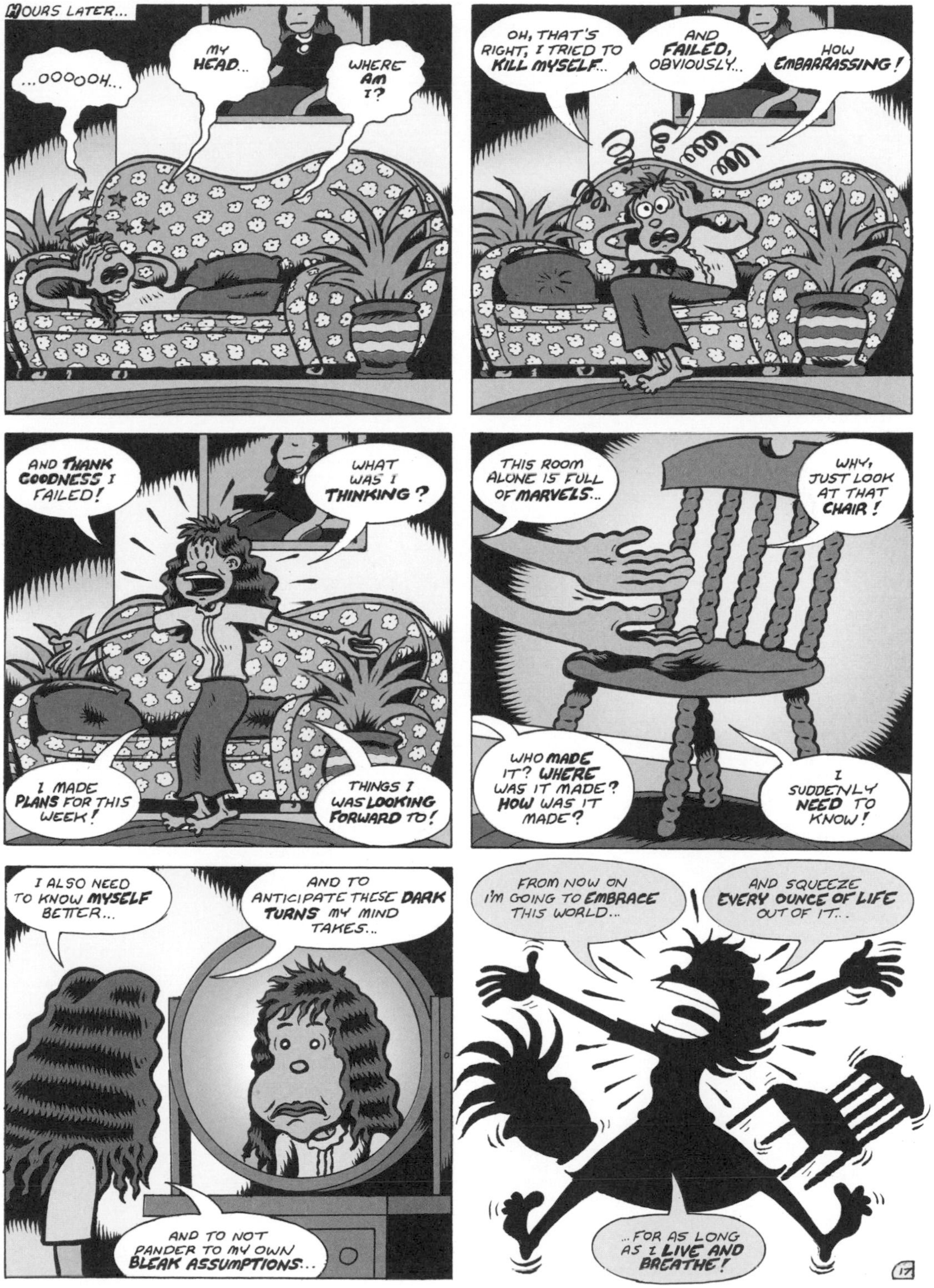
HOURS LATER...
...OOOOOH...
MY HEAD...
WHERE AM I?
OH, THAT'S RIGHT, I TRIED TO KILL MYSELF...
AND FAILED, OBVIOUSLY...
HOW EMBARRASSING!
AND THANK GOODNESS I FAILED!
WHAT WAS I THINKING?
I MADE PLANS FOR THIS WEEK!
THINGS I WAS LOOKING FORWARD TO!
THIS ROOM ALONE IS FULL OF MARVELS...
WHY, JUST LOOK AT THAT CHAIR!
WHO MADE IT? WHERE WAS IT MADE? HOW WAS IT MADE?
I SUDDENLY NEED TO KNOW!
I ALSO NEED TO KNOW MYSELF BETTER...
AND TO ANTICIPATE THESE DARK TURNS MY MIND TAKES...
AND TO NOT PANDER TO MY OWN BLEAK ASSUMPTIONS...
FROM NOW ON I'M GOING TO EMBRACE THIS WORLD...
AND SQUEEZE EVERY OUNCE OF LIFE OUT OF IT...
...FOR AS LONG AS I LIVE AND BREATHE!

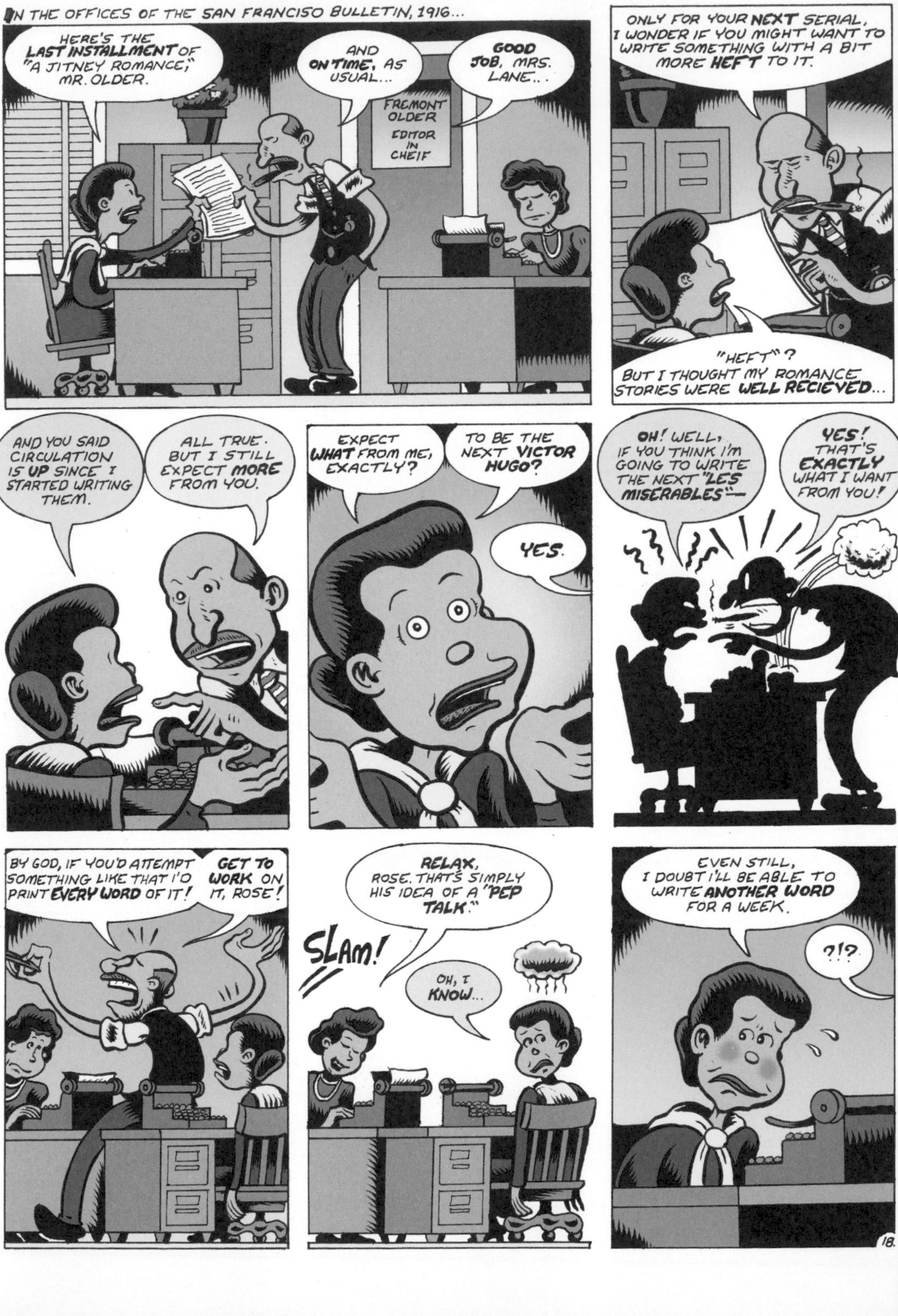
IN THE OFFICES OF THE SAN FRANCISO BULLETIN, 1916...
HERE'S THE LAST INSTALLMENT OF "A JITNEY ROMANCE," MR. OLDER.
AND ON TIME, AS USUAL...
GOOD JOB, MRS. LANE...
FREMONT OLDER EDITOR IN CHEIF
ONLY FOR YOUR NEXT SERIAL, I WONDER IF YOU MIGHT WANT TO WRITE SOMETHING WITH A BIT MORE HEFT TO IT.
"HEFT"? BUT I THOUGHT MY ROMANCE STORIES WERE WELL RECIEVED...
AND YOU SAID CIRCULATION IS UP SINCE I STARTED WRITING THEM.
ALL TRUE. BUT I STILL EXPECT MORE FROM YOU.
EXPECT WHAT FROM ME, EXACTLY?
TO BE THE NEXT VICTOR HUGO?
YES.
OH! WELL, IF YOU THINK I'M GOING TO WRITE THE NEXT "LES MISERABLES"—
YES! THAT'S EXACTLY WHAT I WANT FROM YOU!
BY GOD, IF YOU'D ATTEMPT SOMETHING LIKE THAT I'D PRINT EVERY WORD OF IT!
GET TO WORK ON IT, ROSE!
SLAM!
RELAX, ROSE. THAT'S SIMPLY HIS IDEA OF A "PEP TALK."
OH, I KNOW...
EVEN STILL, I DOUBT I'LL BE ABLE TO WRITE ANOTHER WORD FOR A WEEK.
?!?

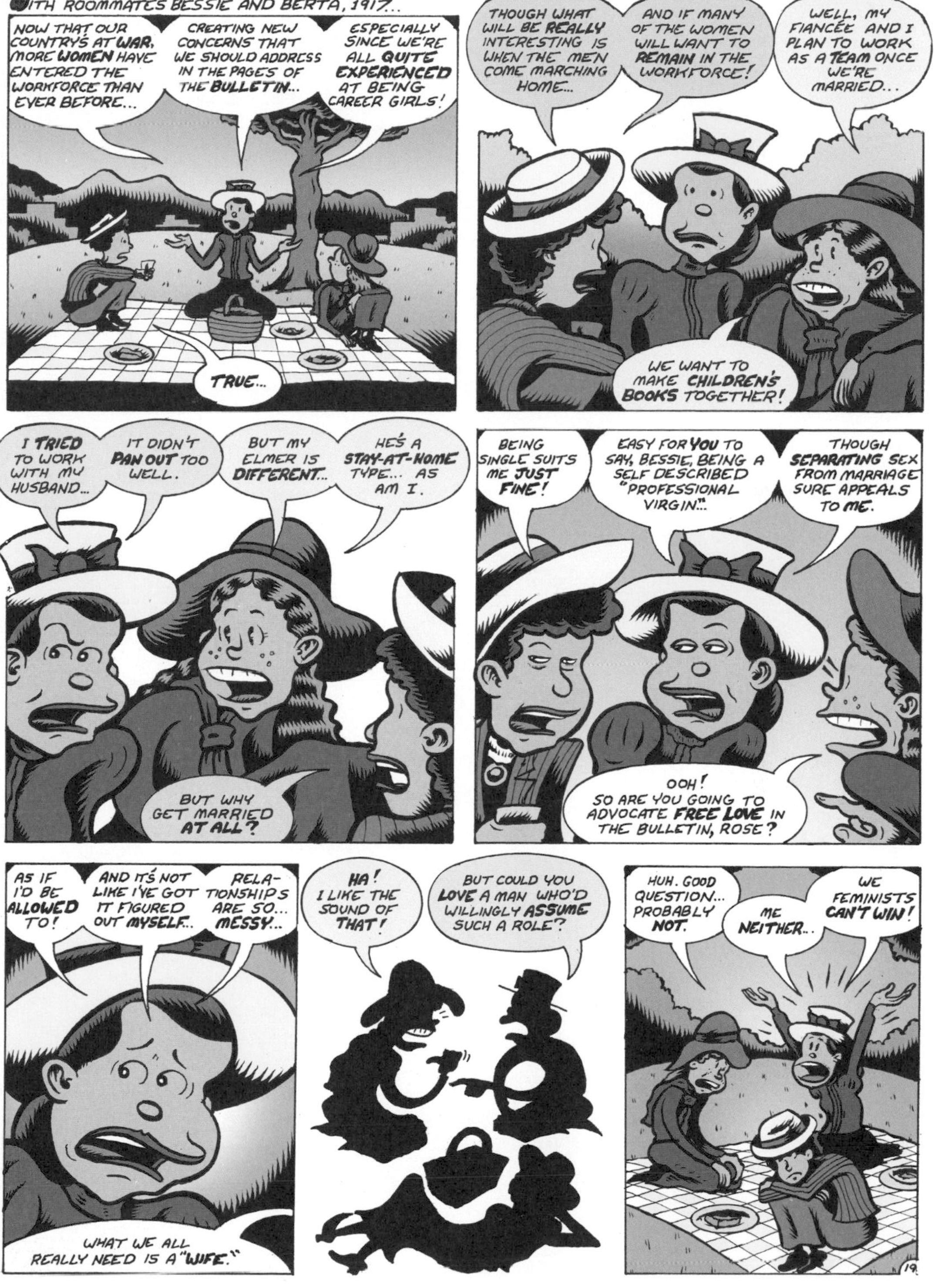
WITH ROOMMATES BESSIE AND BERTA, 1917...
NOW THAT OUR COUNTRY'S AT WAR, MORE WOMEN HAVE ENTERED THE WORKFORCE THAN EVER BEFORE...
CREATING NEW CONCERNS THAT WE SHOULD ADDRESS IN THE PAGES OF THE BULLETIN...
ESPECIALLY SINCE WE'RE ALL QUITE EXPERIENCED AT BEING CAREER GIRLS!
TRUE...
THOUGH WHAT WILL BE REALLY INTERESTING IS WHEN THE MEN COME MARCHING HOME...
AND IF MANY OF THE WOMEN WILL WANT TO REMAIN IN THE WORKFORCE!
WELL, MY FIANCÉE AND I PLAN TO WORK AS A TEAM ONCE WE'RE MARRIED...
WE WANT TO MAKE CHILDREN'S BOOKS TOGETHER!
I TRIED TO WORK WITH MY HUSBAND...
IT DIDN'T PAN OUT TOO WELL.
BUT MY ELMER IS DIFFERENT...
HE'S A STAY-AT-HOME TYPE... AS AM I.
BUT WHY GET MARRIED AT ALL?
BEING SINGLE SUITS ME JUST FINE!
EASY FOR YOU TO SAY, BESSIE, BEING A SELF DESCRIBED "PROFESSIONAL VIRGIN"...
THOUGH SEPARATING SEX FROM MARRIAGE SURE APPEALS TO ME.
OOH! SO ARE YOU GOING TO ADVOCATE FREE LOVE IN THE BULLETIN, ROSE?
AS IF I'D BE ALLOWED TO!
AND IT'S NOT LIKE I'VE GOT IT FIGURED OUT MYSELF...
RELATIONSHIPS ARE SO... MESSY...
WHAT WE ALL REALLY NEED IS A "WIFE."
HA! I LIKE THE SOUND OF THAT!
BUT COULD YOU LOVE A MAN WHO'D WILLINGLY ASSUME SUCH A ROLE?
HUH. GOOD QUESTION... PROBABLY NOT.
ME NEITHER...
WE FEMINISTS CAN'T WIN!

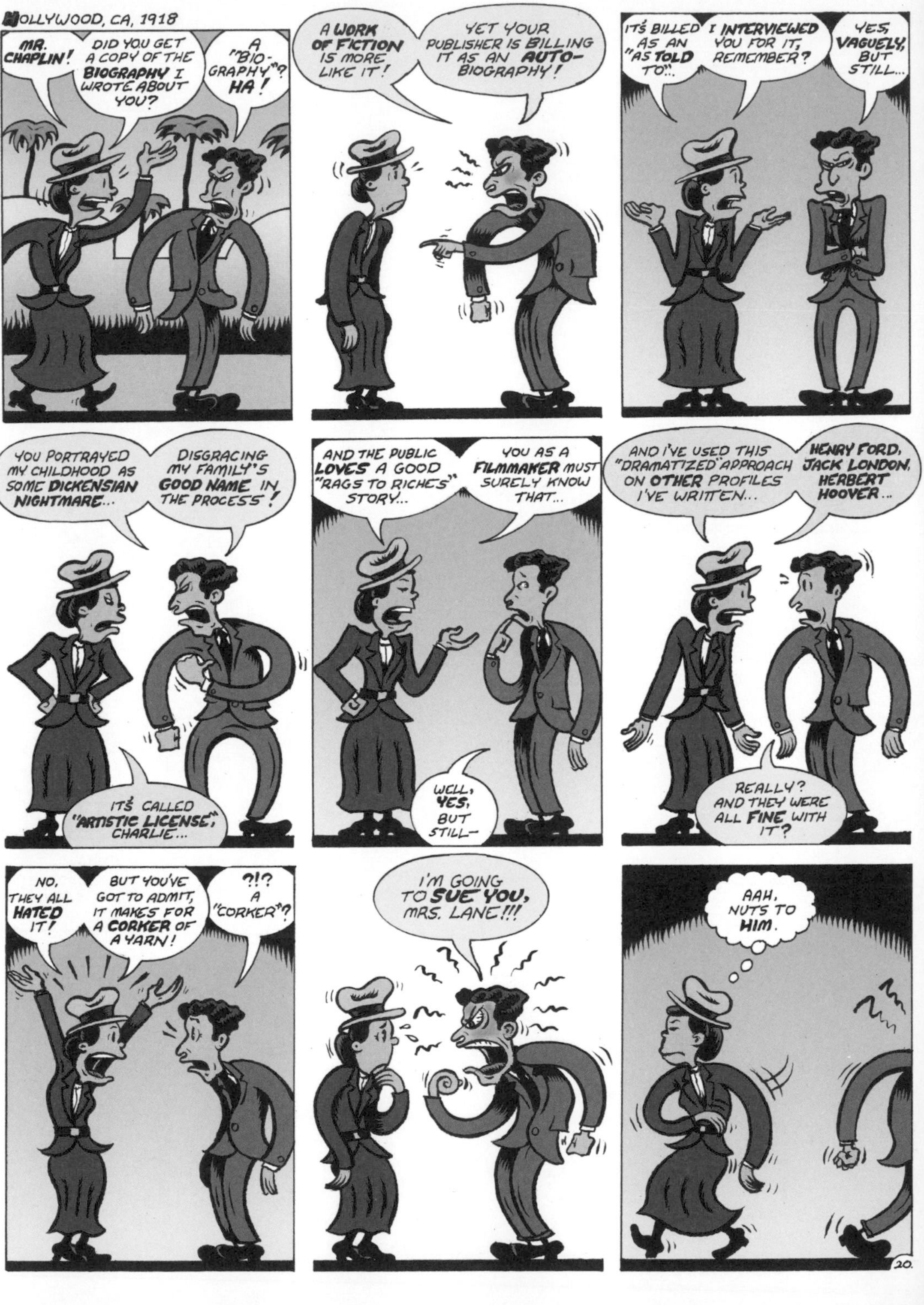
HOLLYWOOD, CA, 1918
MR. CHAPLIN!
DID YOU GET A COPY OF THE BIOGRAPHY I WROTE ABOUT YOU?
A "BIO-GRAPHY"? HA!
A WORK OF FICTION IS MORE LIKE IT!
YET YOUR PUBLISHER IS BILLING IT AS AN AUTO-BIOGRAPHY!
IT'S BILLED AS AN "AS TOLD TO"...
I INTERVIEWED YOU FOR IT, REMEMBER?
YES, VAGUELY, BUT STILL...
YOU PORTRAYED MY CHILDHOOD AS SOME DICKENSIAN NIGHTMARE...
DISGRACING MY FAMILY'S GOOD NAME IN THE PROCESS!
IT'S CALLED "ARTISTIC LICENSE," CHARLIE...
AND THE PUBLIC LOVES A GOOD "RAGS TO RICHES" STORY...
YOU AS A FILMMAKER MUST SURELY KNOW THAT...
WELL, YES, BUT STILL—
AND I'VE USED THIS "DRAMATIZED" APPROACH ON OTHER PROFILES I'VE WRITTEN...
HENRY FORD, JACK LONDON, HERBERT HOOVER...
REALLY? AND THEY WERE ALL FINE WITH IT?
NO, THEY ALL HATED IT!
BUT YOU'VE GOT TO ADMIT, IT MAKES FOR A CORKER OF A YARN!
?!? A "CORKER"?
I'M GOING TO SUE YOU, MRS. LANE!!!
AAH, NUTS TO HIM.

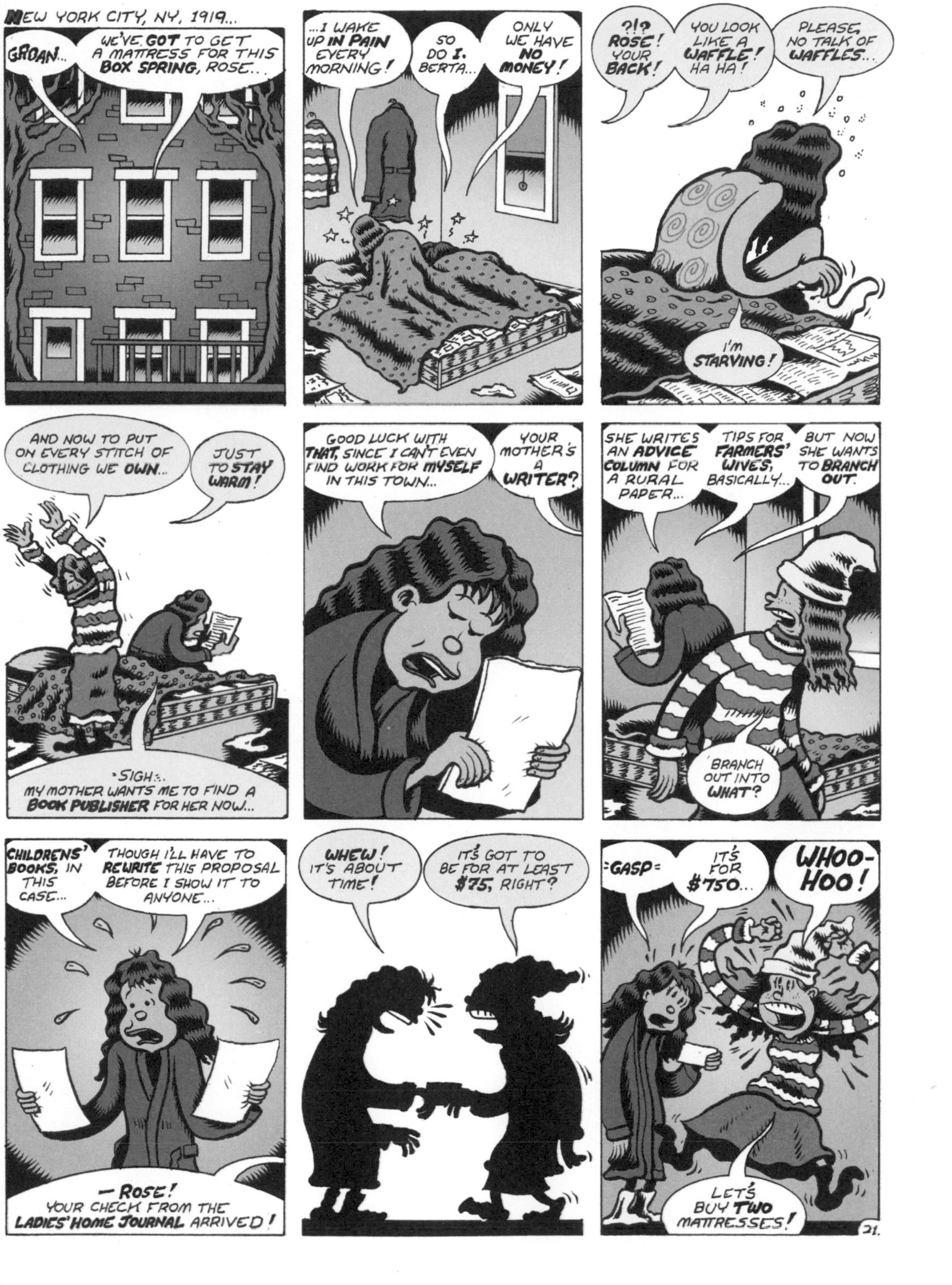
NEW YORK CITY, NY, 1919...
GROAN...
WE'VE GOT TO GET A MATTRESS FOR THIS BOX SPRING, ROSE...
...I WAKE UP IN PAIN EVERY MORNING!
SO DO I, BERTA...
ONLY WE HAVE NO MONEY!
?!? ROSE! YOUR BACK!
YOU LOOK LIKE A WAFFLE! HA HA!
PLEASE, NO TALK OF WAFFLES...
I'M STARVING!
AND NOW TO PUT ON EVERY STITCH OF CLOTHING WE OWN...
JUST TO STAY WARM!
SIGH... MY MOTHER WANTS ME TO FIND A BOOK PUBLISHER FOR HER NOW...
GOOD LUCK WITH THAT, SINCE I CAN'T EVEN FIND WORK FOR MYSELF IN THIS TOWN...
YOUR MOTHER'S A WRITER?
SHE WRITES AN ADVICE COLUMN FOR A RURAL PAPER...
TIPS FOR FARMERS' WIVES, BASICALLY...
BUT NOW SHE WANTS TO BRANCH OUT.
'BRANCH OUT' INTO WHAT?
CHILDRENS' BOOKS, IN THIS CASE...
THOUGH I'LL HAVE TO REWRITE THIS PROPOSAL BEFORE I SHOW IT TO ANYONE...
—ROSE! YOUR CHECK FROM THE LADIES' HOME JOURNAL ARRIVED!
WHEW! IT'S ABOUT TIME!
IT'S GOT TO BE FOR AT LEAST $75, RIGHT?
=GASP=
IT'S FOR $750...
WHOO-HOO!
LET'S BUY TWO MATTRESSES!

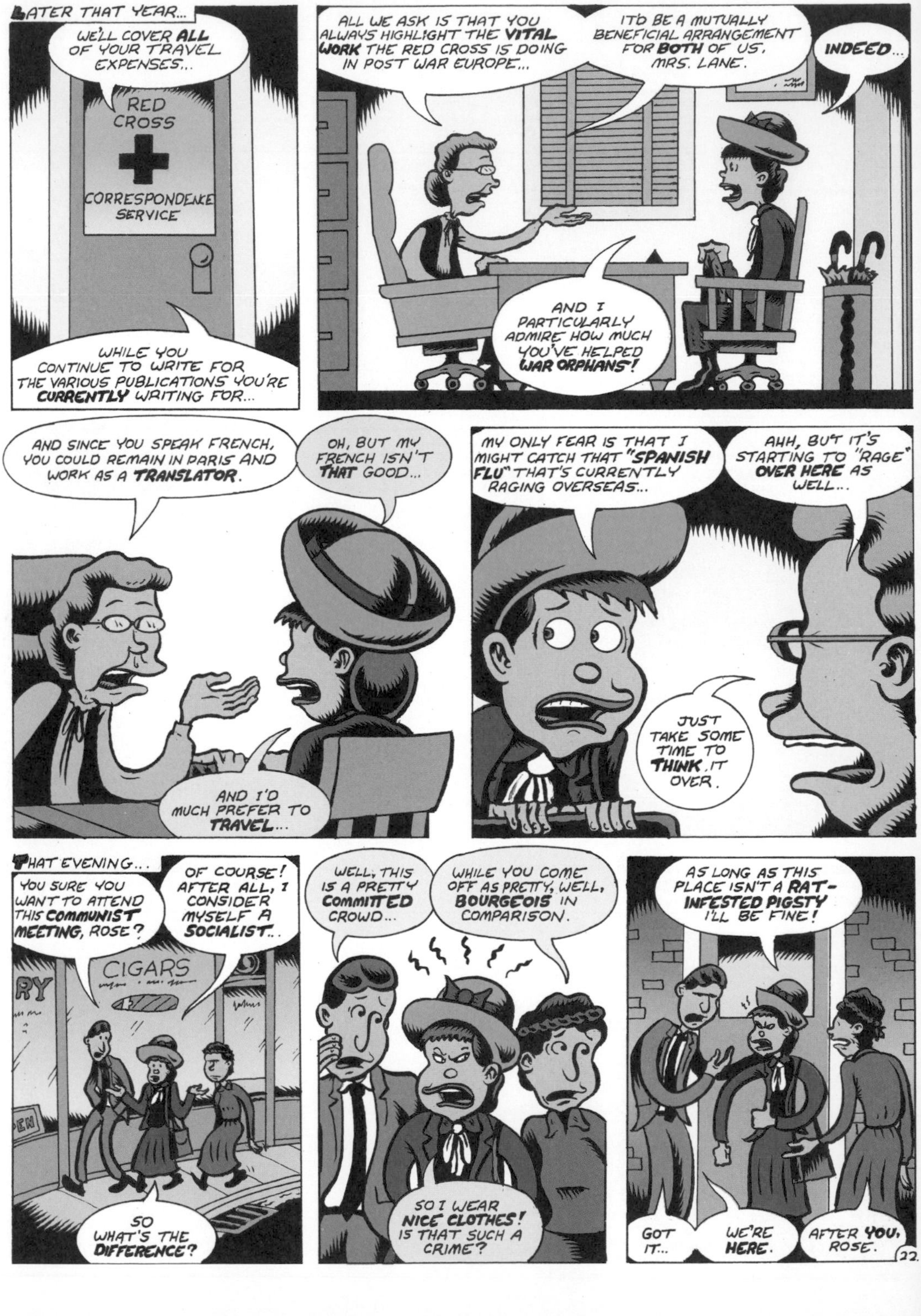
LATER THAT YEAR...
WE'LL COVER ALL OF YOUR TRAVEL EXPENSES...
RED CROSS
CORRESPONDENKE SERVICE
WHILE YOU CONTINUE TO WRITE FOR THE VARIOUS PUBLICATIONS YOU'RE CURRENTLY WRITING FOR...
ALL WE ASK IS THAT YOU ALWAYS HIGHLIGHT THE VITAL WORK THE RED CROSS IS DOING IN POST WAR EUROPE...
IT'D BE A MUTUALLY BENEFICIAL ARRANGEMENT FOR BOTH OF US, MRS. LANE.
INDEED...
AND I PARTICULARLY ADMIRE HOW MUCH YOU'VE HELPED WAR ORPHANS!
AND SINCE YOU SPEAK FRENCH, YOU COULD REMAIN IN PARIS AND WORK AS A TRANSLATOR.
OH, BUT MY FRENCH ISN'T THAT GOOD...
AND I'D MUCH PREFER TO TRAVEL...
MY ONLY FEAR IS THAT I MIGHT CATCH THAT "SPANISH FLU" THAT'S CURRENTLY RAGING OVERSEAS...
AHH, BUT IT'S STARTING TO "RAGE" OVER HERE AS WELL...
JUST TAKE SOME TIME TO THINK IT OVER.
THAT EVENING...
YOU SURE YOU WANT TO ATTEND THIS COMMUNIST MEETING, ROSE?
OF COURSE! AFTER ALL, I CONSIDER MYSELF A SOCIALIST...
CIGARS
SO WHAT'S THE DIFFERENCE?
WELL, THIS IS A PRETTY COMMITTED CROWD...
WHILE YOU COME OFF AS PRETTY, WELL, BOURGEOIS IN COMPARISON.
SO I WEAR NICE CLOTHES! IS THAT SUCH A CRIME?
AS LONG AS THIS PLACE ISN'T A RAT-INFESTED PIGSTY I'LL BE FINE!
GOT IT...
WE'RE HERE.
AFTER YOU, ROSE.

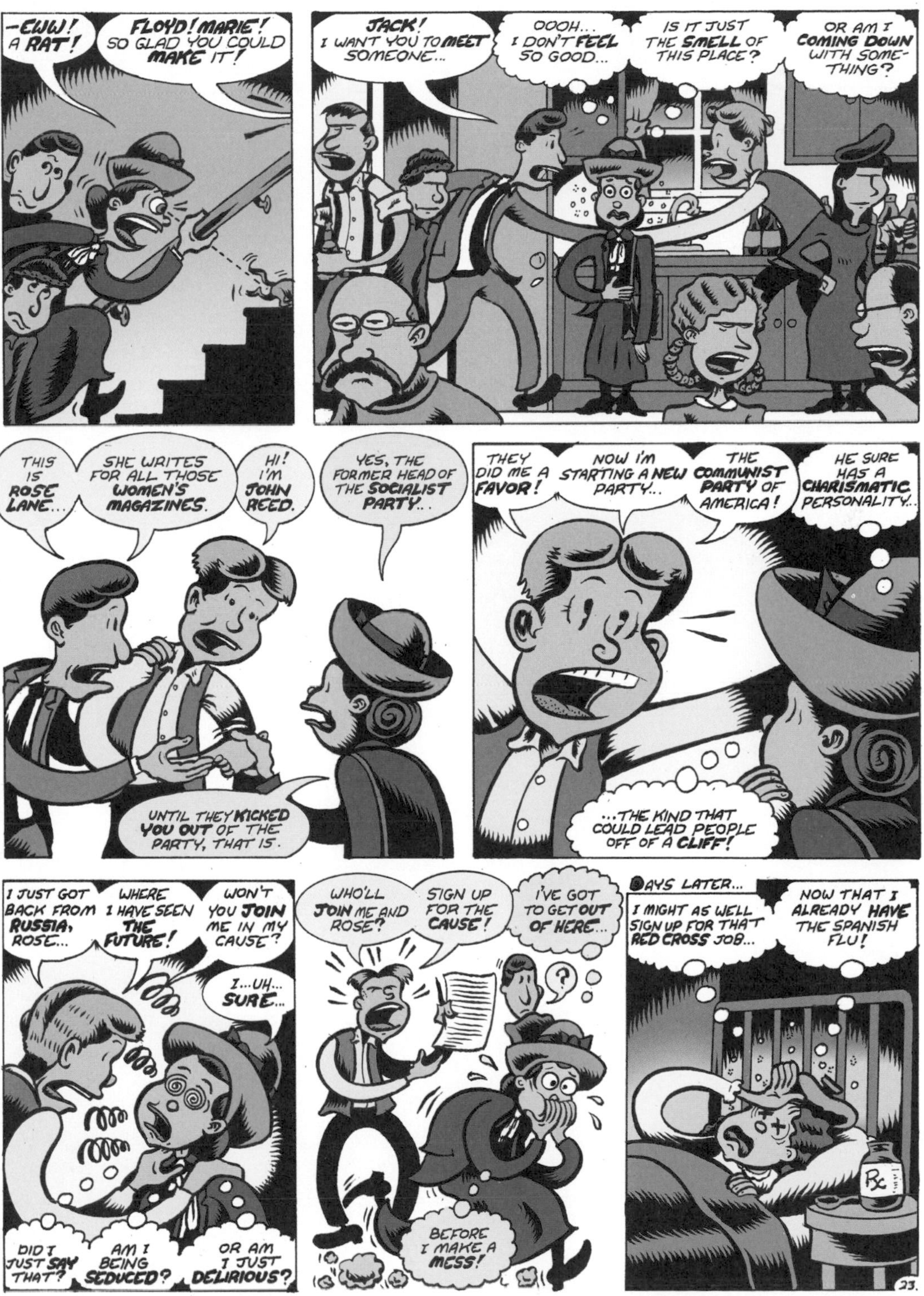
-EWW! A RAT!
FLOYD! MARIE! SO GLAD YOU COULD MAKE IT!
JACK! I WANT YOU TO MEET SOMEONE...
OOOH... I DON'T FEEL SO GOOD...
IS IT JUST THE SMELL OF THIS PLACE?
OR AM I COMING DOWN WITH SOME-THING?
THIS IS ROSE LANE...
SHE WRITES FOR ALL THOSE WOMEN'S MAGAZINES.
HI! I'M JOHN REED.
YES, THE FORMER HEAD OF THE SOCIALIST PARTY...
UNTIL THEY KICKED YOU OUT OF THE PARTY, THAT IS.
THEY DID ME A FAVOR!
NOW I'M STARTING A NEW PARTY...
THE COMMUNIST PARTY OF AMERICA!
HE SURE HAS A CHARISMATIC PERSONALITY...
...THE KIND THAT COULD LEAD PEOPLE OFF OF A CLIFF!
I JUST GOT BACK FROM RUSSIA, ROSE...
WHERE I HAVE SEEN THE FUTURE!
WON'T YOU JOIN ME IN MY CAUSE?
I...UH... SURE...
DID I JUST SAY THAT?
AM I BEING SEDUCED?
OR AM I JUST DELIRIOUS?
WHO'LL JOIN ME AND ROSE?
SIGN UP FOR THE CAUSE!
I'VE GOT TO GET OUT OF HERE...
?
BEFORE I MAKE A MESS!
DAYS LATER...
I MIGHT AS WELL SIGN UP FOR THAT RED CROSS JOB...
NOW THAT I ALREADY HAVE THE SPANISH FLU!
Rx

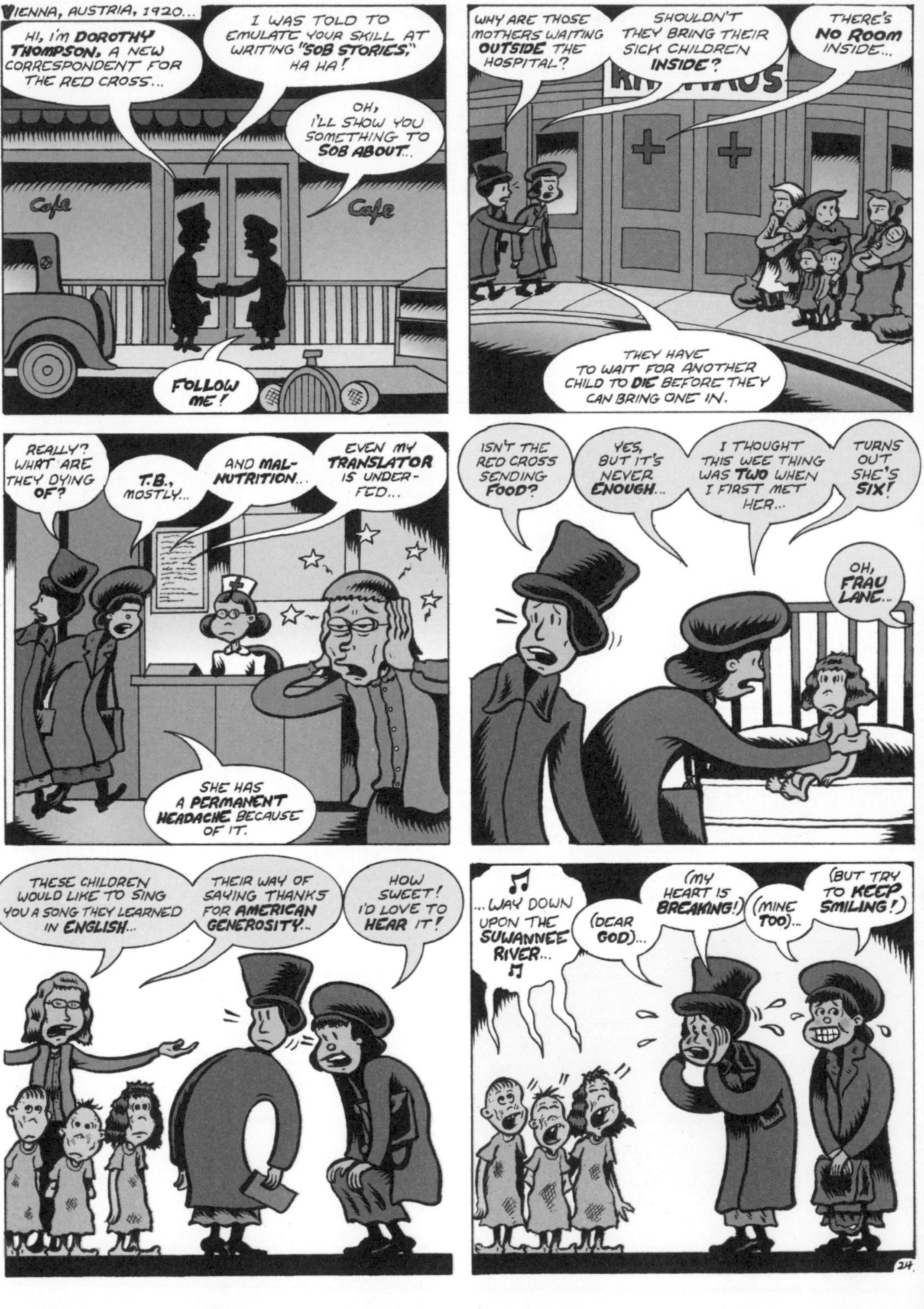
VIENNA, AUSTRIA, 1920...
HI, I'M DOROTHY THOMPSON, A NEW CORRESPONDENT FOR THE RED CROSS...
I WAS TOLD TO EMULATE YOUR SKILL AT WRITING "SOB STORIES," HA HA!
OH, I'LL SHOW YOU SOMETHING TO SOB ABOUT...
Cafe
Cafe
FOLLOW ME!
WHY ARE THOSE MOTHERS WAITING OUTSIDE THE HOSPITAL?
SHOULDN'T THEY BRING THEIR SICK CHILDREN INSIDE?
THERE'S NO ROOM INSIDE...
THEY HAVE TO WAIT FOR ANOTHER CHILD TO DIE BEFORE THEY CAN BRING ONE IN.
REALLY? WHAT ARE THEY DYING OF?
T.B., MOSTLY...
AND MAL-NUTRITION...
EVEN MY TRANSLATOR IS UNDER-FED...
SHE HAS A PERMANENT HEADACHE BECAUSE OF IT.
ISN'T THE RED CROSS SENDING FOOD?
YES, BUT IT'S NEVER ENOUGH...
I THOUGHT THIS WEE THING WAS TWO WHEN I FIRST MET HER...
TURNS OUT SHE'S SIX!
OH, FRAU LANE...
THESE CHILDREN WOULD LIKE TO SING YOU A SONG THEY LEARNED IN ENGLISH...
THEIR WAY OF SAYING THANKS FOR AMERICAN GENEROSITY...
HOW SWEET! I'D LOVE TO HEAR IT!
...WAY DOWN UPON THE SUWANNEE RIVER...
(DEAR GOD)...
(MY HEART IS BREAKING!)
(MINE TOO)...
(BUT TRY TO KEEP SMILING!)

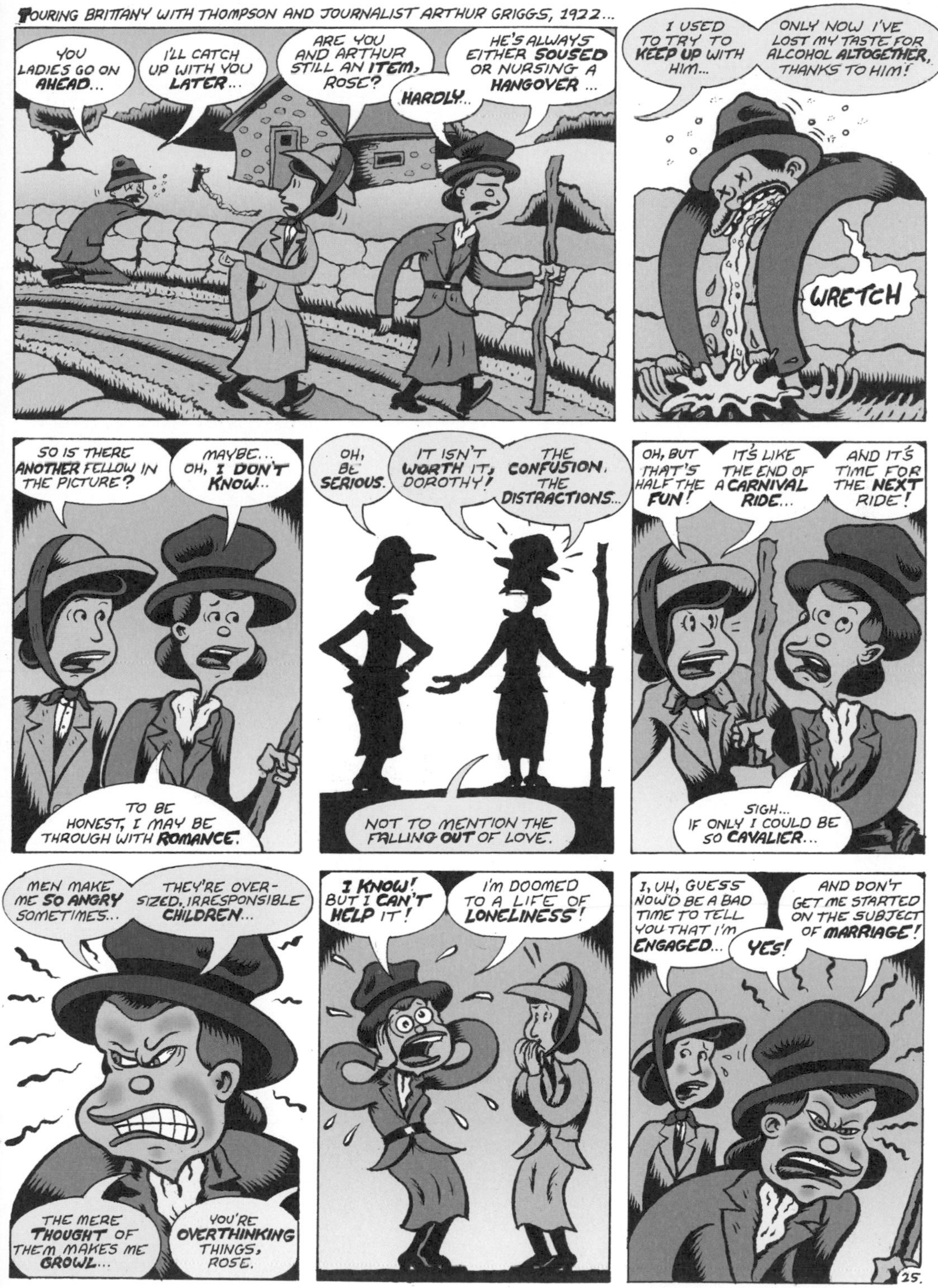
TOURING BRITTANY WITH THOMPSON AND JOURNALIST ARTHUR GRIGGS, 1922...
YOU LADIES GO ON AHEAD...
I'LL CATCH UP WITH YOU LATER...
ARE YOU AND ARTHUR STILL AN ITEM, ROSE?
HARDLY...
HE'S ALWAYS EITHER SOUSED OR NURSING A HANGOVER...
I USED TO TRY TO KEEP UP WITH HIM...
ONLY NOW I'VE LOST MY TASTE FOR ALCOHOL ALTOGETHER, THANKS TO HIM!
WRETCH
SO IS THERE ANOTHER FELLOW IN THE PICTURE?
MAYBE... OH, I DON'T KNOW...
TO BE HONEST, I MAY BE THROUGH WITH ROMANCE.
OH, BE SERIOUS.
IT ISN'T WORTH IT, DOROTHY!
THE CONFUSION. THE DISTRACTIONS...
NOT TO MENTION THE FALLING OUT OF LOVE.
OH, BUT THAT'S HALF THE FUN!
IT'S LIKE THE END OF A CARNIVAL RIDE...
AND IT'S TIME FOR THE NEXT RIDE!
SIGH... IF ONLY I COULD BE SO CAVALIER...
MEN MAKE ME SO ANGRY SOMETIMES...
THEY'RE OVER-SIZED, IRRESPONSIBLE CHILDREN...
THE MERE THOUGHT OF THEM MAKES ME GROWL...
YOU'RE OVERTHINKING THINGS, ROSE.
I KNOW! BUT I CAN'T HELP IT!
I'M DOOMED TO A LIFE OF LONELINESS!
I, UH, GUESS NOW'D BE A BAD TIME TO TELL YOU THAT I'M ENGAGED...
YES!
AND DON'T GET ME STARTED ON THE SUBJECT OF MARRIAGE!

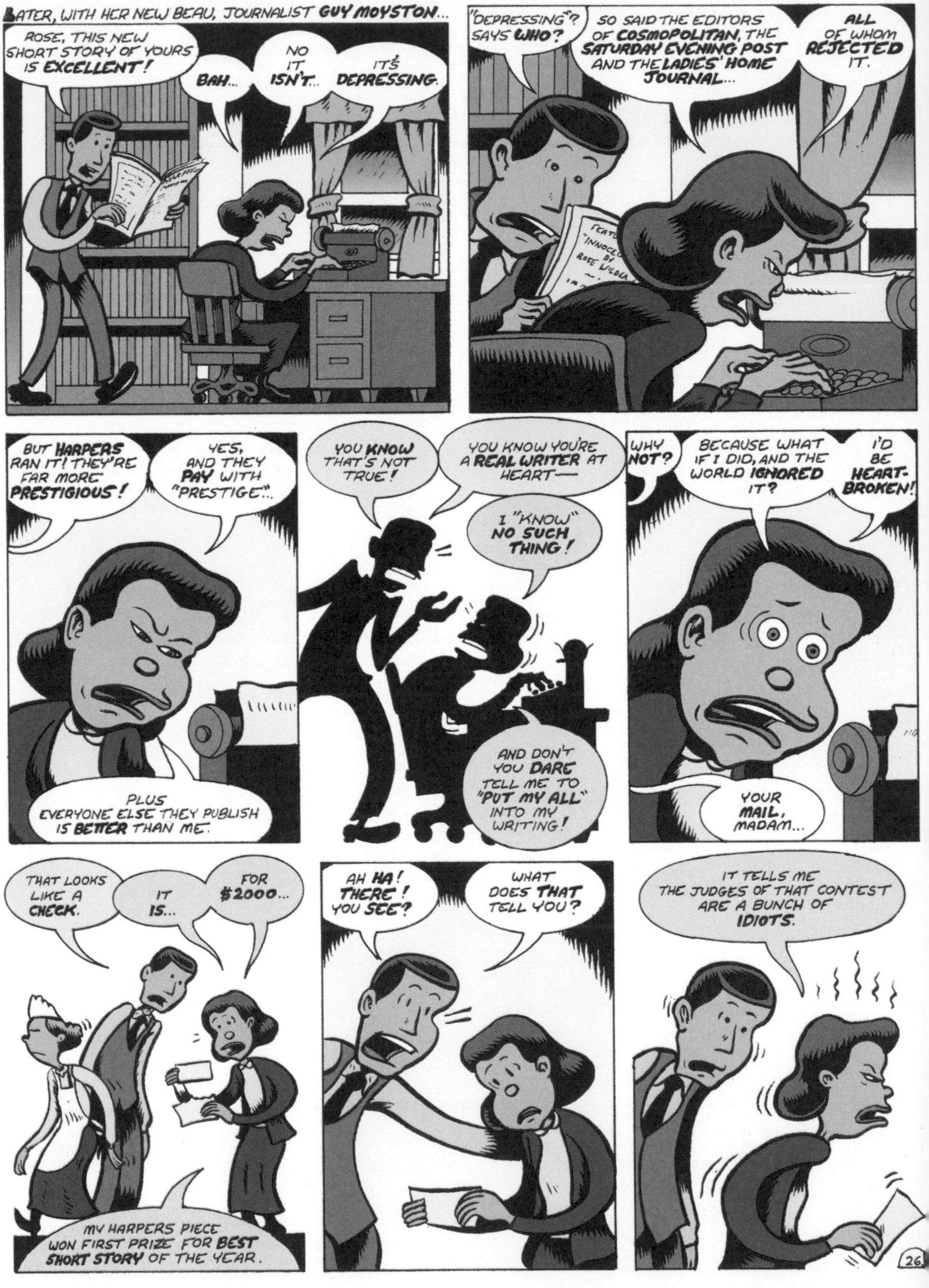
LATER, WITH HER NEW BEAU, JOURNALIST GUY MOYSTON...
ROSE, THIS NEW SHORT STORY OF YOURS IS EXCELLENT!
BAH...
NO IT ISN'T...
IT'S DEPRESSING.
"DEPRESSING"? SAYS WHO?
SO SAID THE EDITORS OF COSMOPOLITAN, THE SATURDAY EVENING POST AND THE LADIES' HOME JOURNAL...
ALL OF WHOM REJECTED IT.
BUT HARPERS RAN IT! THEY'RE FAR MORE PRESTIGIOUS!
YES, AND THEY PAY WITH "PRESTIGE"...
PLUS EVERYONE ELSE THEY PUBLISH IS BETTER THAN ME.
YOU KNOW THAT'S NOT TRUE!
YOU KNOW YOU'RE A REAL WRITER AT HEART—
I "KNOW" NO SUCH THING!
AND DON'T YOU DARE TELL ME TO "PUT MY ALL" INTO MY WRITING!
WHY NOT?
BECAUSE WHAT IF I DID, AND THE WORLD IGNORED IT?
I'D BE HEART-BROKEN!
YOUR MAIL, MADAM...
THAT LOOKS LIKE A CHECK.
IT IS...
FOR $2000...
MY HARPERS PIECE WON FIRST PRIZE FOR BEST SHORT STORY OF THE YEAR.
AH HA! THERE! YOU SEE?
WHAT DOES THAT TELL YOU?
IT TELLS ME THE JUDGES OF THAT CONTEST ARE A BUNCH OF IDIOTS.

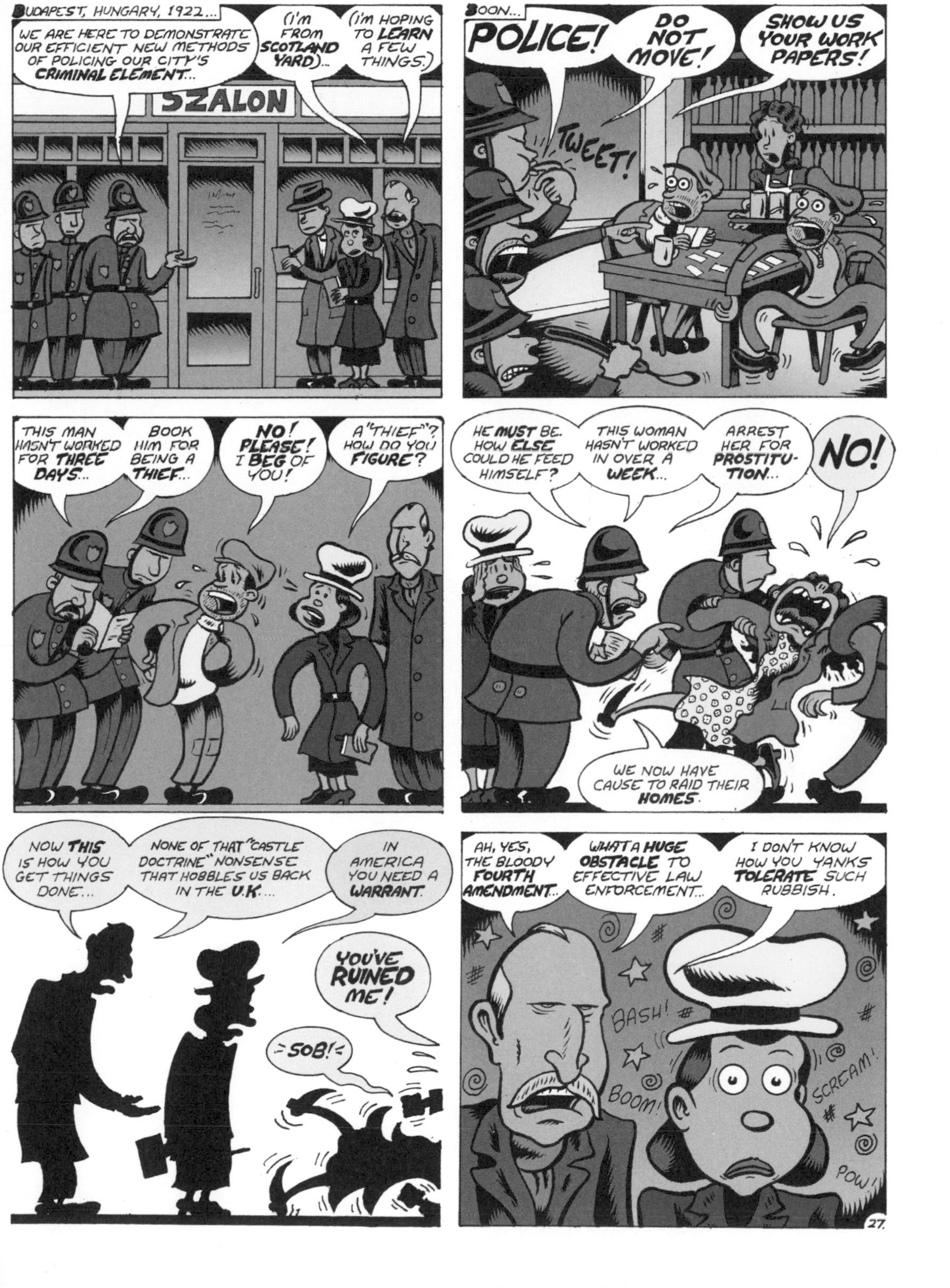
BUDAPEST, HUNGARY, 1922...
WE ARE HERE TO DEMONSTRATE OUR EFFICIENT NEW METHODS OF POLICING OUR CITY'S CRIMINAL ELEMENT...
(I'M FROM SCOTLAND YARD)...
(I'M HOPING TO LEARN A FEW THINGS.)
SZALON
SOON...
POLICE!
DO NOT MOVE!
SHOW US YOUR WORK PAPERS!
TWEET!
THIS MAN HASN'T WORKED FOR THREE DAYS...
BOOK HIM FOR BEING A THIEF...
NO! PLEASE! I BEG OF YOU!
A "THIEF"? HOW DO YOU FIGURE?
HE MUST BE. HOW ELSE COULD HE FEED HIMSELF?
THIS WOMAN HASN'T WORKED IN OVER A WEEK...
ARREST HER FOR PROSTITUTION...
NO!
WE NOW HAVE CAUSE TO RAID THEIR HOMES.
NOW THIS IS HOW YOU GET THINGS DONE...
NONE OF THAT "CASTLE DOCTRINE" NONSENSE THAT HOBBLES US BACK IN THE U.K....
IN AMERICA YOU NEED A WARRANT.
YOU'VE RUINED ME!
SOB!
AH, YES, THE BLOODY FOURTH AMENDMENT...
WHAT A HUGE OBSTACLE TO EFFECTIVE LAW ENFORCEMENT...
I DON'T KNOW HOW YOU YANKS TOLERATE SUCH RUBBISH.
BASH!
BOOM!
SCREAM!
POW!

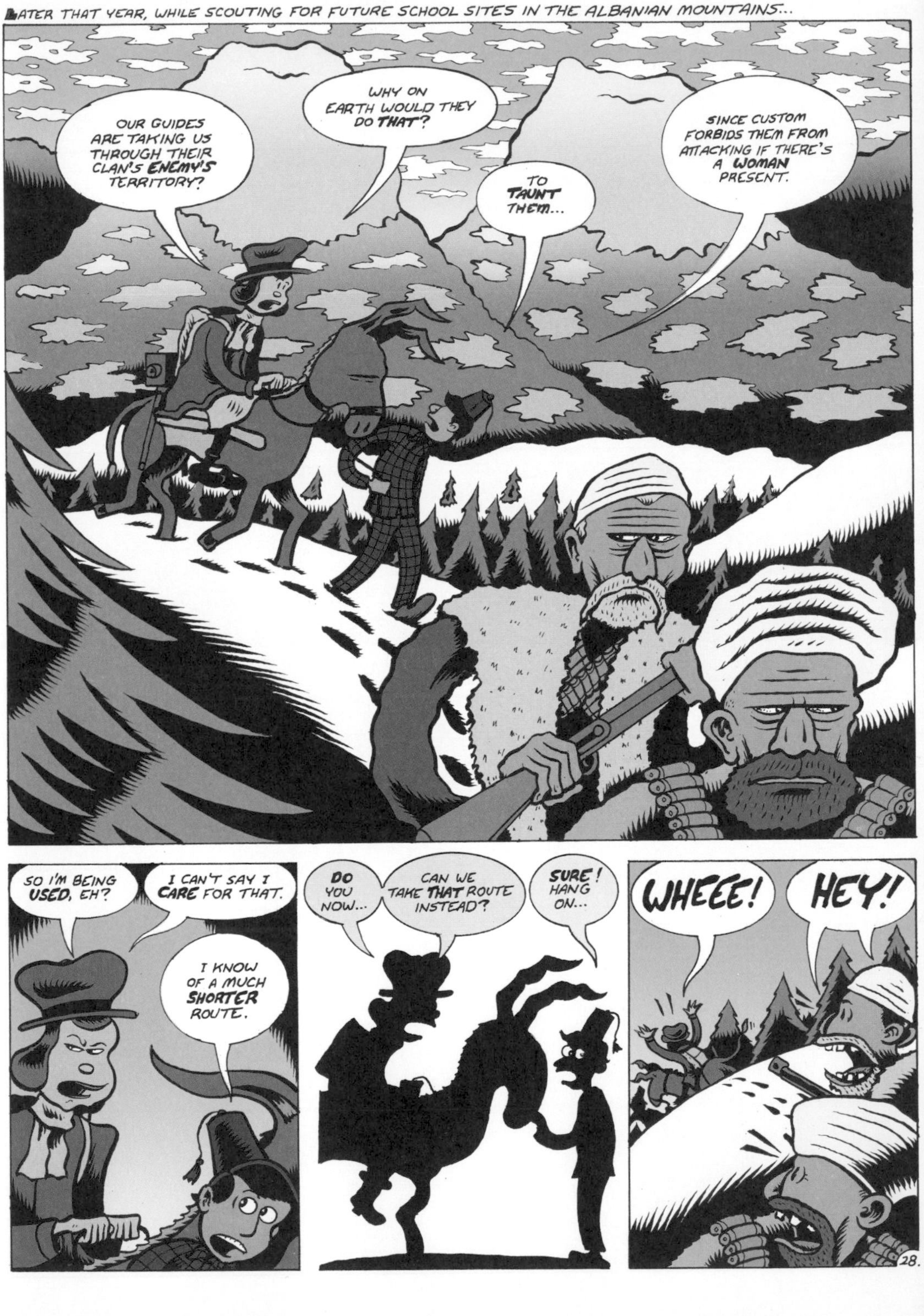
LATER THAT YEAR, WHILE SCOUTING FOR FUTURE SCHOOL SITES IN THE ALBANIAN MOUNTAINS...
OUR GUIDES ARE TAKING US THROUGH THEIR CLAN'S ENEMY'S TERRITORY?
WHY ON EARTH WOULD THEY DO THAT?
TO TAUNT THEM...
SINCE CUSTOM FORBIDS THEM FROM ATTACKING IF THERE'S A WOMAN PRESENT.
SO I'M BEING USED, EH?
I CAN'T SAY I CARE FOR THAT.
I KNOW OF A MUCH SHORTER ROUTE.
DO YOU NOW...
CAN WE TAKE THAT ROUTE INSTEAD?
SURE! HANG ON...
WHEEE!
HEY!

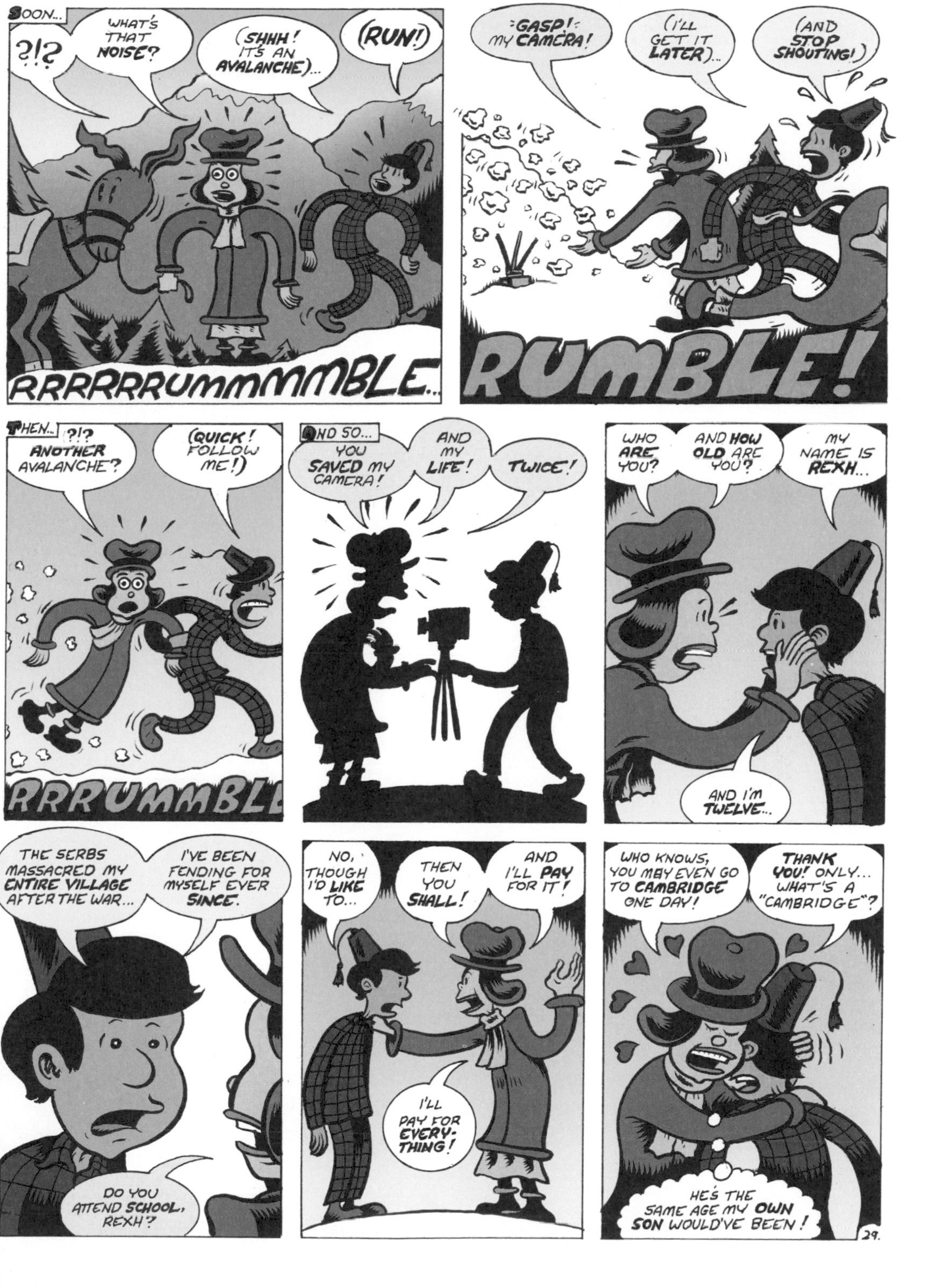
SOON...
?!?
WHAT'S THAT NOISE?
(SHHH! IT'S AN AVALANCHE)...
(RUN!)
RRRRRRUMMMMBLE...
:GASP!: MY CAMERA!
(I'LL GET IT LATER)...
(AND STOP SHOUTING!)
RUMBLE!
THEN...
?!? ANOTHER AVALANCHE?
(QUICK! FOLLOW ME!)
RRRUMMBLE
AND SO...
YOU SAVED MY CAMERA!
AND MY LIFE!
TWICE!
WHO ARE YOU?
AND HOW OLD ARE YOU?
MY NAME IS REXH...
AND I'M TWELVE...
THE SERBS MASSACRED MY ENTIRE VILLAGE AFTER THE WAR...
I'VE BEEN FENDING FOR MYSELF EVER SINCE.
DO YOU ATTEND SCHOOL, REXH?
NO, THOUGH I'D LIKE TO...
THEN YOU SHALL!
AND I'LL PAY FOR IT!
I'LL PAY FOR EVERY-THING!
WHO KNOWS, YOU MAY EVEN GO TO CAMBRIDGE ONE DAY!
THANK YOU! ONLY... WHAT'S A "CAMBRIDGE"?
HE'S THE SAME AGE MY OWN SON WOULD'VE BEEN!

ARMENIA, 1923: SIGNS OF THE RECENT GENOCIDE ARE STILL **EVERYWHERE**...

SUCH AS HOMES THAT HAD BEEN TORN APART TO USE THE WOOD FOR FUEL, ONLY TO HAVE THEIR INHABITANTS DIE FROM **EXPOSURE**.

THE ONLY REMAINING SURVIVORS WERE **SORE-INFESTED CHILDREN** WHO LIVED ON ROOTS AND WORMS...

AND WHO SCREAMED LIKE CAUGHT ANIMALS WHEN AID WORKERS PULLED THEM FROM THEIR **HIDING PLACES**.

AT THE FOOT OF A CLIFF LIE A PILE OF **HUMAN REMAINS**...

ONLY THESE VICTIMS WERE **TATARS** — PUSH TO THEIR DEATHS BY THEIR ARMENIAN NEIGHBORS!

MEANWHILE, A GROUP OF ARMENIAN MONKS **GOURGED THEMSELVES** EVERY EVENING, WHILE STARVING CHILDEN BANGED AT THE DOOR, BEGGING FOR **SCRAPS**.

DO YOU HAVE YOUR **CAMERA** WITH YOU?

A PHOTO OF THOSE STARVING BRATS WOULD BE GOOD FOR **FUNDRAISING**.

BANG-BANG-BANG

WHILE AMERICAN AID WORKERS TEACH THE LOCALS BETTER FARMING TECHNIQUES, SOVIET BUREAUCRATS RIDE OFF WITH THE **RESULTS**...

AT LEAST THEY'RE BETTER THAN THE **TSARS**.

ARE THEY?

THE FARMERS ARE PROMISED "RE-DISTRIBUTION," BUT THEY KNOW THEY ARE DOOMED TO **STARVE**.

THESE IDEOLOGICALLY DRIVEN CIVIL SERVANTS KNOW **NOTHING** ABOUT AGRICULTURE, YET THEY ARE SURE TO PREVAIL...

WE ORDERED EVERY-ONE TO GROW WHEAT LAST YEAR...

ONLY NOW WE HAVE **TOO MUCH** WHEAT...

SO THIS YEAR: **NO MORE WHEAT**!

GHAAA!!! NOOoo...

SOMEONE IS BEING **TORTURED** BACK THERE!

DID HE TRY TO GROW **WHEAT**?

SINCE WE WESTERNERS WILL ALL LEAVE EVENTUALLY, WHILE THE RUSSIANS ARE **HERE TO STAY**!

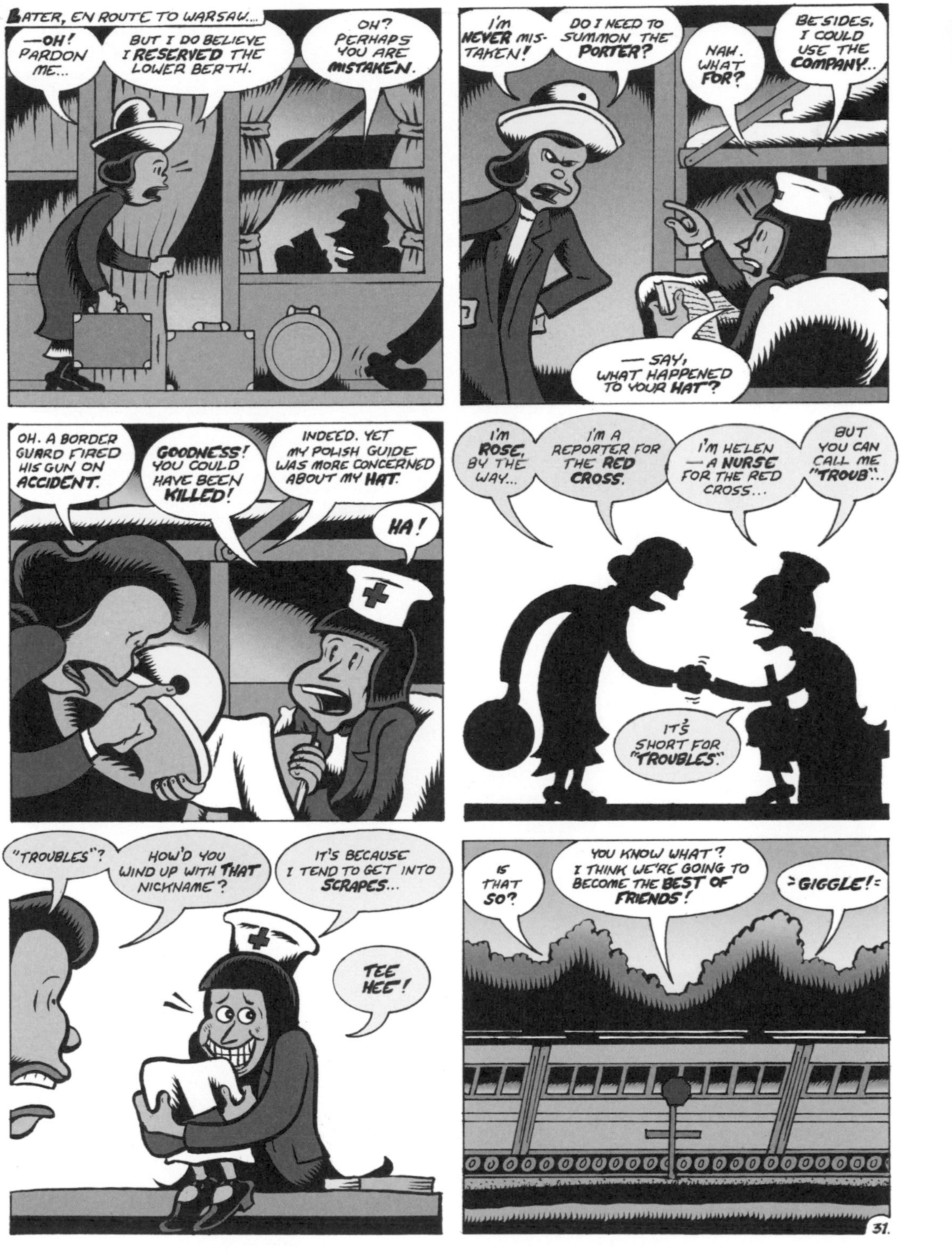
LATER, EN ROUTE TO WARSAW...
—OH! PARDON ME...
BUT I DO BELIEVE I RESERVED THE LOWER BERTH.
OH? PERHAPS YOU ARE MISTAKEN.
I'M NEVER MISTAKEN!
DO I NEED TO SUMMON THE PORTER?
NAH. WHAT FOR?
BESIDES, I COULD USE THE COMPANY...
— SAY, WHAT HAPPENED TO YOUR HAT?
OH. A BORDER GUARD FIRED HIS GUN ON ACCIDENT.
GOODNESS! YOU COULD HAVE BEEN KILLED!
INDEED. YET MY POLISH GUIDE WAS MORE CONCERNED ABOUT MY HAT.
HA!
I'M ROSE, BY THE WAY...
I'M A REPORTER FOR THE RED CROSS.
I'M HELEN — A NURSE FOR THE RED CROSS...
BUT YOU CAN CALL ME "TROUB"...
IT'S SHORT FOR "TROUBLES".
"TROUBLES"?
HOW'D YOU WIND UP WITH THAT NICKNAME?
IT'S BECAUSE I TEND TO GET INTO SCRAPES...
TEE HEE!
IS THAT SO?
YOU KNOW WHAT? I THINK WE'RE GOING TO BECOME THE BEST OF FRIENDS!
=GIGGLE!=

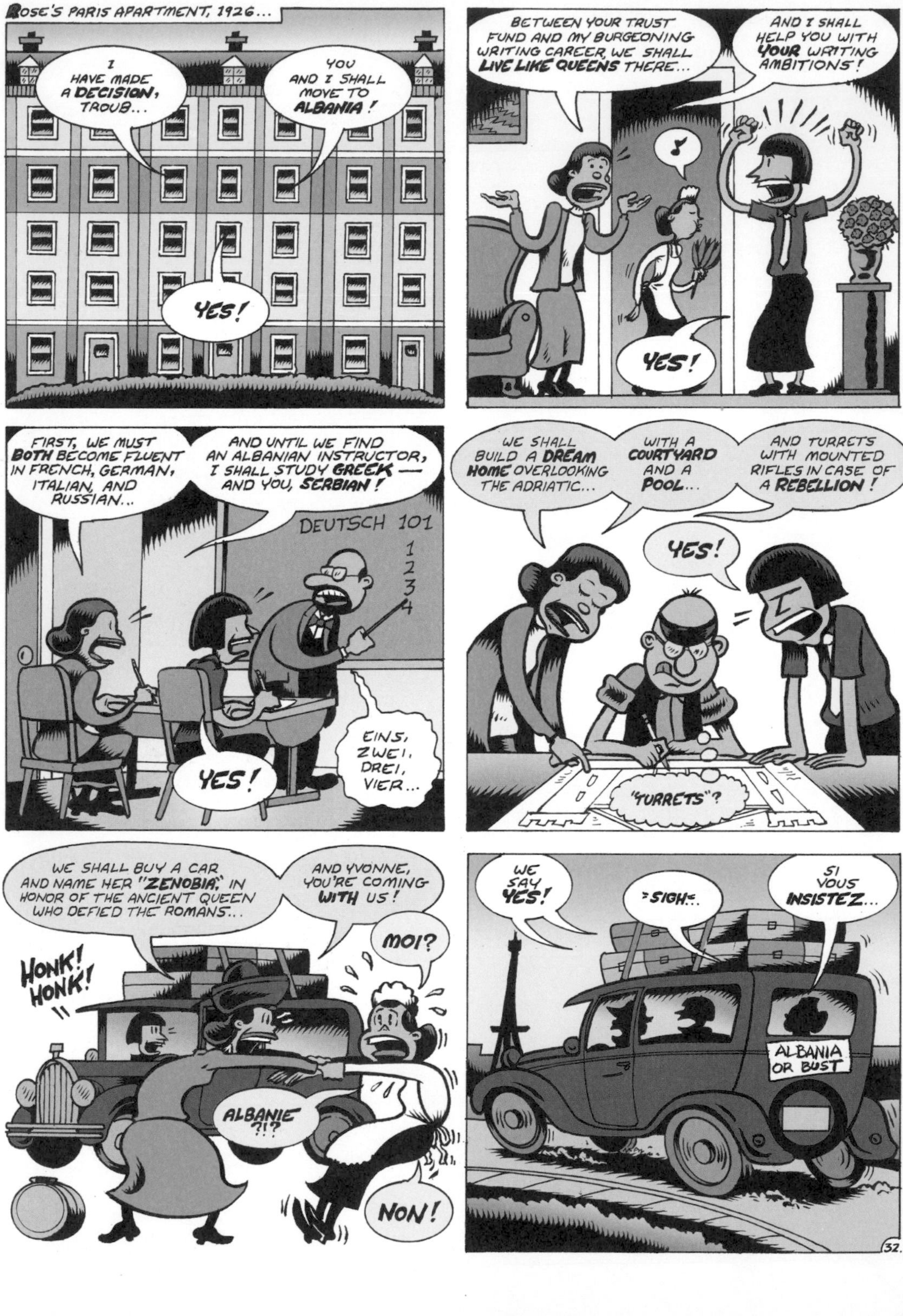
ROSE'S PARIS APARTMENT, 1926...
I HAVE MADE A DECISION, TROUB...
YOU AND I SHALL MOVE TO ALBANIA!
YES!
BETWEEN YOUR TRUST FUND AND MY BURGEONING WRITING CAREER, WE SHALL LIVE LIKE QUEENS THERE...
AND I SHALL HELP YOU WITH YOUR WRITING AMBITIONS!
YES!
FIRST, WE MUST BOTH BECOME FLUENT IN FRENCH, GERMAN, ITALIAN, AND RUSSIAN...
AND UNTIL WE FIND AN ALBANIAN INSTRUCTOR, I SHALL STUDY GREEK — AND YOU, SERBIAN!
DEUTSCH 101
1 2 3 4
YES!
EINS, ZWEI, DREI, VIER...
WE SHALL BUILD A DREAM HOME OVERLOOKING THE ADRIATIC...
WITH A COURTYARD AND A POOL...
AND TURRETS WITH MOUNTED RIFLES IN CASE OF A REBELLION!
YES!
"TURRETS"?
WE SHALL BUY A CAR AND NAME HER "ZENOBIA," IN HONOR OF THE ANCIENT QUEEN WHO DEFIED THE ROMANS...
AND YVONNE, YOU'RE COMING WITH US!
HONK! HONK!
MOI?
ALBANIE ?!?
NON!
WE SAY YES!
SIGH...
SI VOUS INSISTEZ...
ALBANIA OR BUST

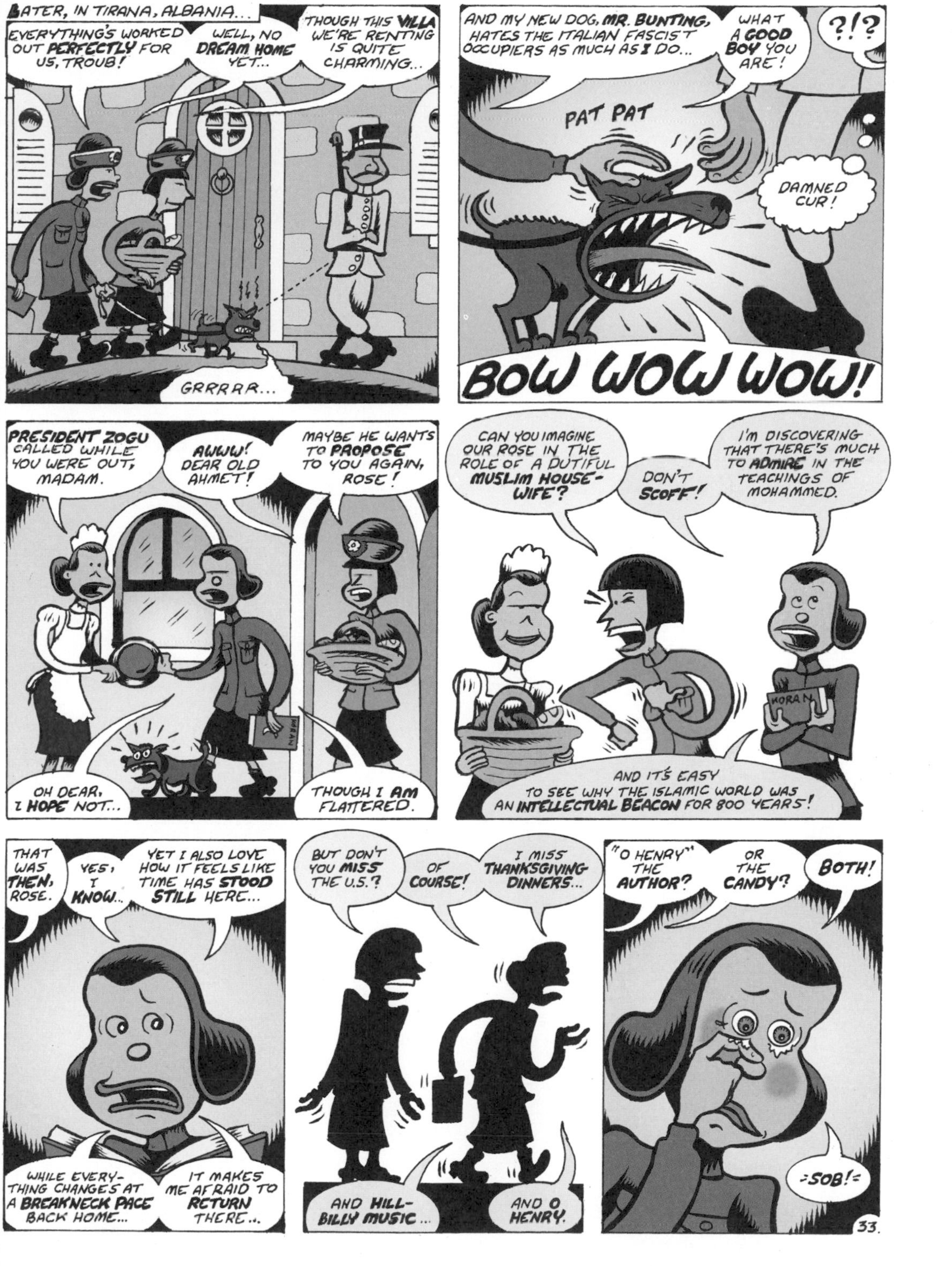
LATER, IN TIRANA, ALBANIA...
EVERYTHING'S WORKED OUT PERFECTLY FOR US, TROUB!
WELL, NO DREAM HOME YET...
THOUGH THIS VILLA WE'RE RENTING IS QUITE CHARMING...
GRRRRR...
AND MY NEW DOG, MR. BUNTING, HATES THE ITALIAN FASCIST OCCUPIERS AS MUCH AS I DO...
WHAT A GOOD BOY YOU ARE!
?!?
PAT PAT
DAMNED CUR!
BOW WOW WOW!
PRESIDENT ZOGU CALLED WHILE YOU WERE OUT, MADAM.
AWWW! DEAR OLD AHMET!
MAYBE HE WANTS TO PROPOSE TO YOU AGAIN, ROSE!
OH DEAR, I HOPE NOT...
THOUGH I AM FLATTERED.
CAN YOU IMAGINE OUR ROSE IN THE ROLE OF A DUTIFUL MUSLIM HOUSE-WIFE?
DON'T SCOFF!
I'M DISCOVERING THAT THERE'S MUCH TO ADMIRE IN THE TEACHINGS OF MOHAMMED.
KORAN
AND IT'S EASY TO SEE WHY THE ISLAMIC WORLD WAS AN INTELLECTUAL BEACON FOR 800 YEARS!
THAT WAS THEN, ROSE.
YES, I KNOW...
YET I ALSO LOVE HOW IT FEELS LIKE TIME HAS STOOD STILL HERE...
WHILE EVERY-THING CHANGES AT A BREAKNECK PACE BACK HOME...
IT MAKES ME AFRAID TO RETURN THERE...
BUT DON'T YOU MISS THE U.S.?
OF COURSE!
I MISS THANKSGIVING DINNERS...
AND HILL-BILLY MUSIC...
AND O HENRY.
"O HENRY" THE AUTHOR?
OR THE CANDY?
BOTH!
=SOB!=

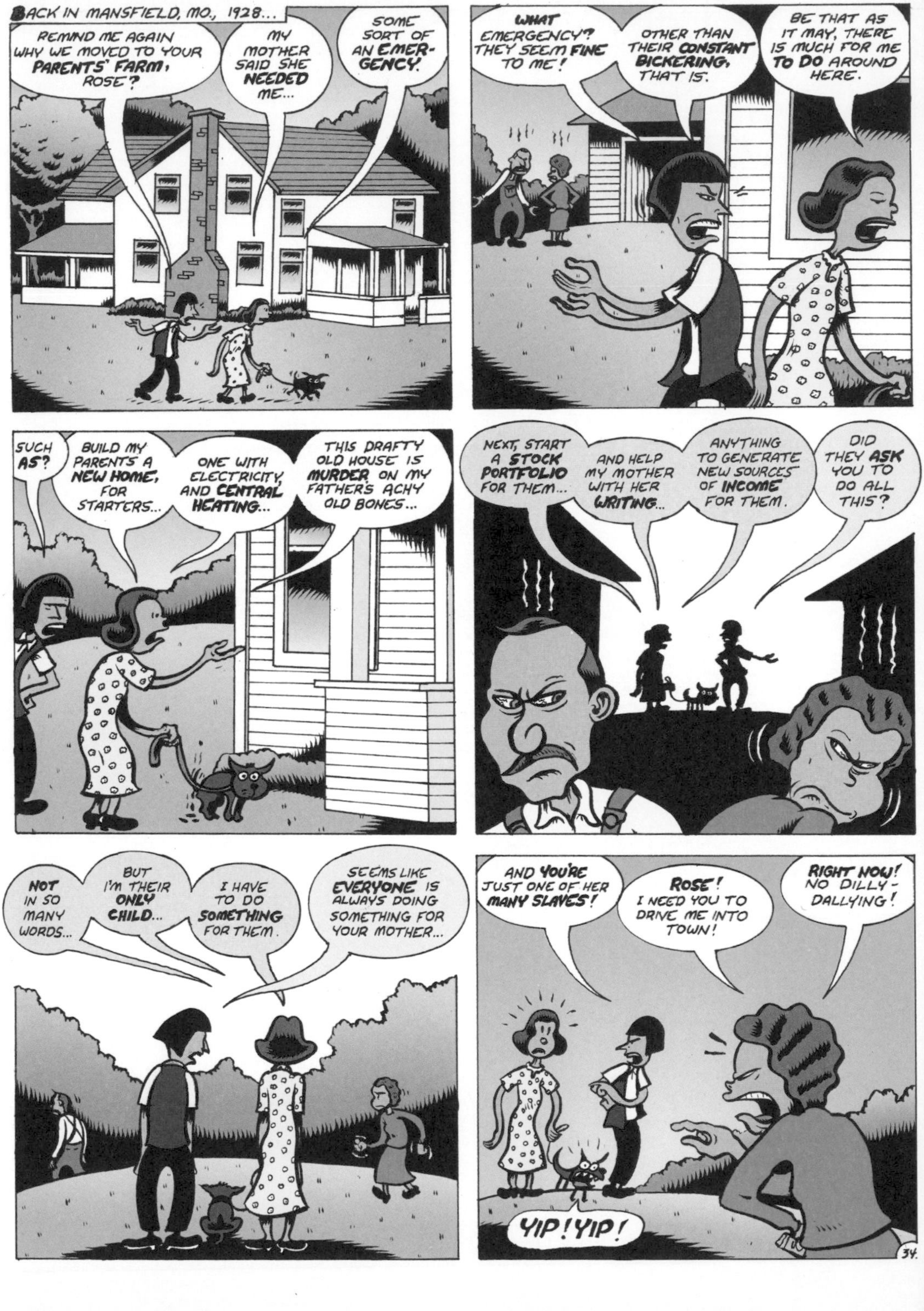
BACK IN MANSFIELD, MO., 1928...
REMIND ME AGAIN WHY WE MOVED TO YOUR PARENTS' FARM, ROSE?
MY MOTHER SAID SHE NEEDED ME...
SOME SORT OF AN EMERGENCY.
WHAT EMERGENCY? THEY SEEM FINE TO ME!
OTHER THAN THEIR CONSTANT BICKERING, THAT IS.
BE THAT AS IT MAY, THERE IS MUCH FOR ME TO DO AROUND HERE.
SUCH AS?
BUILD MY PARENTS A NEW HOME, FOR STARTERS...
ONE WITH ELECTRICITY, AND CENTRAL HEATING...
THIS DRAFTY OLD HOUSE IS MURDER ON MY FATHER'S ACHY OLD BONES...
NEXT, START A STOCK PORTFOLIO FOR THEM...
AND HELP MY MOTHER WITH HER WRITING...
ANYTHING TO GENERATE NEW SOURCES OF INCOME FOR THEM.
DID THEY ASK YOU TO DO ALL THIS?
NOT IN SO MANY WORDS...
BUT I'M THEIR ONLY CHILD...
I HAVE TO DO SOMETHING FOR THEM.
SEEMS LIKE EVERYONE IS ALWAYS DOING SOMETHING FOR YOUR MOTHER...
AND YOU'RE JUST ONE OF HER MANY SLAVES!
ROSE! I NEED YOU TO DRIVE ME INTO TOWN!
RIGHT NOW! NO DILLY-DALLYING!
YIP! YIP!

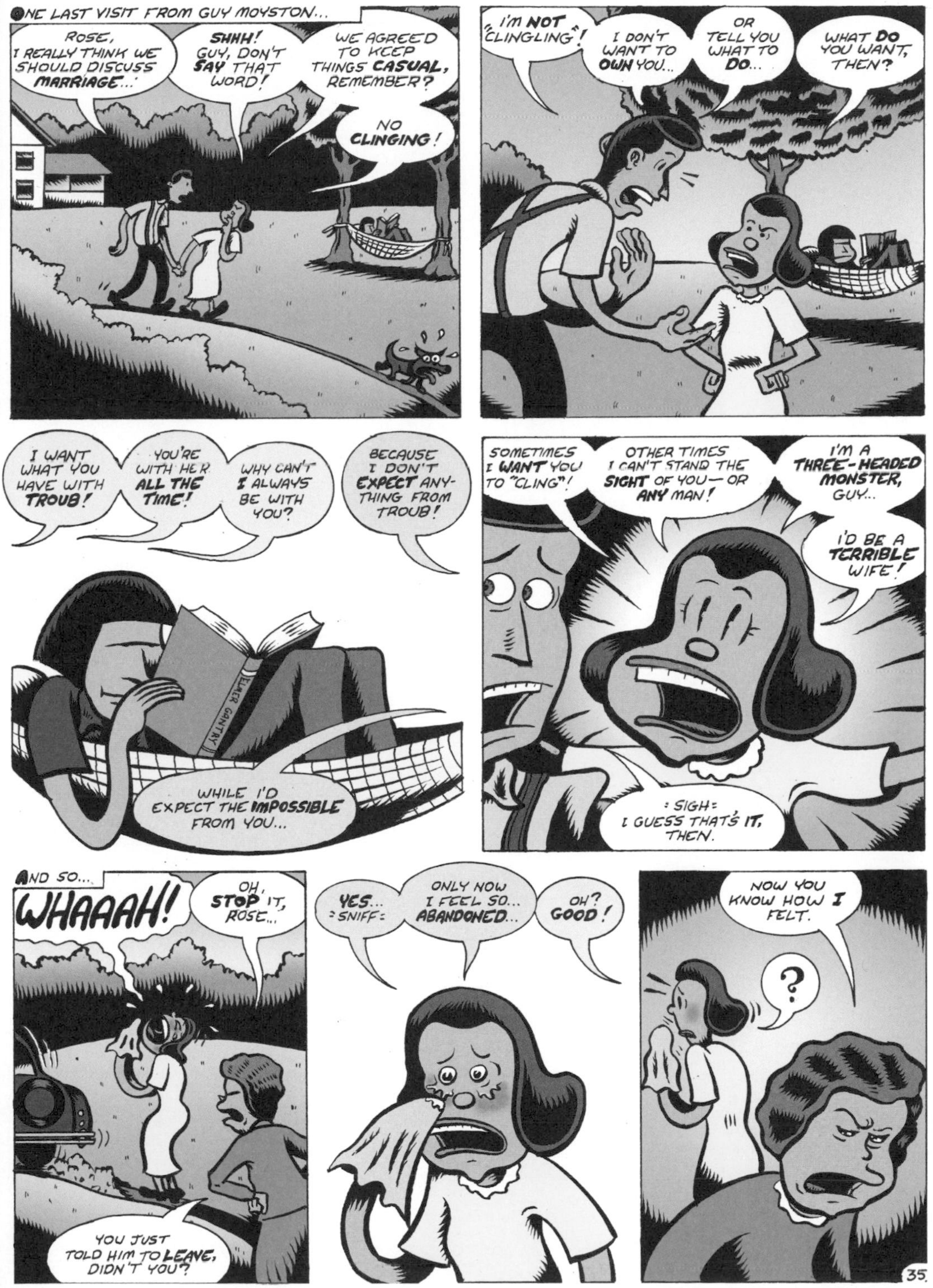
ONE LAST VISIT FROM GUY MOYSTON...
ROSE, I REALLY THINK WE SHOULD DISCUSS MARRIAGE...
SHHH! GUY, DON'T SAY THAT WORD!
WE AGREED TO KEEP THINGS CASUAL, REMEMBER?
NO CLINGING!
I'M NOT "CLINGLING"!
I DON'T WANT TO OWN YOU...
OR TELL YOU WHAT TO DO...
WHAT DO YOU WANT, THEN?
I WANT WHAT YOU HAVE WITH TROUB!
YOU'RE WITH HER ALL THE TIME!
WHY CAN'T I ALWAYS BE WITH YOU?
BECAUSE I DON'T EXPECT ANY-THING FROM TROUB!
ELMER GANTRY
WHILE I'D EXPECT THE IMPOSSIBLE FROM YOU...
SOMETIMES I WANT YOU TO "CLING"!
OTHER TIMES I CAN'T STAND THE SIGHT OF YOU— OR ANY MAN!
I'M A THREE-HEADED MONSTER, GUY...
I'D BE A TERRIBLE WIFE!
:SIGH: I GUESS THAT'S IT, THEN.
AND SO...
WHAAAH!
OH, STOP IT, ROSE...
YOU JUST TOLD HIM TO LEAVE, DIDN'T YOU?
YES... :SNIFF:
ONLY NOW I FEEL SO... ABANDONED...
OH? GOOD!
NOW YOU KNOW HOW I FELT.
?

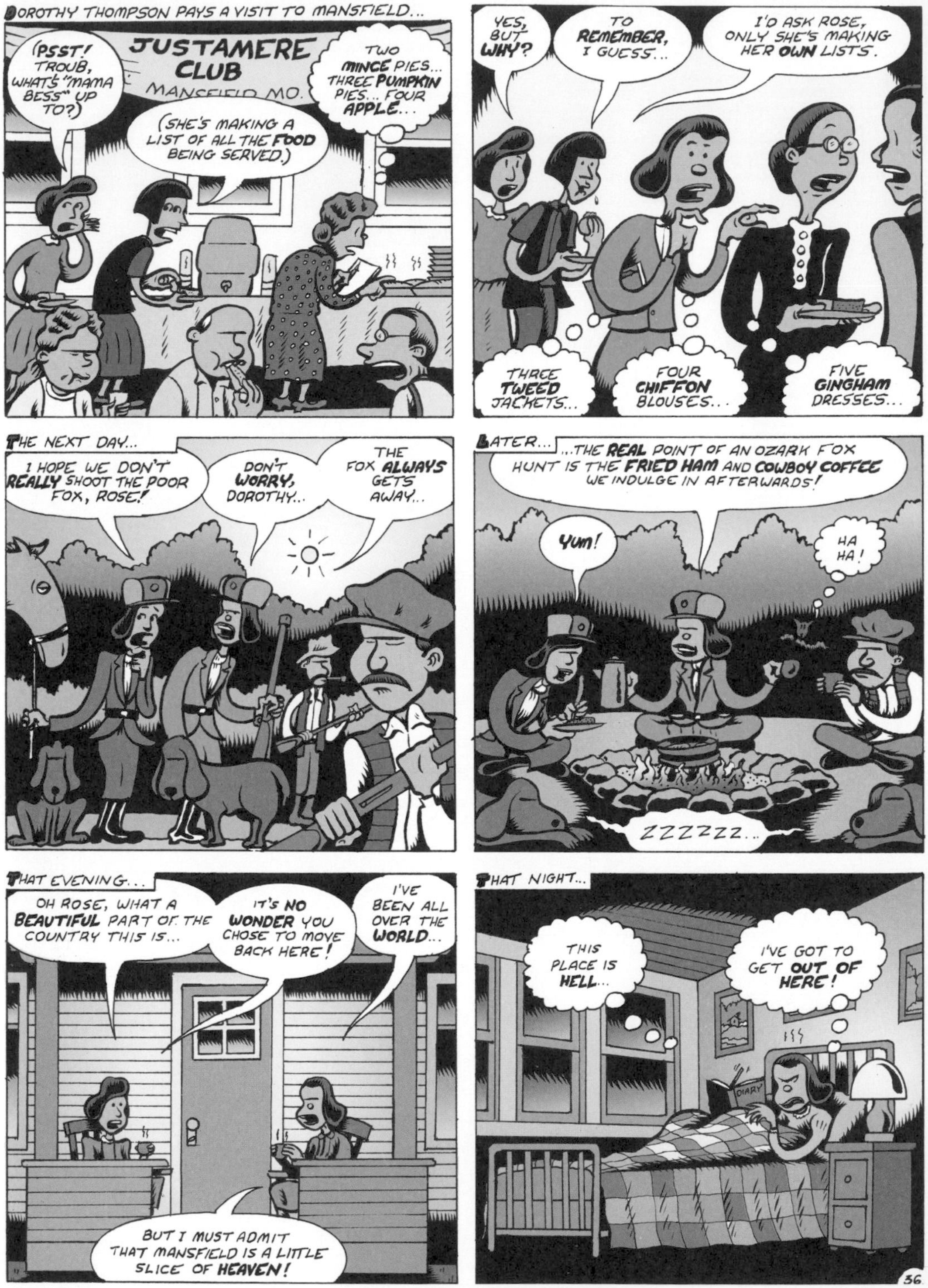
DOROTHY THOMPSON PAYS A VISIT TO MANSFIELD...
JUSTAMERE CLUB MANSFIELD MO.
(PSST! TROUB, WHAT'S "MAMA BESS" UP TO?)
(SHE'S MAKING A LIST OF ALL THE FOOD BEING SERVED.)
TWO MINCE PIES... THREE PUMPKIN PIES... FOUR APPLE...
YES, BUT WHY?
TO REMEMBER, I GUESS...
I'D ASK ROSE, ONLY SHE'S MAKING HER OWN LISTS.
THREE TWEED JACKETS...
FOUR CHIFFON BLOUSES...
FIVE GINGHAM DRESSES...
THE NEXT DAY...
I HOPE WE DON'T REALLY SHOOT THE POOR FOX, ROSE!
DON'T WORRY, DOROTHY...
THE FOX ALWAYS GETS AWAY...
LATER...
...THE REAL POINT OF AN OZARK FOX HUNT IS THE FRIED HAM AND COWBOY COFFEE WE INDULGE IN AFTERWARDS!
YUM!
HA HA!
ZZZZZZ...
THAT EVENING...
OH ROSE, WHAT A BEAUTIFUL PART OF THE COUNTRY THIS IS...
IT'S NO WONDER YOU CHOSE TO MOVE BACK HERE!
I'VE BEEN ALL OVER THE WORLD...
BUT I MUST ADMIT THAT MANSFIELD IS A LITTLE SLICE OF HEAVEN!
THAT NIGHT...
THIS PLACE IS HELL...
I'VE GOT TO GET OUT OF HERE!
DIARY

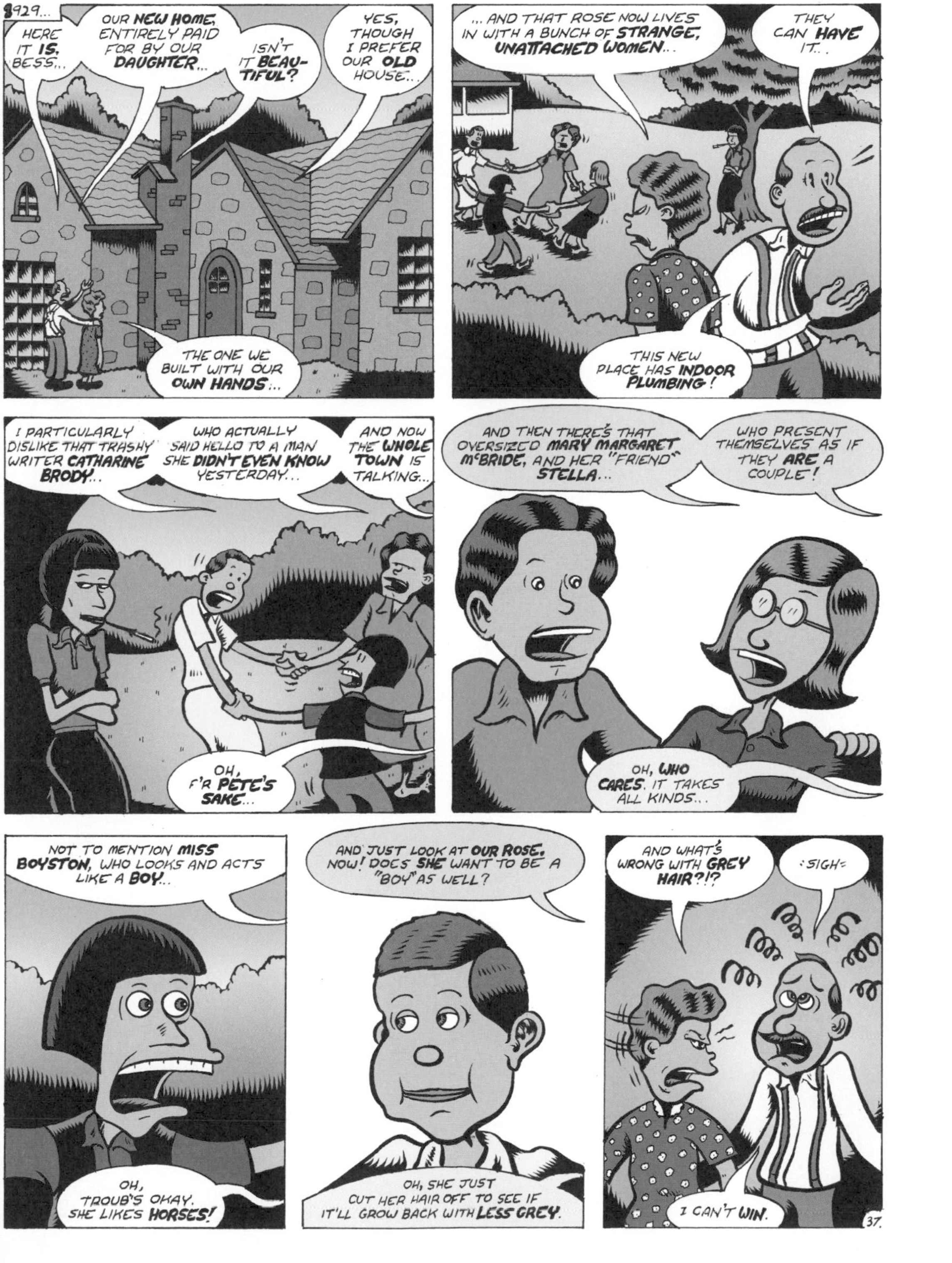
1929...
HERE IT IS, BESS...
OUR NEW HOME, ENTIRELY PAID FOR BY OUR DAUGHTER...
ISN'T IT BEAUTIFUL?
YES, THOUGH I PREFER OUR OLD HOUSE...
THE ONE WE BUILT WITH OUR OWN HANDS...
... AND THAT ROSE NOW LIVES IN WITH A BUNCH OF STRANGE, UNATTACHED WOMEN...
THEY CAN HAVE IT...
THIS NEW PLACE HAS INDOOR PLUMBING!
I PARTICULARLY DISLIKE THAT TRASHY WRITER CATHARINE BRODY...
WHO ACTUALLY SAID HELLO TO A MAN SHE DIDN'T EVEN KNOW YESTERDAY...
AND NOW THE WHOLE TOWN IS TALKING...
OH, F'R PETE'S SAKE...
AND THEN THERE'S THAT OVERSIZED MARY MARGARET M^cBRIDE, AND HER "FRIEND" STELLA...
WHO PRESENT THEMSELVES AS IF THEY ARE A COUPLE!
OH, WHO CARES. IT TAKES ALL KINDS...
NOT TO MENTION MISS BOYSTON, WHO LOOKS AND ACTS LIKE A BOY...
OH, TROUB'S OKAY. SHE LIKES HORSES!
AND JUST LOOK AT OUR ROSE, NOW! DOES SHE WANT TO BE A "BOY" AS WELL?
OH, SHE JUST CUT HER HAIR OFF TO SEE IF IT'LL GROW BACK WITH LESS GREY.
AND WHAT'S WRONG WITH GREY HAIR?!?
=SIGH=
I CAN'T WIN.

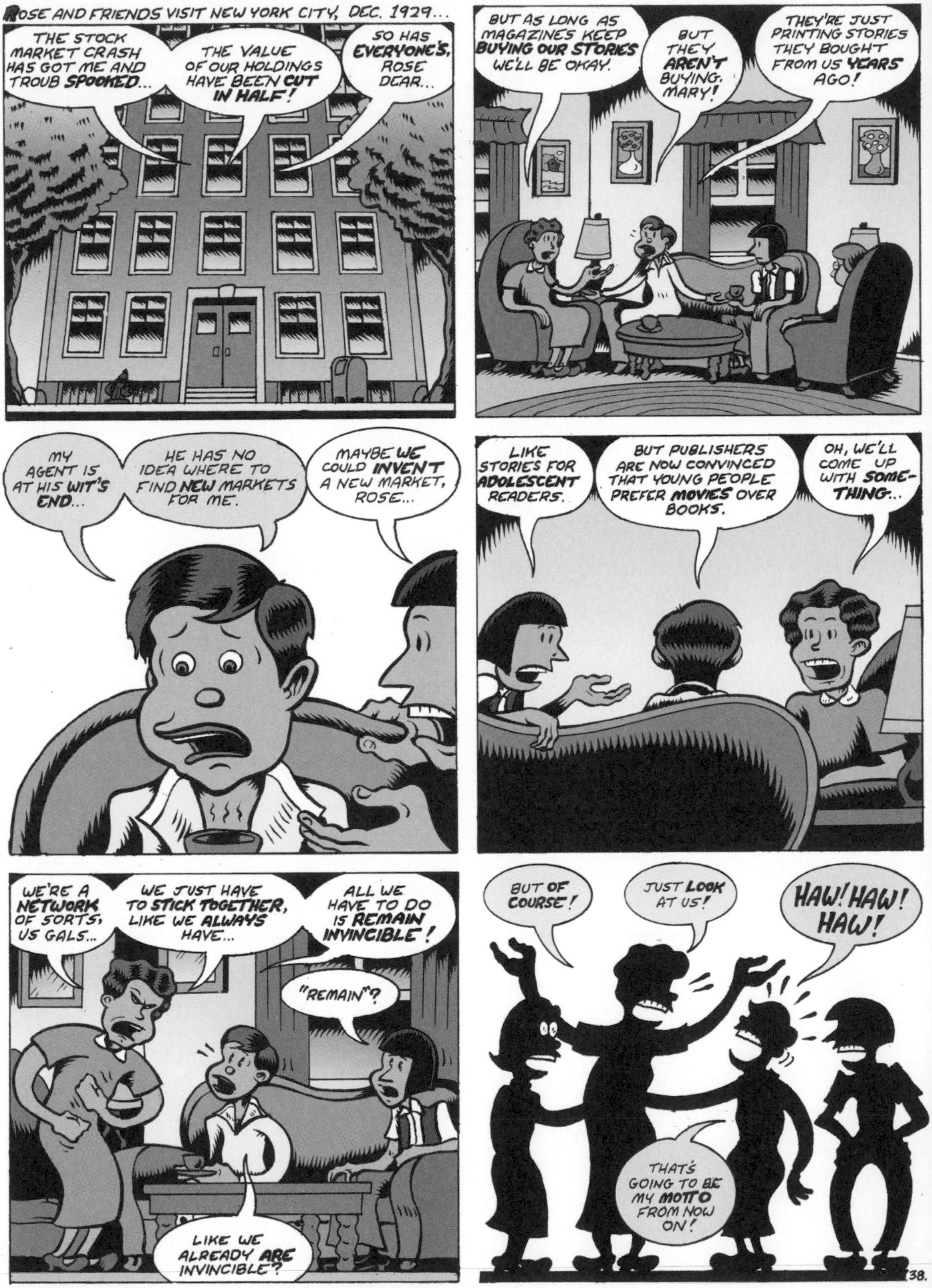
ROSE AND FRIENDS VISIT NEW YORK CITY, DEC. 1929...
THE STOCK MARKET CRASH HAS GOT ME AND TROUB SPOOKED...
THE VALUE OF OUR HOLDINGS HAVE BEEN CUT IN HALF!
SO HAS EVERYONE'S, ROSE DEAR...
BUT AS LONG AS MAGAZINES KEEP BUYING OUR STORIES WE'LL BE OKAY.
BUT THEY AREN'T BUYING, MARY!
THEY'RE JUST PRINTING STORIES THEY BOUGHT FROM US YEARS AGO!
MY AGENT IS AT HIS WIT'S END...
HE HAS NO IDEA WHERE TO FIND NEW MARKETS FOR ME.
MAYBE WE COULD INVENT A NEW MARKET, ROSE...
LIKE STORIES FOR ADOLESCENT READERS.
BUT PUBLISHERS ARE NOW CONVINCED THAT YOUNG PEOPLE PREFER MOVIES OVER BOOKS.
OH, WE'LL COME UP WITH SOMETHING...
WE'RE A NETWORK OF SORTS, US GALS...
WE JUST HAVE TO STICK TOGETHER, LIKE WE ALWAYS HAVE...
ALL WE HAVE TO DO IS REMAIN INVINCIBLE!
"REMAIN"?
LIKE WE ALREADY ARE INVINCIBLE?
BUT OF COURSE!
JUST LOOK AT US!
HAW! HAW! HAW!
THAT'S GOING TO BE MY MOTTO FROM NOW ON!

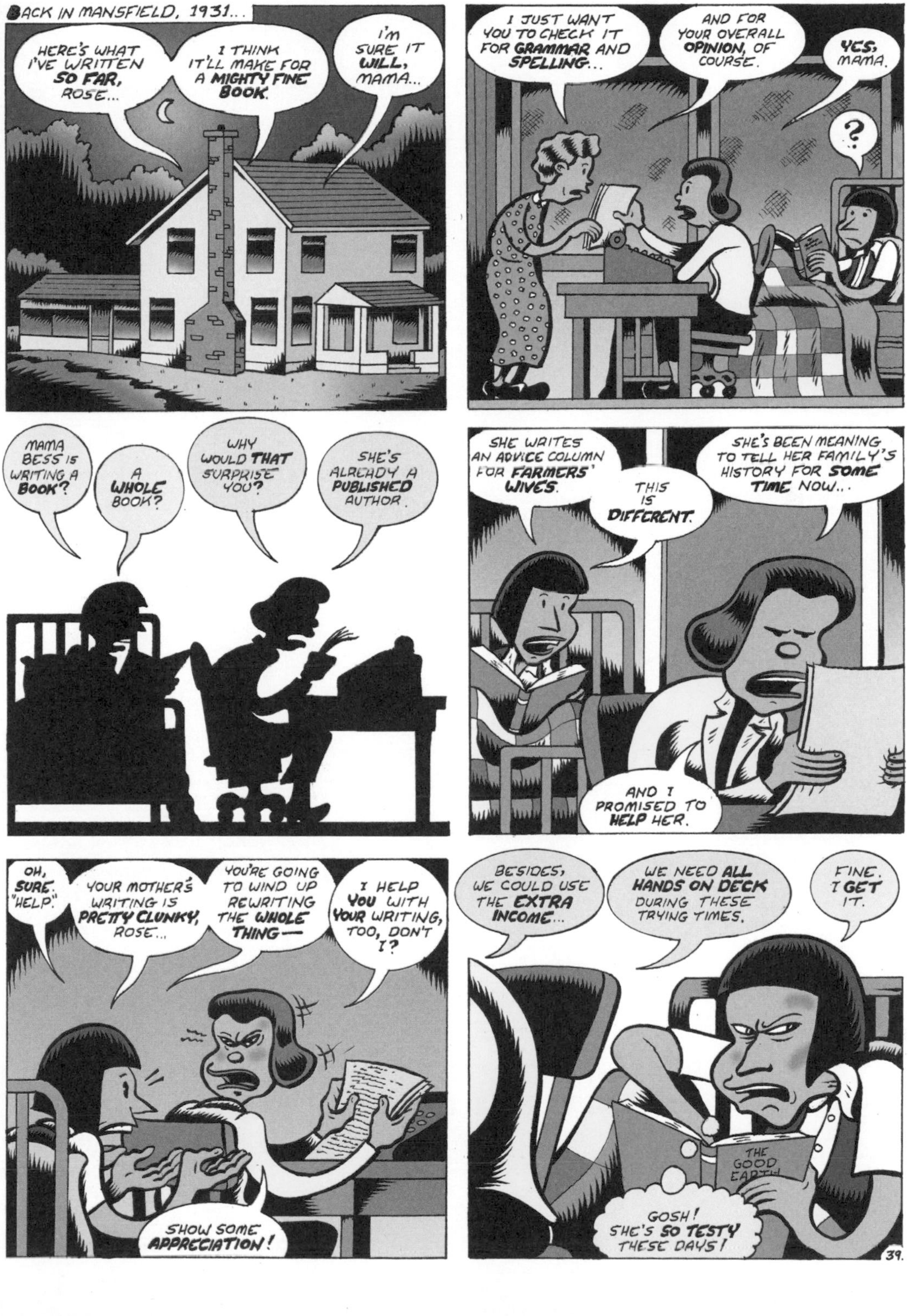
BACK IN MANSFIELD, 1931...
HERE'S WHAT I'VE WRITTEN SO FAR, ROSE...
I THINK IT'LL MAKE FOR A MIGHTY FINE BOOK.
I'M SURE IT WILL, MAMA...
I JUST WANT YOU TO CHECK IT FOR GRAMMAR AND SPELLING...
AND FOR YOUR OVERALL OPINION, OF COURSE.
YES, MAMA.
?
MAMA BESS IS WRITING A BOOK?
A WHOLE BOOK?
WHY WOULD THAT SURPRISE YOU?
SHE'S ALREADY A PUBLISHED AUTHOR.
SHE WRITES AN ADVICE COLUMN FOR FARMERS' WIVES.
THIS IS DIFFERENT.
SHE'S BEEN MEANING TO TELL HER FAMILY'S HISTORY FOR SOME TIME NOW...
AND I PROMISED TO HELP HER.
OH, SURE. "HELP."
YOUR MOTHER'S WRITING IS PRETTY CLUNKY, ROSE...
YOU'RE GOING TO WIND UP REWRITING THE WHOLE THING—
I HELP YOU WITH YOUR WRITING, TOO, DON'T I?
SHOW SOME APPRECIATION!
BESIDES, WE COULD USE THE EXTRA INCOME...
WE NEED ALL HANDS ON DECK DURING THESE TRYING TIMES.
FINE. I GET IT.
THE GOOD EARTH
GOSH! SHE'S SO TESTY THESE DAYS!

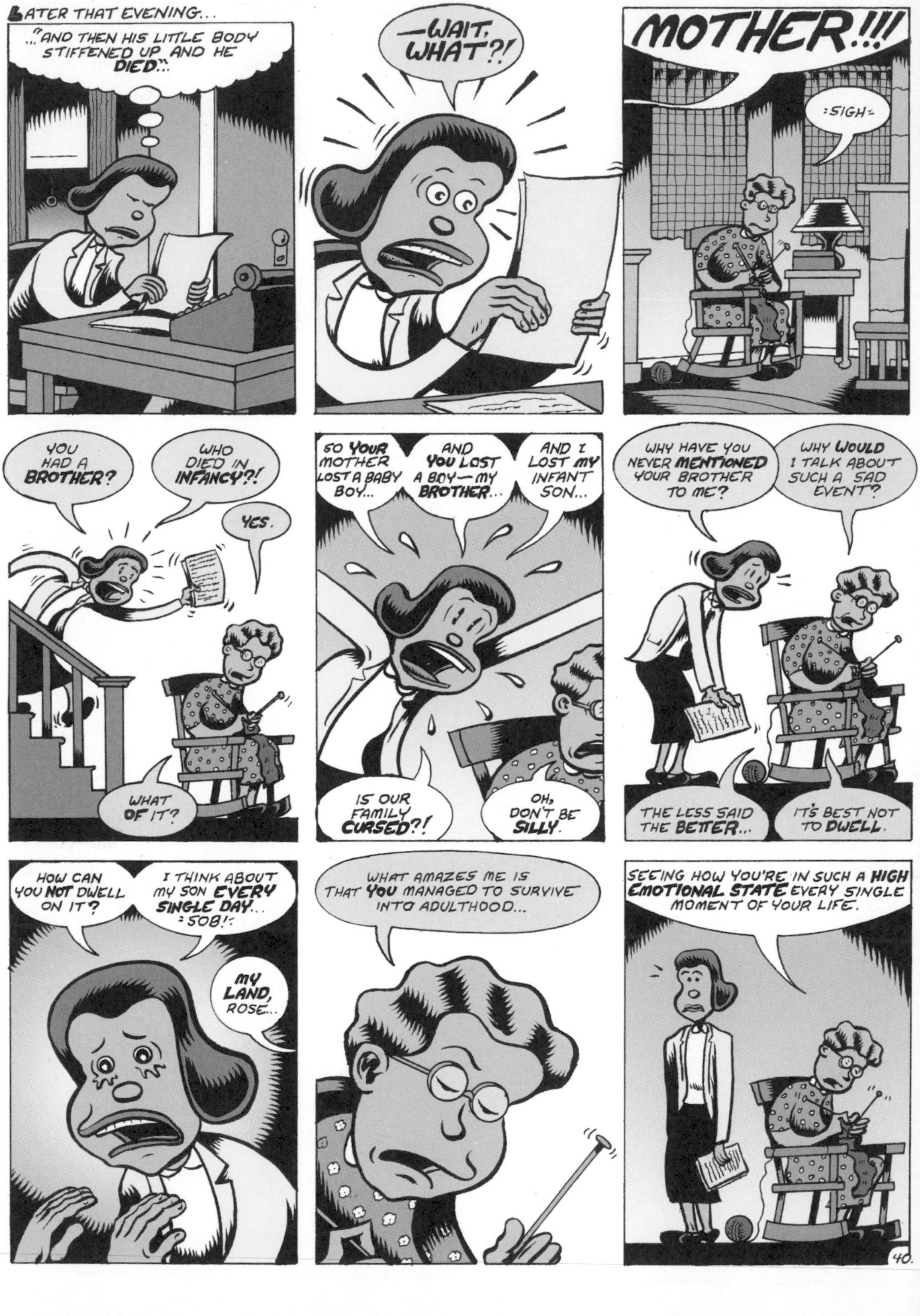
LATER THAT EVENING...
..."AND THEN HIS LITTLE BODY STIFFENED UP AND HE DIED"...
—WAIT, WHAT?!
MOTHER!!!
=SIGH=
YOU HAD A BROTHER?
WHO DIED IN INFANCY?!
YES.
WHAT OF IT?
SO YOUR MOTHER LOST A BABY BOY...
AND YOU LOST A BOY—MY BROTHER...
AND I LOST MY INFANT SON...
IS OUR FAMILY CURSED?!
OH, DON'T BE SILLY.
WHY HAVE YOU NEVER MENTIONED YOUR BROTHER TO ME?
WHY WOULD I TALK ABOUT SUCH A SAD EVENT?
THE LESS SAID THE BETTER...
IT'S BEST NOT TO DWELL.
HOW CAN YOU NOT DWELL ON IT?
I THINK ABOUT MY SON EVERY SINGLE DAY... =SOB!=
MY LAND, ROSE...
WHAT AMAZES ME IS THAT YOU MANAGED TO SURVIVE INTO ADULTHOOD...
SEEING HOW YOU'RE IN SUCH A HIGH EMOTIONAL STATE EVERY SINGLE MOMENT OF YOUR LIFE.

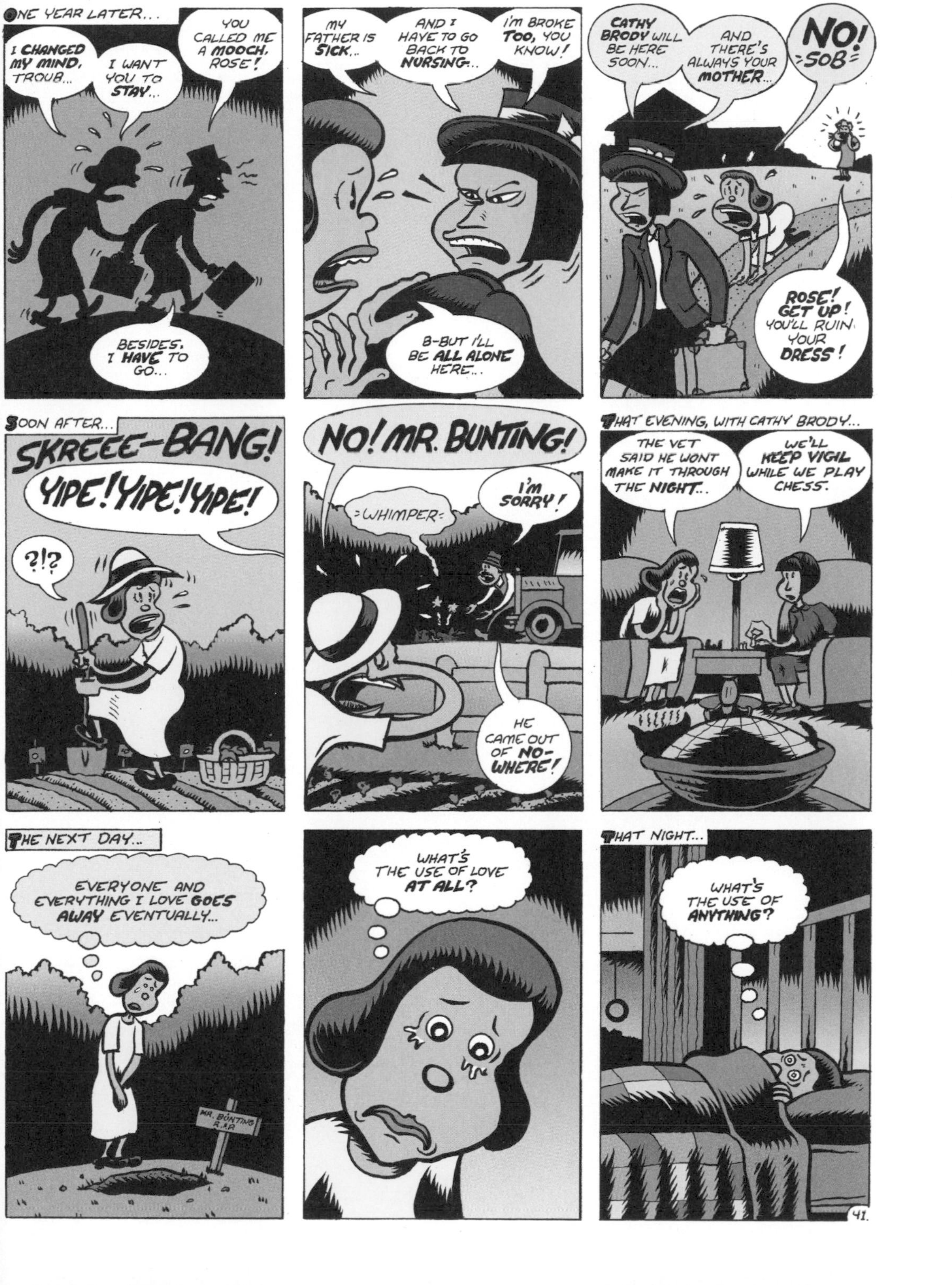
ONE YEAR LATER...
I CHANGED MY MIND, TROUB...
I WANT YOU TO STAY...
YOU CALLED ME A MOOCH, ROSE!
BESIDES, I HAVE TO GO...
MY FATHER IS SICK...
AND I HAVE TO GO BACK TO NURSING...
I'M BROKE TOO, YOU KNOW!
B-BUT I'LL BE ALL ALONE HERE...
CATHY BRODY WILL BE HERE SOON...
AND THERE'S ALWAYS YOUR MOTHER...
NO! SOB
ROSE! GET UP! YOU'LL RUIN YOUR DRESS!
SOON AFTER...
SKREEE-BANG!
YIPE! YIPE! YIPE!
?!?
NO! MR. BUNTING!
WHIMPER
I'M SORRY!
HE CAME OUT OF NO-WHERE!
THAT EVENING, WITH CATHY BRODY...
THE VET SAID HE WONT MAKE IT THROUGH THE NIGHT...
WE'LL KEEP VIGIL WHILE WE PLAY CHESS.
THE NEXT DAY...
EVERYONE AND EVERYTHING I LOVE GOES AWAY EVENTUALLY...
MR. BUNTING R.I.P.
WHAT'S THE USE OF LOVE AT ALL?
THAT NIGHT...
WHAT'S THE USE OF ANYTHING?

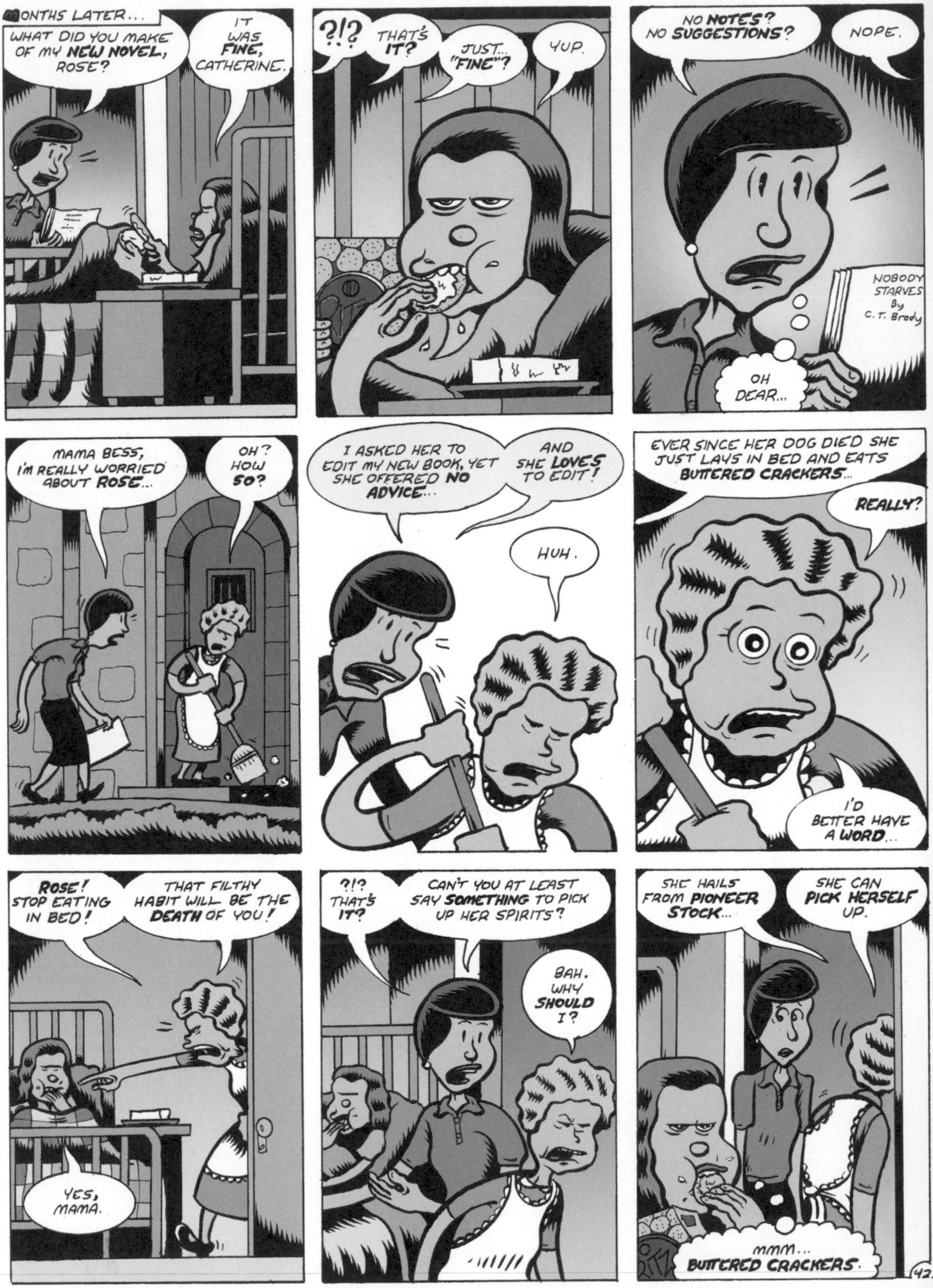
MONTHS LATER...
WHAT DID YOU MAKE OF MY NEW NOVEL, ROSE?
IT WAS FINE, CATHERINE.
?!?
THAT'S IT?
JUST... "FINE"?
YUP.
NO NOTES? NO SUGGESTIONS?
NOPE.
OH DEAR...
NOBODY STARVES By C.T. Brody
MAMA BESS, I'M REALLY WORRIED ABOUT ROSE...
OH? HOW SO?
I ASKED HER TO EDIT MY NEW BOOK, YET SHE OFFERED NO ADVICE...
AND SHE LOVES TO EDIT!
HUH.
EVER SINCE HER DOG DIED SHE JUST LAYS IN BED AND EATS BUTTERED CRACKERS...
REALLY?
I'D BETTER HAVE A WORD...
ROSE! STOP EATING IN BED!
THAT FILTHY HABIT WILL BE THE DEATH OF YOU!
YES, MAMA.
?!? THAT'S IT?
CAN'T YOU AT LEAST SAY SOMETHING TO PICK UP HER SPIRITS?
BAH. WHY SHOULD I?
SHE HAILS FROM PIONEER STOCK...
SHE CAN PICK HERSELF UP.
MMM... BUTTERED CRACKERS.

Panel 1:
SOON AFTER... THE EDITOR AT HARPERS **LOVES** YOUR BOOK, MAMA...

BUT SHE DOES HAVE A **FEW NOTES**...

HARPERS?

I THOUGHT **KNOPF** WAS GOING TO PUBLISH IT.

Panel 2:

KNOPF KILLED THEIR **JUVENILE** DEPARTMENT...

"JUVENILE"? MY BOOK IS A **MEMOIR!**

HOW CAN YOU **STAND** ALL THIS NONSENSE?

Panel 3:

AT LEAST **SOMEONE** IS PUBLISHING IT...

BEGGARS CAN'T BE **CHOOSERS** THESE DAYS...

I AM **NOT** A BEGGAR.

Panel 4:

DULY NOTED... ANYHOW, SHE SUGGESTS YOU HAVE THE STORY COVER AN **ENTIRE YEAR**, RATHER THAN JUST ONE WINTER.

WHY?

Panel 5:

TO MAKE IT **LONGER**, FOR ONE THING...

AND TO SHARE **MORE DETAILS** REGARDING YOUR PARENTS' SEASONAL ROUTINES.

MY LAND... I HOPE I CAN **REMEMBER** IT ALL...

Panel 6:

SHE ALSO WANTS YOU TO AVOID THE SUBJECT OF **DEATH**...

THEY FEAR IT MIGHT BE TOO UPSETTING FOR **CHILDREN**...

BUT **I** DEALT WITH DEATH AS A CHILD!

I'M THE CHILD IN MY **BOOK!**

Panel 7:

SHE ALSO WANTS TO CHANGE THE **TITLE**...

SHE SUGGESTS "LITTLE HOUSE IN THE **BIG WOODS**"...

TELL HER THIS IS **MY** BOOK! **MINE!**

Panel 8:

WHY, THE **NERVE** OF SOME PEOPLE...

Panel 9:

I'LL TELL HER THE NEW TITLE IS **FINE**.

SLAM

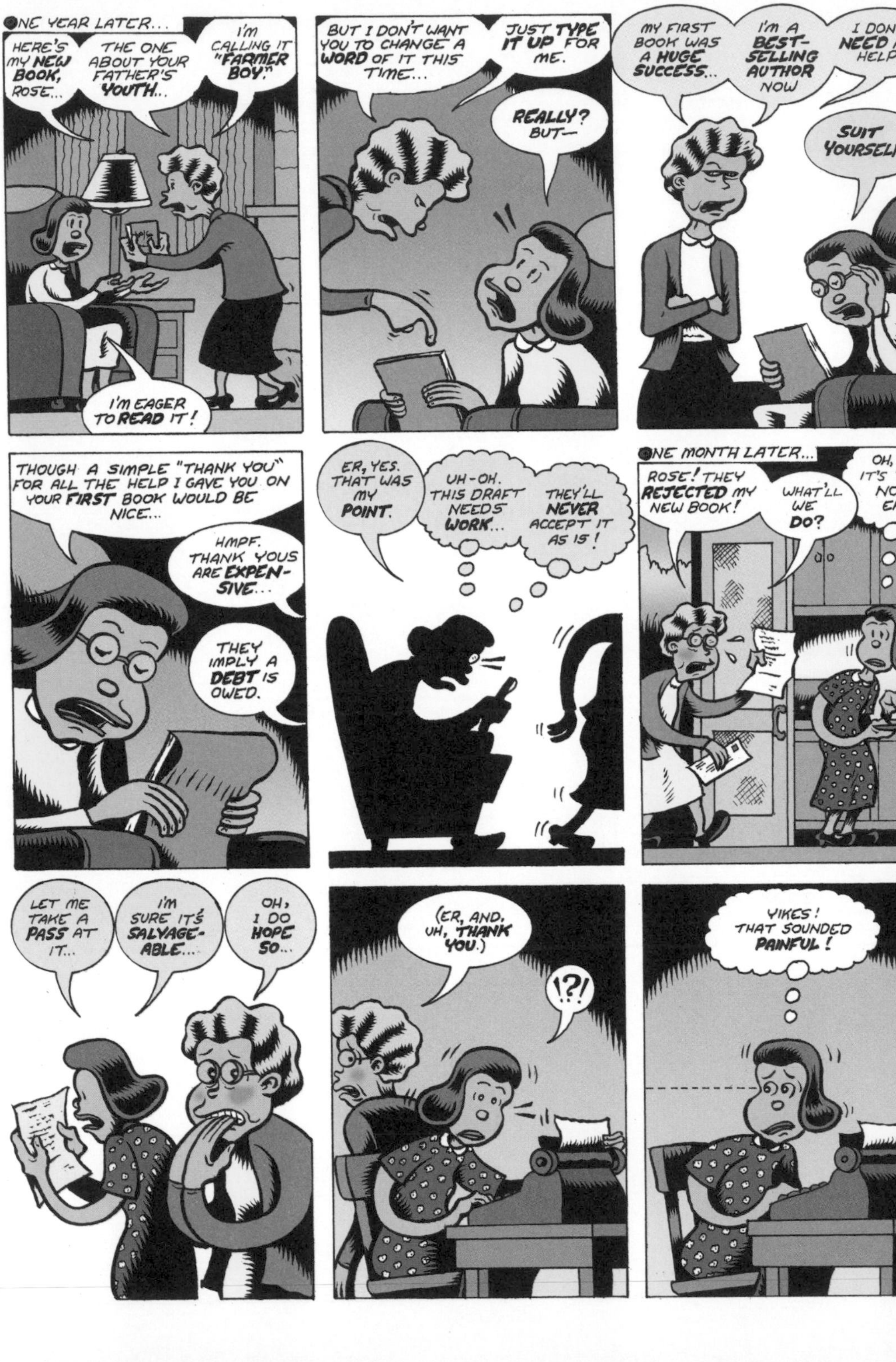
ONE YEAR LATER...
HERE'S MY NEW BOOK, ROSE...
THE ONE ABOUT YOUR FATHER'S YOUTH...
I'M CALLING IT "FARMER BOY."
I'M EAGER TO READ IT!
BUT I DON'T WANT YOU TO CHANGE A WORD OF IT THIS TIME...
JUST TYPE IT UP FOR ME.
REALLY? BUT—
MY FIRST BOOK WAS A HUGE SUCCESS...
I'M A BEST-SELLING AUTHOR NOW
I DON'T NEED ANY HELP.
SUIT YOURSELF...
THOUGH A SIMPLE "THANK YOU" FOR ALL THE HELP I GAVE YOU ON YOUR FIRST BOOK WOULD BE NICE...
HMPF. THANK YOUS ARE EXPEN-SIVE...
THEY IMPLY A DEBT IS OWED.
ER, YES. THAT WAS MY POINT.
UH-OH. THIS DRAFT NEEDS WORK...
THEY'LL NEVER ACCEPT IT AS IS!
ONE MONTH LATER...
ROSE! THEY REJECTED MY NEW BOOK!
WHAT'LL WE DO?
OH, SO IT'S "WE" NOW, EH?
LET ME TAKE A PASS AT IT...
I'M SURE IT'S SALVAGE-ABLE...
OH, I DO HOPE SO...
(ER, AND, UH, THANK YOU.)
!?!
YIKES! THAT SOUNDED PAINFUL!

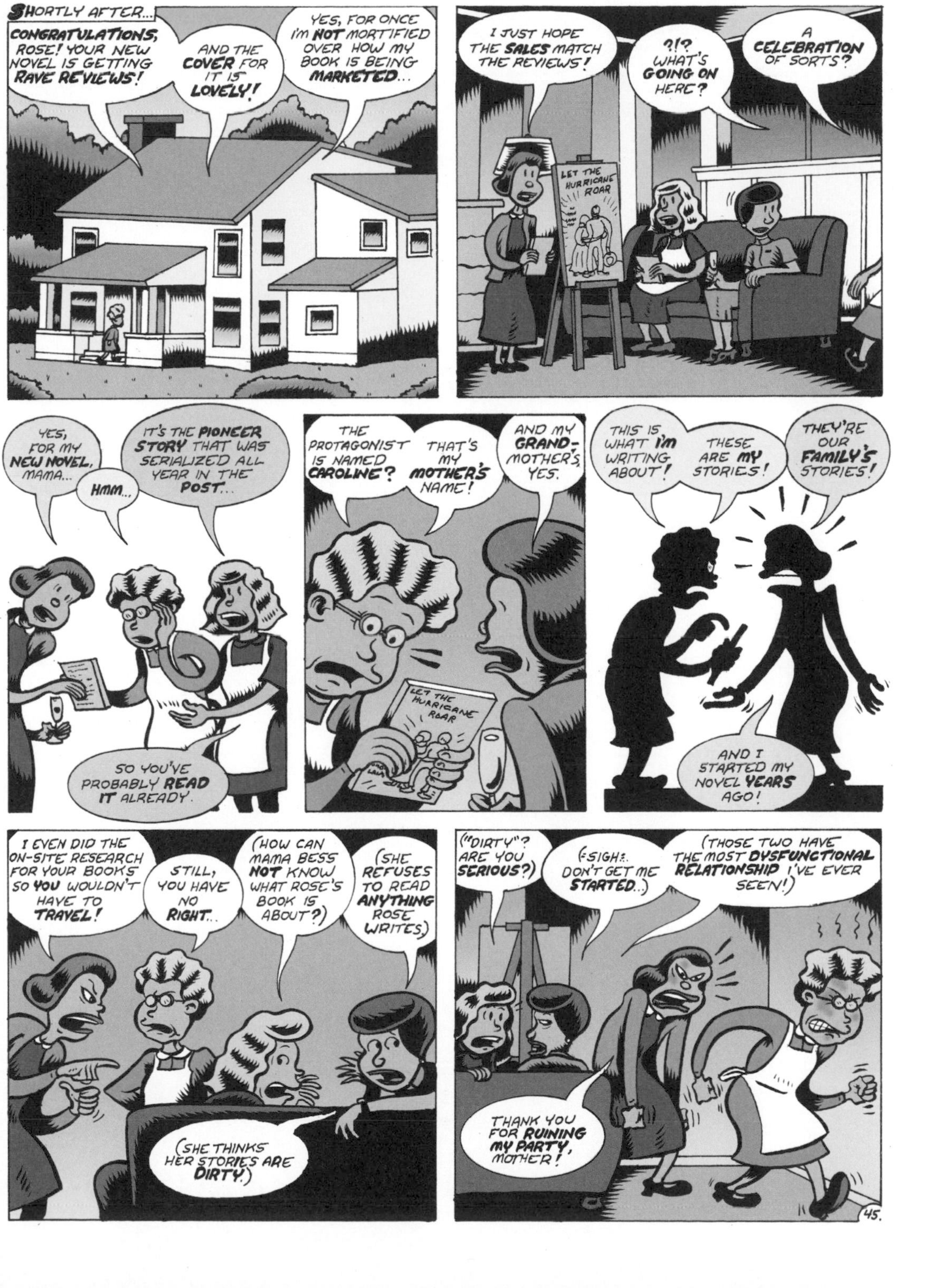

SHORTLY AFTER...
CONGRATULATIONS, ROSE! YOUR NEW NOVEL IS GETTING RAVE REVIEWS!
AND THE COVER FOR IT IS LOVELY!
YES, FOR ONCE I'M NOT MORTIFIED OVER HOW MY BOOK IS BEING MARKETED...
I JUST HOPE THE SALES MATCH THE REVIEWS!
?!? WHAT'S GOING ON HERE?
A CELEBRATION OF SORTS?
LET THE HURRICANE ROAR
YES, FOR MY NEW NOVEL, MAMA...
HMM...
IT'S THE PIONEER STORY THAT WAS SERIALIZED ALL YEAR IN THE POST...
SO YOU'VE PROBABLY READ IT ALREADY.
THE PROTAGONIST IS NAMED CAROLINE?
THAT'S MY MOTHER'S NAME!
AND MY GRAND-MOTHER'S, YES.
LET THE HURRICANE ROAR
THIS IS WHAT I'M WRITING ABOUT!
THESE ARE MY STORIES!
THEY'RE OUR FAMILY'S STORIES!
AND I STARTED MY NOVEL YEARS AGO!
I EVEN DID THE ON-SITE RESEARCH FOR YOUR BOOKS SO YOU WOULDN'T HAVE TO TRAVEL!
STILL, YOU HAVE NO RIGHT...
(HOW CAN MAMA BESS NOT KNOW WHAT ROSE'S BOOK IS ABOUT?)
(SHE REFUSES TO READ ANYTHING ROSE WRITES.)
(SHE THINKS HER STORIES ARE DIRTY.)
("DIRTY"? ARE YOU SERIOUS?)
(-SIGH-. DON'T GET ME STARTED...)
(THOSE TWO HAVE THE MOST DYSFUNCTIONAL RELATIONSHIP I'VE EVER SEEN!)
THANK YOU FOR RUINING MY PARTY, MOTHER!

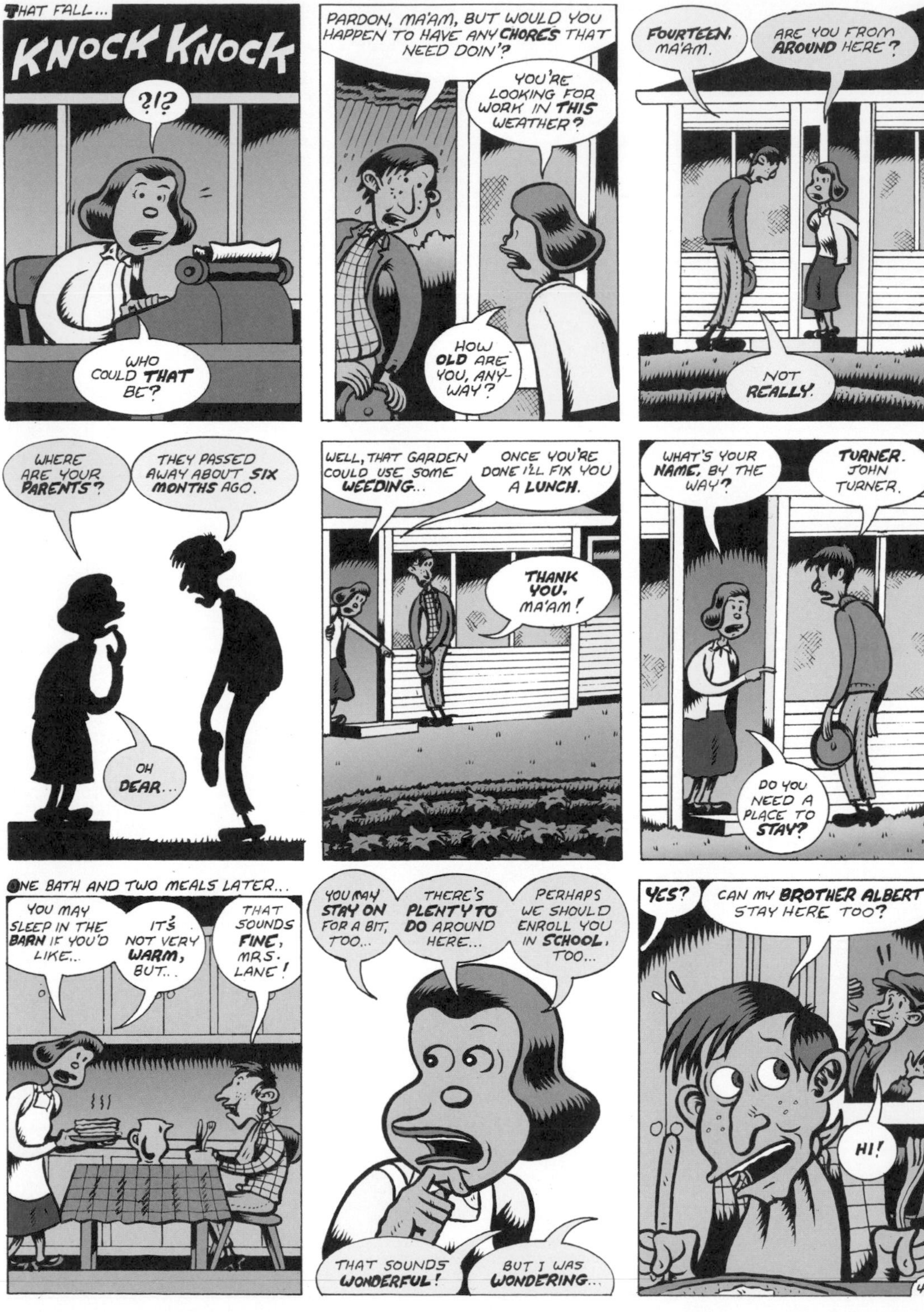
THAT FALL...
KNOCK KNOCK
?!?
WHO COULD THAT BE?
PARDON, MA'AM, BUT WOULD YOU HAPPEN TO HAVE ANY CHORES THAT NEED DOIN'?
YOU'RE LOOKING FOR WORK IN THIS WEATHER?
HOW OLD ARE YOU, ANY-WAY?
FOURTEEN, MA'AM.
ARE YOU FROM AROUND HERE?
NOT REALLY.
WHERE ARE YOUR PARENTS?
THEY PASSED AWAY ABOUT SIX MONTHS AGO.
OH DEAR...
WELL, THAT GARDEN COULD USE SOME WEEDING...
ONCE YOU'RE DONE I'LL FIX YOU A LUNCH.
THANK YOU, MA'AM!
WHAT'S YOUR NAME, BY THE WAY?
TURNER. JOHN TURNER.
DO YOU NEED A PLACE TO STAY?
ONE BATH AND TWO MEALS LATER...
YOU MAY SLEEP IN THE BARN IF YOU'D LIKE...
IT'S NOT VERY WARM, BUT...
THAT SOUNDS FINE, MRS. LANE!
YOU MAY STAY ON FOR A BIT, TOO...
THERE'S PLENTY TO DO AROUND HERE...
PERHAPS WE SHOULD ENROLL YOU IN SCHOOL, TOO...
THAT SOUNDS WONDERFUL!
BUT I WAS WONDERING...
YES?
CAN MY BROTHER ALBERT STAY HERE TOO?
HI!

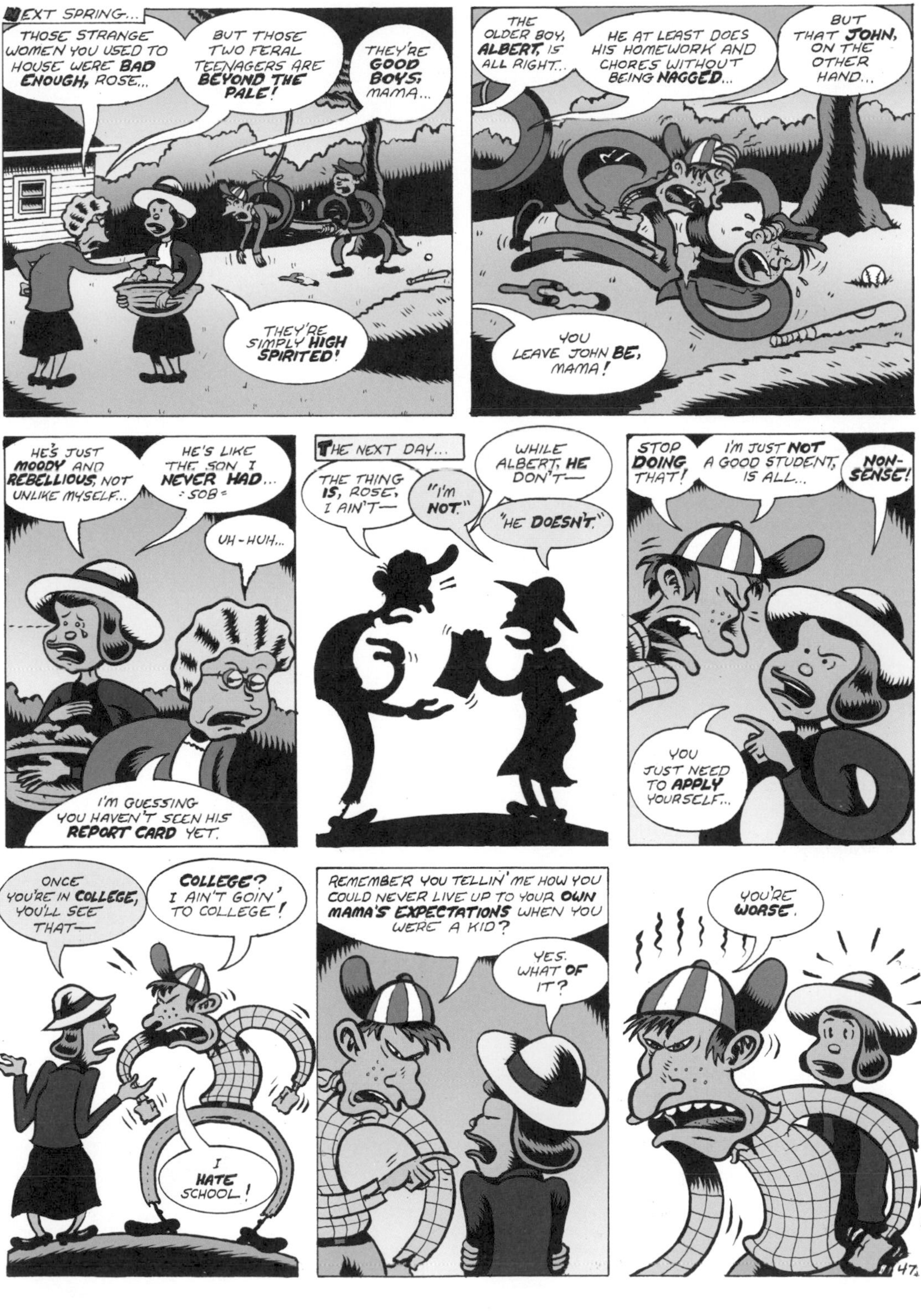
NEXT SPRING...
THOSE STRANGE WOMEN YOU USED TO HOUSE WERE BAD ENOUGH, ROSE...
BUT THOSE TWO FERAL TEENAGERS ARE BEYOND THE PALE!
THEY'RE GOOD BOYS, MAMA...
THEY'RE SIMPLY HIGH SPIRITED!
THE OLDER BOY, ALBERT, IS ALL RIGHT...
HE AT LEAST DOES HIS HOMEWORK AND CHORES WITHOUT BEING NAGGED...
BUT THAT JOHN, ON THE OTHER HAND...
YOU LEAVE JOHN BE, MAMA!
HE'S JUST MOODY AND REBELLIOUS, NOT UNLIKE MYSELF...
HE'S LIKE THE SON I NEVER HAD... =SOB=
UH-HUH...
I'M GUESSING YOU HAVEN'T SEEN HIS REPORT CARD YET.
THE NEXT DAY...
THE THING IS, ROSE, I AIN'T—
"I'M NOT."
WHILE ALBERT, HE DON'T—
"HE DOESN'T."
STOP DOING THAT!
I'M JUST NOT A GOOD STUDENT, IS ALL...
NON-SENSE!
YOU JUST NEED TO APPLY YOURSELF...
ONCE YOU'RE IN COLLEGE, YOU'LL SEE THAT—
COLLEGE?, I AIN'T GOIN' TO COLLEGE!
I HATE SCHOOL!
REMEMBER YOU TELLIN' ME HOW YOU COULD NEVER LIVE UP TO YOUR OWN MAMA'S EXPECTATIONS WHEN YOU WERE A KID?
YES. WHAT OF IT?
YOU'RE WORSE.

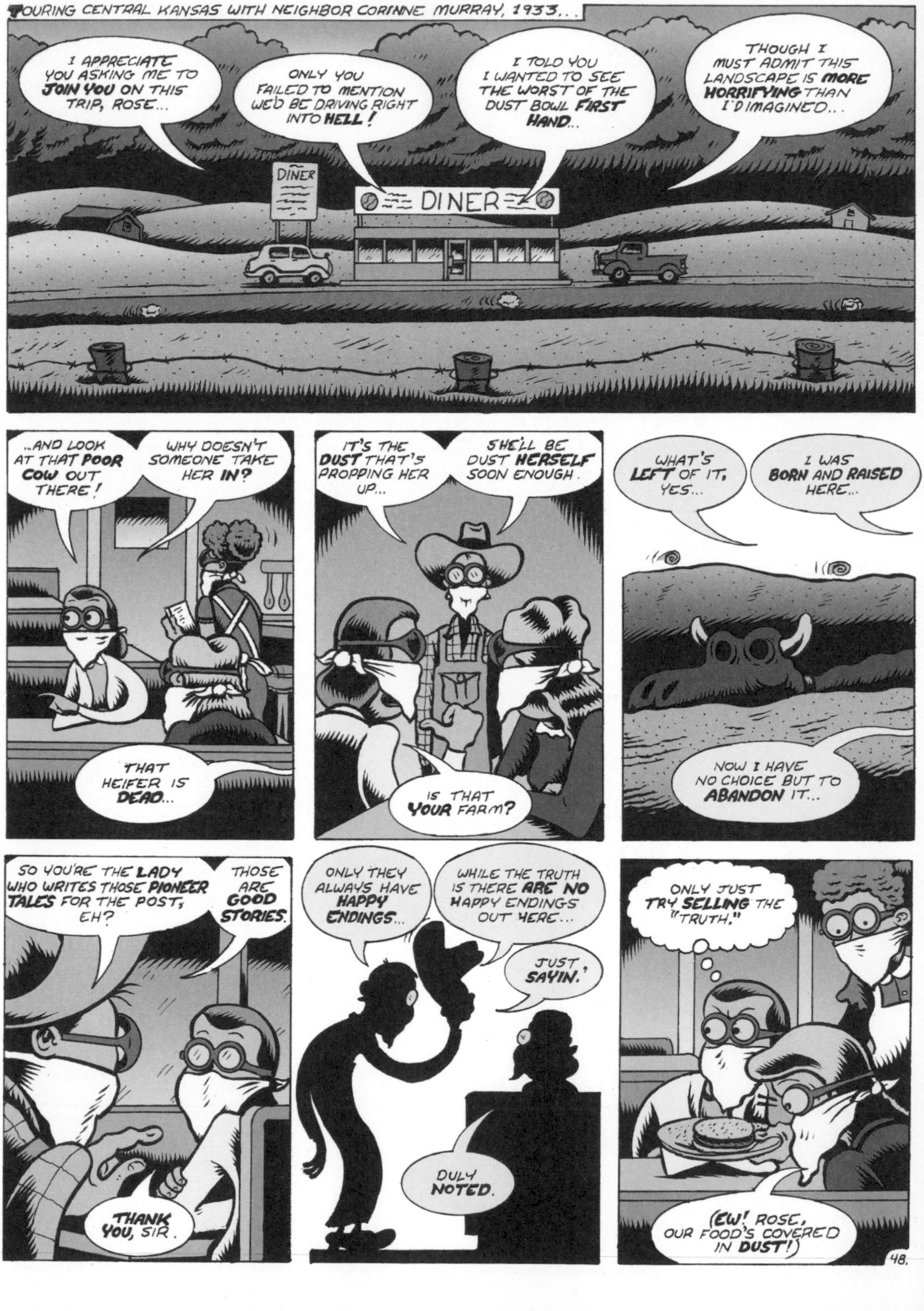
TOURING CENTRAL KANSAS WITH NEIGHBOR CORINNE MURRAY, 1933...
I APPRECIATE YOU ASKING ME TO JOIN YOU ON THIS TRIP, ROSE...
ONLY YOU FAILED TO MENTION WE'D BE DRIVING RIGHT INTO HELL!
I TOLD YOU I WANTED TO SEE THE WORST OF THE DUST BOWL FIRST HAND...
THOUGH I MUST ADMIT THIS LANDSCAPE IS MORE HORRIFYING THAN I'D IMAGINED...
DINER
DINER
..AND LOOK AT THAT POOR COW OUT THERE!
WHY DOESN'T SOMEONE TAKE HER IN?
THAT HEIFER IS DEAD...
IT'S THE DUST THAT'S PROPPING HER UP...
SHE'LL BE DUST HERSELF SOON ENOUGH.
IS THAT YOUR FARM?
WHAT'S LEFT OF IT, YES...
I WAS BORN AND RAISED HERE...
NOW I HAVE NO CHOICE BUT TO ABANDON IT...
SO YOU'RE THE LADY WHO WRITES THOSE PIONEER TALES FOR THE POST, EH?
THOSE ARE GOOD STORIES.
THANK YOU, SIR.
ONLY THEY ALWAYS HAVE HAPPY ENDINGS...
WHILE THE TRUTH IS THERE ARE NO HAPPY ENDINGS OUT HERE...
JUST SAYIN.'
DULY NOTED.
ONLY JUST TRY SELLING THE "TRUTH."
(EW! ROSE, OUR FOOD'S COVERED IN DUST!)

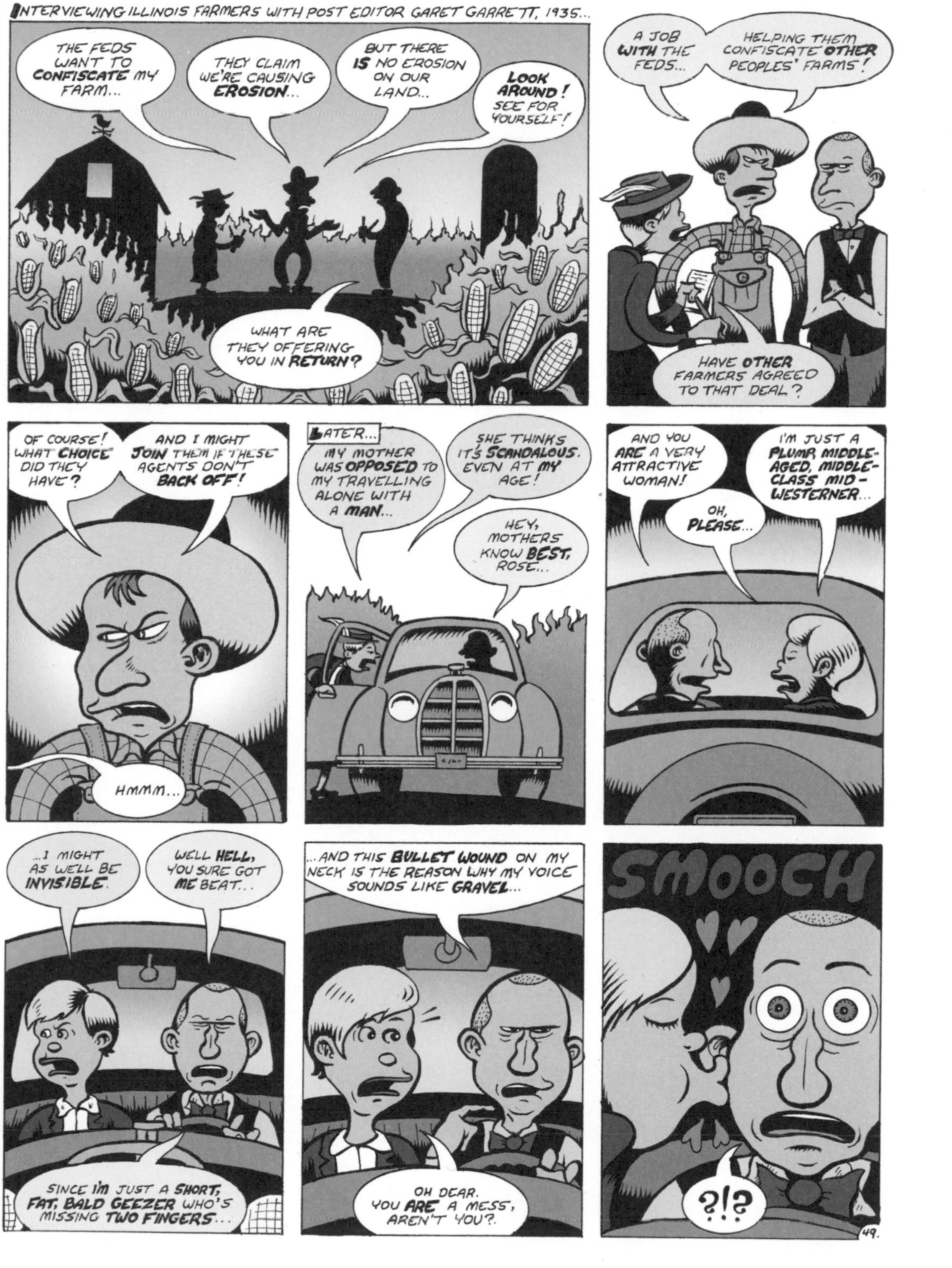
INTERVIEWING ILLINOIS FARMERS WITH POST EDITOR GARET GARRETT, 1935...
THE FEDS WANT TO CONFISCATE MY FARM...
THEY CLAIM WE'RE CAUSING EROSION...
BUT THERE IS NO EROSION ON OUR LAND...
LOOK AROUND! SEE FOR YOURSELF!
WHAT ARE THEY OFFERING YOU IN RETURN?
A JOB WITH THE FEDS...
HELPING THEM CONFISCATE OTHER PEOPLES' FARMS!
HAVE OTHER FARMERS AGREED TO THAT DEAL?
OF COURSE! WHAT CHOICE DID THEY HAVE?
AND I MIGHT JOIN THEM IF THESE AGENTS DON'T BACK OFF!
HMMM...
LATER...
MY MOTHER WAS OPPOSED TO MY TRAVELLING ALONE WITH A MAN...
SHE THINKS IT'S SCANDALOUS. EVEN AT MY AGE!
HEY, MOTHERS KNOW BEST, ROSE...
AND YOU ARE A VERY ATTRACTIVE WOMAN!
OH, PLEASE...
I'M JUST A PLUMP, MIDDLE-AGED, MIDDLE-CLASS MID-WESTERNER...
...I MIGHT AS WELL BE INVISIBLE.
WELL HELL, YOU SURE GOT ME BEAT...
SINCE I'M JUST A SHORT, FAT, BALD GEEZER WHO'S MISSING TWO FINGERS...
...AND THIS BULLET WOUND ON MY NECK IS THE REASON WHY MY VOICE SOUNDS LIKE GRAVEL...
OH DEAR. YOU ARE A MESS, AREN'T YOU?.
SMOOCH
?!?

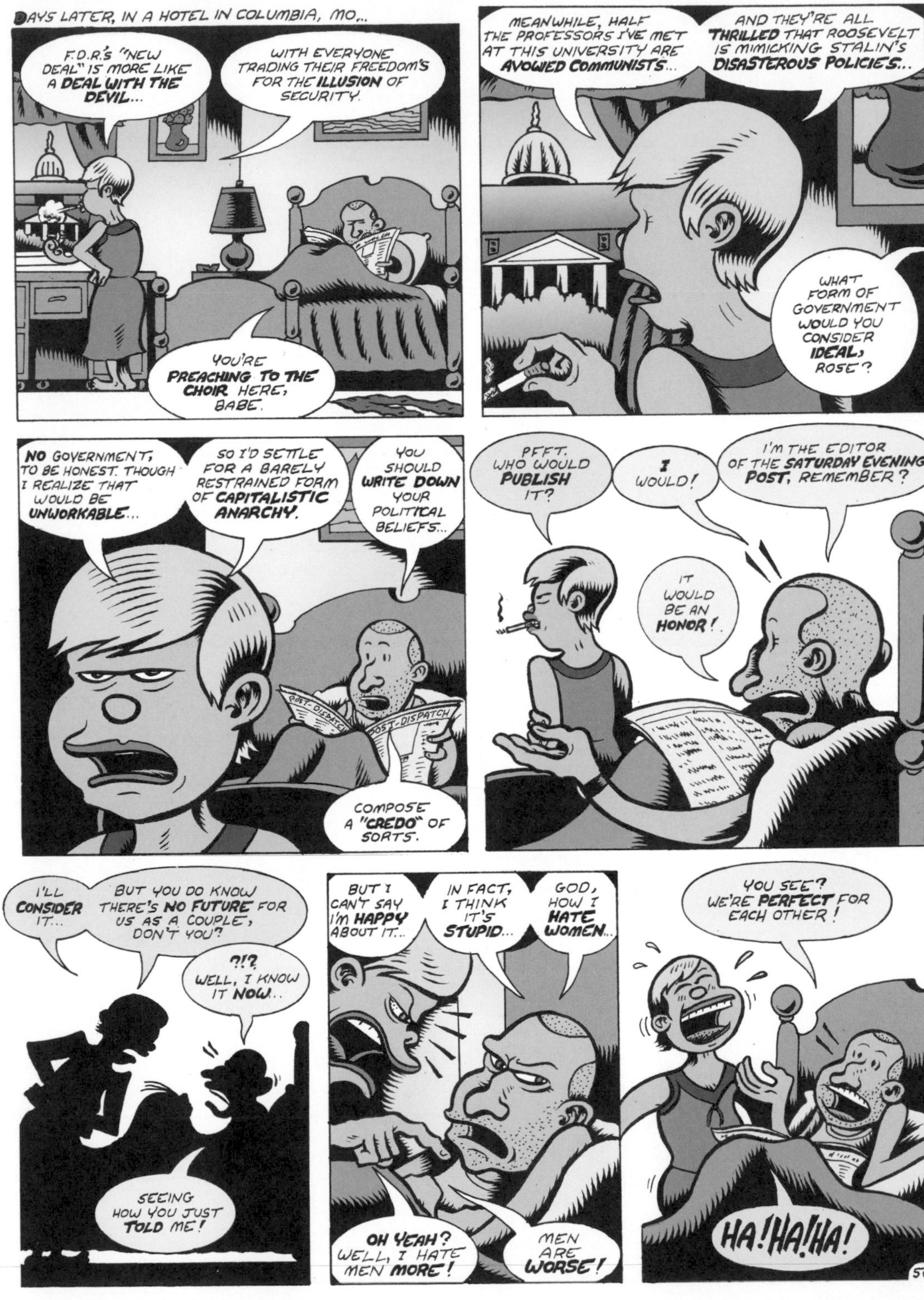
DAYS LATER, IN A HOTEL IN COLUMBIA, MO...
F.D.R.'S "NEW DEAL" IS MORE LIKE A DEAL WITH THE DEVIL...
WITH EVERYONE TRADING THEIR FREEDOM'S FOR THE ILLUSION OF SECURITY.
YOU'RE PREACHING TO THE CHOIR HERE, BABE.
MEANWHILE, HALF THE PROFESSORS I'VE MET AT THIS UNIVERSITY ARE AVOWED COMMUNISTS...
AND THEY'RE ALL THRILLED THAT ROOSEVELT IS MIMICKING STALIN'S DISASTEROUS POLICIES...
WHAT FORM OF GOVERNMENT WOULD YOU CONSIDER IDEAL, ROSE?
NO GOVERNMENT, TO BE HONEST. THOUGH I REALIZE THAT WOULD BE UNWORKABLE...
SO I'D SETTLE FOR A BARELY RESTRAINED FORM OF CAPITALISTIC ANARCHY.
YOU SHOULD WRITE DOWN YOUR POLITICAL BELIEFS...
POST-DISPATCH
POST-DISPATCH
COMPOSE A "CREDO" OF SORTS.
PFFT. WHO WOULD PUBLISH IT?
I WOULD!
I'M THE EDITOR OF THE SATURDAY EVENING POST, REMEMBER?
IT WOULD BE AN HONOR!
I'LL CONSIDER IT...
BUT YOU DO KNOW THERE'S NO FUTURE FOR US AS A COUPLE, DON'T YOU?
?!? WELL, I KNOW IT NOW...
SEEING HOW YOU JUST TOLD ME!
BUT I CAN'T SAY I'M HAPPY ABOUT IT...
IN FACT, I THINK IT'S STUPID...
GOD, HOW I HATE WOMEN...
OH YEAH? WELL, I HATE MEN MORE!
MEN ARE WORSE!
YOU SEE? WE'RE PERFECT FOR EACH OTHER!
HA!HA!HA!

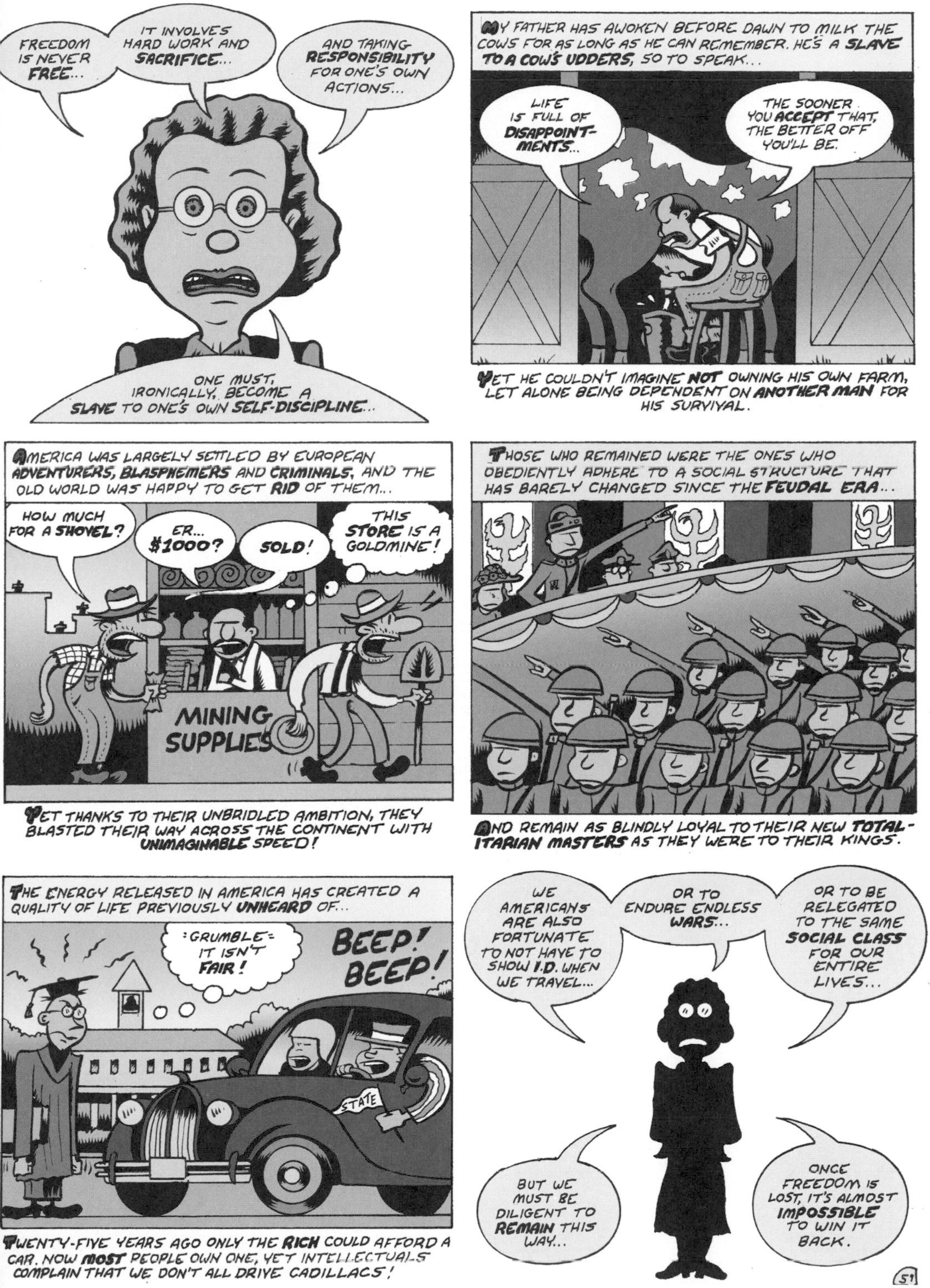

FREEDOM IS NEVER FREE...
IT INVOLVES HARD WORK AND SACRIFICE...
AND TAKING RESPONSIBILITY FOR ONE'S OWN ACTIONS...
ONE MUST, IRONICALLY, BECOME A SLAVE TO ONE'S OWN SELF-DISCIPLINE...
MY FATHER HAS AWOKEN BEFORE DAWN TO MILK THE COWS FOR AS LONG AS HE CAN REMEMBER. HE'S A SLAVE TO A COW'S UDDERS, SO TO SPEAK...
LIFE IS FULL OF DISAPPOINT-MENTS...
THE SOONER YOU ACCEPT THAT, THE BETTER OFF YOU'LL BE.
YET HE COULDN'T IMAGINE NOT OWNING HIS OWN FARM, LET ALONE BEING DEPENDENT ON ANOTHER MAN FOR HIS SURVIVAL.
AMERICA WAS LARGELY SETTLED BY EUROPEAN ADVENTURERS, BLASPHEMERS AND CRIMINALS, AND THE OLD WORLD WAS HAPPY TO GET RID OF THEM...
HOW MUCH FOR A SHOVEL?
ER... $1000?
SOLD!
THIS STORE IS A GOLDMINE!
MINING SUPPLIES
YET THANKS TO THEIR UNBRIDLED AMBITION, THEY BLASTED THEIR WAY ACROSS THE CONTINENT WITH UNIMAGINABLE SPEED!
THOSE WHO REMAINED WERE THE ONES WHO OBEDIENTLY ADHERE TO A SOCIAL STRUCTURE THAT HAS BARELY CHANGED SINCE THE FEUDAL ERA...
AND REMAIN AS BLINDLY LOYAL TO THEIR NEW TOTAL-ITARIAN MASTERS AS THEY WERE TO THEIR KINGS.
THE ENERGY RELEASED IN AMERICA HAS CREATED A QUALITY OF LIFE PREVIOUSLY UNHEARD OF...
=GRUMBLE= IT ISN'T FAIR!
BEEP! BEEP!
STATE
TWENTY-FIVE YEARS AGO ONLY THE RICH COULD AFFORD A CAR. NOW MOST PEOPLE OWN ONE, YET INTELLECTUALS COMPLAIN THAT WE DON'T ALL DRIVE CADILLACS!
WE AMERICANS ARE ALSO FORTUNATE TO NOT HAVE TO SHOW I.D. WHEN WE TRAVEL...
OR TO ENDURE ENDLESS WARS...
OR TO BE RELEGATED TO THE SAME SOCIAL CLASS FOR OUR ENTIRE LIVES...
BUT WE MUST BE DILIGENT TO REMAIN THIS WAY...
ONCE FREEDOM IS LOST, IT'S ALMOST IMPOSSIBLE TO WIN IT BACK.

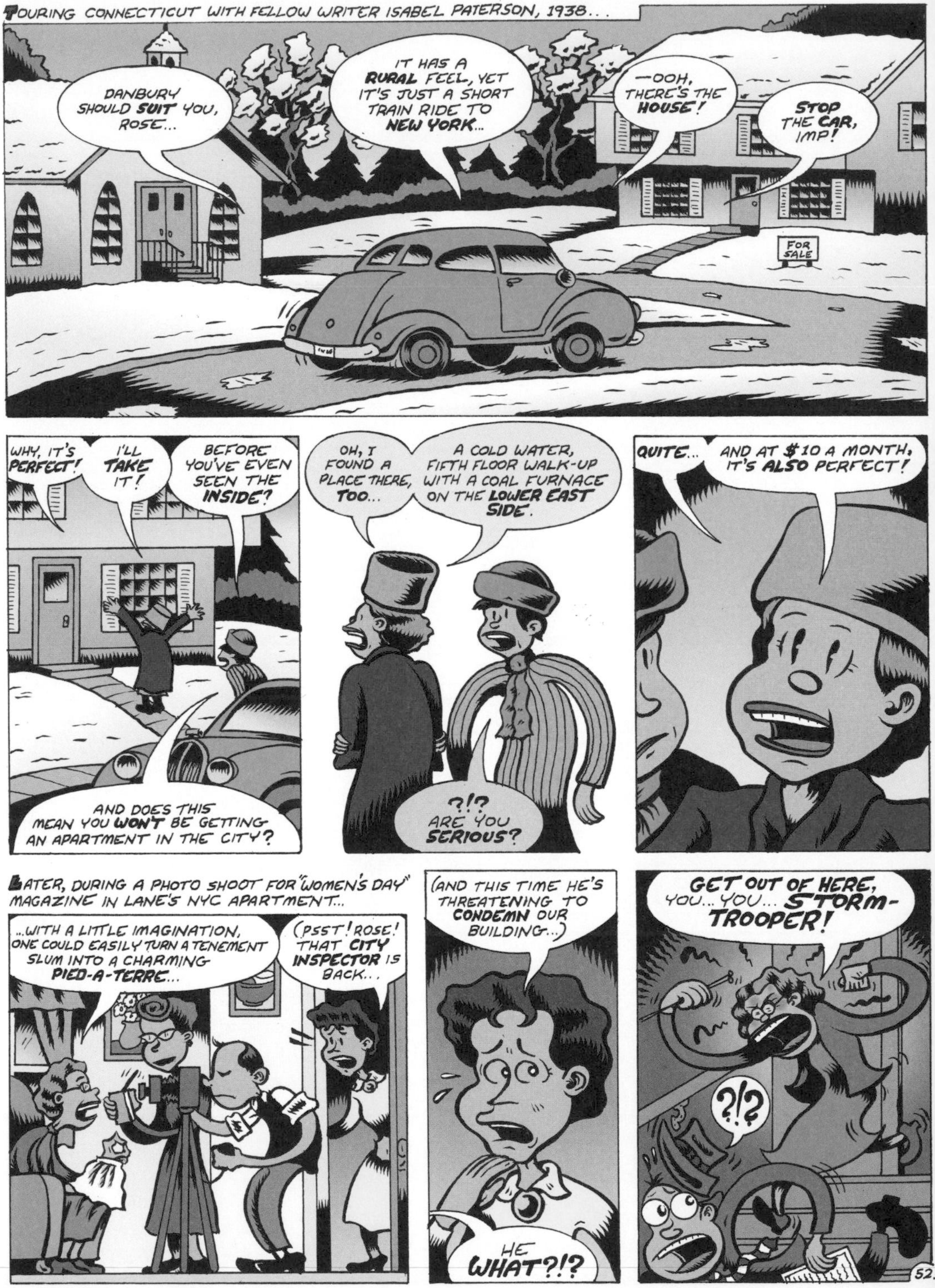

TOURING CONNECTICUT WITH FELLOW WRITER ISABEL PATERSON, 1938...
DANBURY SHOULD SUIT YOU, ROSE...
IT HAS A RURAL FEEL, YET IT'S JUST A SHORT TRAIN RIDE TO NEW YORK...
—OOH, THERE'S THE HOUSE!
STOP THE CAR, IMP!
FOR SALE
WHY, IT'S PERFECT!
I'LL TAKE IT!
BEFORE YOU'VE EVEN SEEN THE INSIDE?
AND DOES THIS MEAN YOU WON'T BE GETTING AN APARTMENT IN THE CITY?
OH, I FOUND A PLACE THERE, TOO...
A COLD WATER, FIFTH FLOOR WALK-UP WITH A COAL FURNACE ON THE LOWER EAST SIDE.
?!? ARE YOU SERIOUS?
QUITE...
AND AT $10 A MONTH, IT'S ALSO PERFECT!
LATER, DURING A PHOTO SHOOT FOR "WOMEN'S DAY" MAGAZINE IN LANE'S NYC APARTMENT...
...WITH A LITTLE IMAGINATION, ONE COULD EASILY TURN A TENEMENT SLUM INTO A CHARMING PIED-A-TERRE...
(PSST! ROSE! THAT CITY INSPECTOR IS BACK...
(AND THIS TIME HE'S THREATENING TO CONDEMN OUR BUILDING...)
HE WHAT?!?
GET OUT OF HERE, YOU... YOU... STORM-TROOPER!
?!?

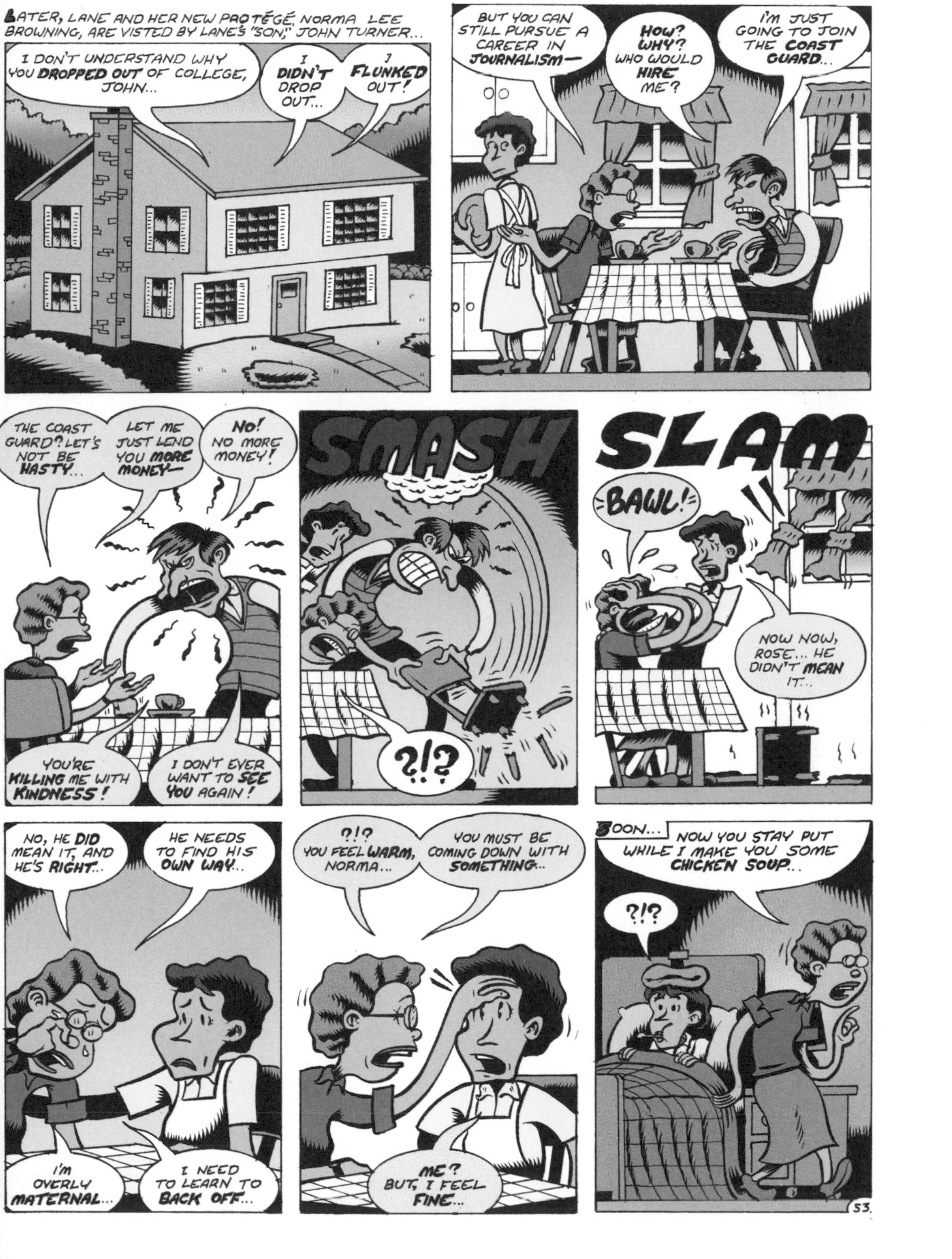
LATER, LANE AND HER NEW PROTÉGÉ, NORMA LEE BROWNING, ARE VISTED BY LANE'S "SON," JOHN TURNER...
I DON'T UNDERSTAND WHY YOU DROPPED OUT OF COLLEGE, JOHN...
I DIDN'T DROP OUT...
I FLUNKED OUT!
BUT YOU CAN STILL PURSUE A CAREER IN JOURNALISM—
HOW? WHY? WHO WOULD HIRE ME?
I'M JUST GOING TO JOIN THE COAST GUARD...
THE COAST GUARD? LET'S NOT BE HASTY...
LET ME JUST LEND YOU MORE MONEY—
NO! NO MORE MONEY!
YOU'RE KILLING ME WITH KINDNESS!
I DON'T EVER WANT TO SEE YOU AGAIN!
SMASH
?!?
SLAM
BAWL!
NOW NOW, ROSE... HE DIDN'T MEAN IT...
NO, HE DID MEAN IT, AND HE'S RIGHT...
HE NEEDS TO FIND HIS OWN WAY...
I'M OVERLY MATERNAL...
I NEED TO LEARN TO BACK OFF...
?!? YOU FEEL WARM, NORMA...
YOU MUST BE COMING DOWN WITH SOMETHING...
ME? BUT, I FEEL FINE...
SOON...
NOW YOU STAY PUT WHILE I MAKE YOU SOME CHICKEN SOUP...
?!?

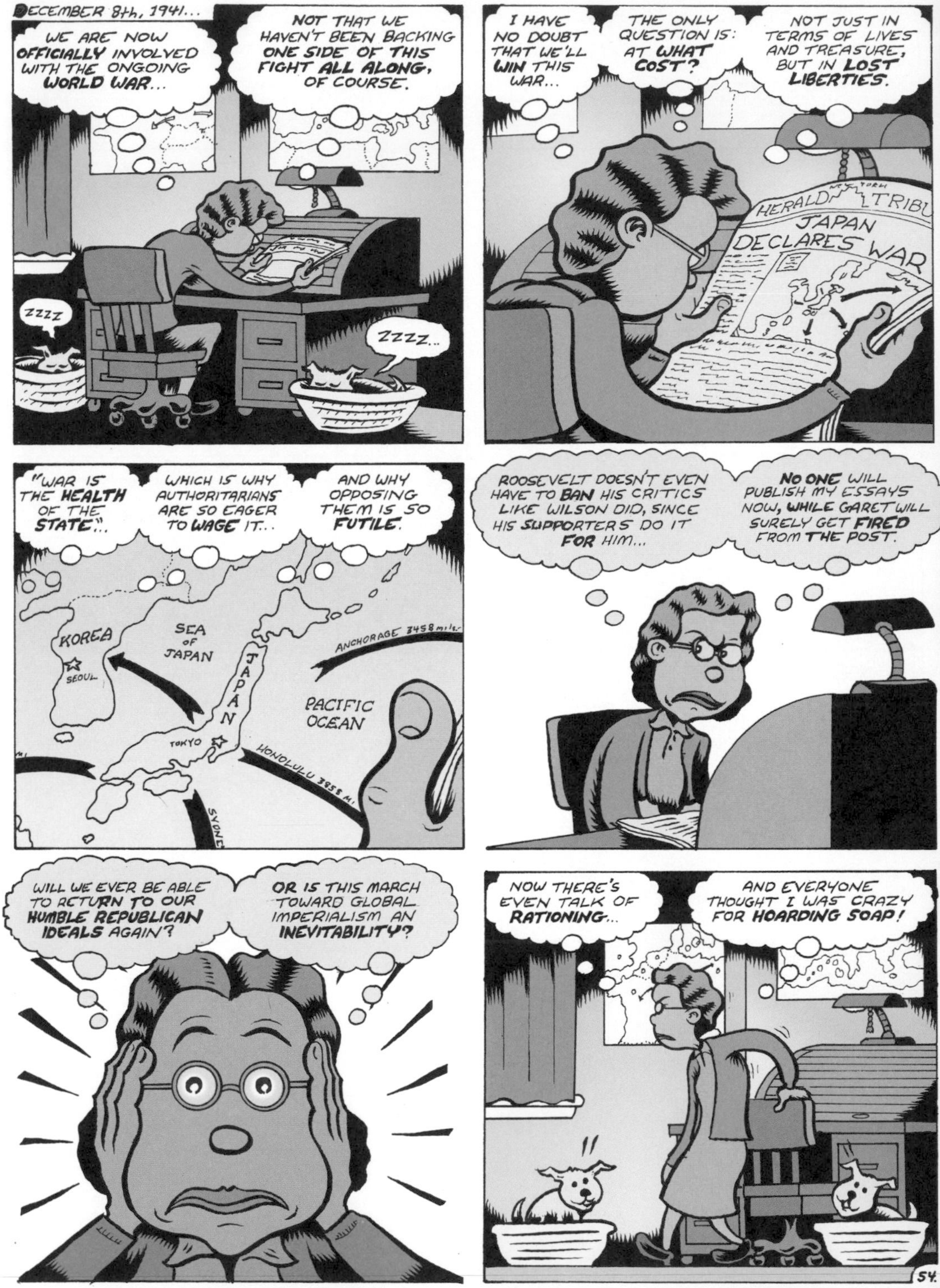
DECEMBER 8th, 1941...
WE ARE NOW OFFICIALLY INVOLVED WITH THE ONGOING WORLD WAR...
NOT THAT WE HAVEN'T BEEN BACKING ONE SIDE OF THIS FIGHT ALL ALONG, OF COURSE.
ZZZZ
ZZZZ...
I HAVE NO DOUBT THAT WE'LL WIN THIS WAR...
THE ONLY QUESTION IS: AT WHAT COST?
NOT JUST IN TERMS OF LIVES AND TREASURE, BUT IN LOST LIBERTIES.
HERALD TRIBU
JAPAN DECLARES WAR
"WAR IS THE HEALTH OF THE STATE"...
WHICH IS WHY AUTHORITARIANS ARE SO EAGER TO WAGE IT...
AND WHY OPPOSING THEM IS SO FUTILE.
KOREA
SEOUL
SEA OF JAPAN
JAPAN
TOKYO
ANCHORAGE 3458 miles
PACIFIC OCEAN
HONOLULU 3958 MI
ROOSEVELT DOESN'T EVEN HAVE TO BAN HIS CRITICS LIKE WILSON DID, SINCE HIS SUPPORTERS DO IT FOR HIM...
NO ONE WILL PUBLISH MY ESSAYS NOW, WHILE GARET WILL SURELY GET FIRED FROM THE POST.
WILL WE EVER BE ABLE TO RETURN TO OUR HUMBLE REPUBLICAN IDEALS AGAIN?
OR IS THIS MARCH TOWARD GLOBAL IMPERIALISM AN INEVITABILITY?
NOW THERE'S EVEN TALK OF RATIONING...
AND EVERYONE THOUGHT I WAS CRAZY FOR HOARDING SOAP!

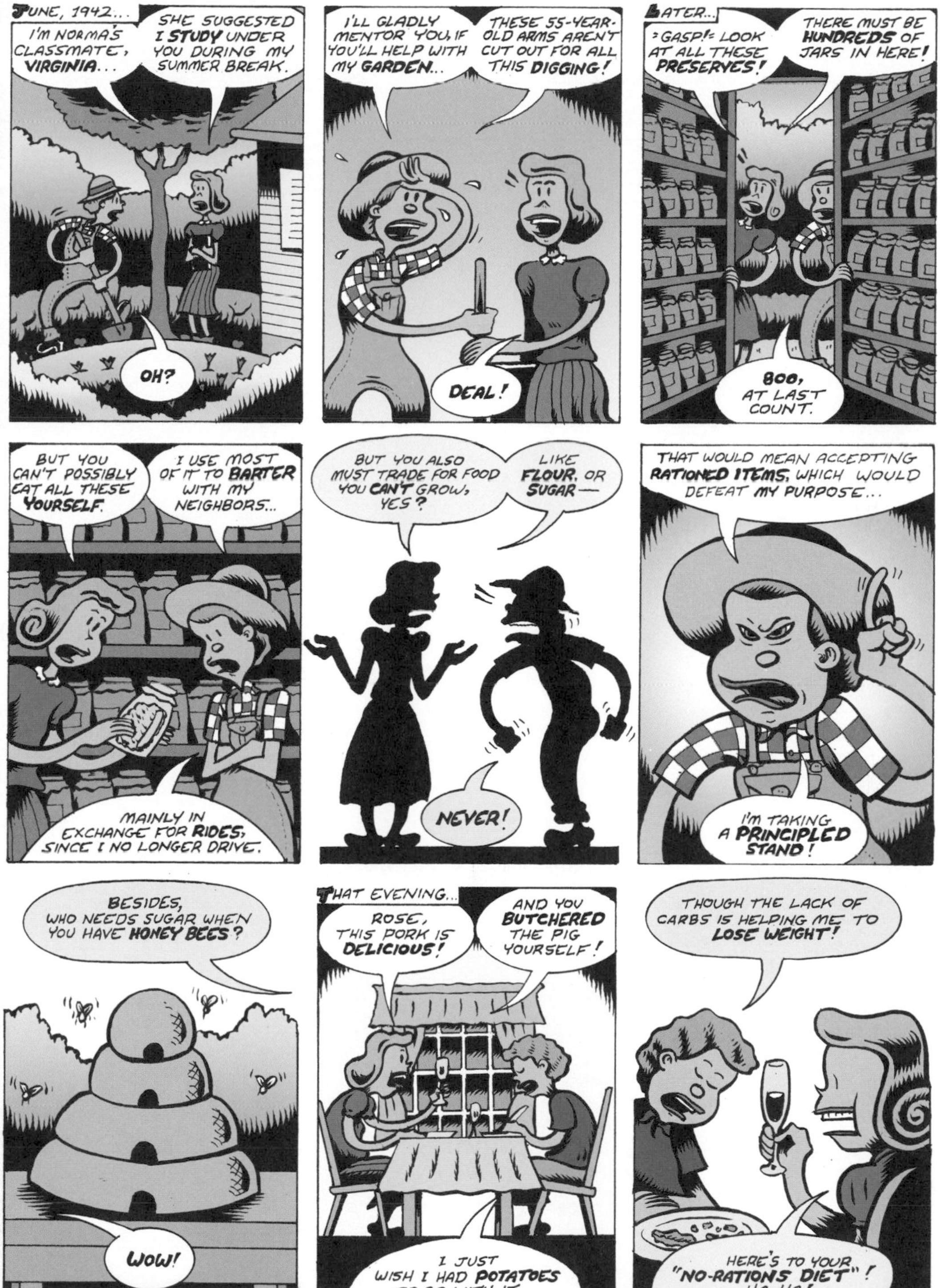
JUNE, 1942...
I'M NORMA'S CLASSMATE, VIRGINIA...
SHE SUGGESTED I STUDY UNDER YOU DURING MY SUMMER BREAK.
OH?
I'LL GLADLY MENTOR YOU, IF YOU'LL HELP WITH MY GARDEN...
THESE 55-YEAR-OLD ARMS AREN'T CUT OUT FOR ALL THIS DIGGING!
DEAL!
LATER...
=GASP!= LOOK AT ALL THESE PRESERVES!
THERE MUST BE HUNDREDS OF JARS IN HERE!
800, AT LAST COUNT.
BUT YOU CAN'T POSSIBLY EAT ALL THESE YOURSELF.
I USE MOST OF IT TO BARTER WITH MY NEIGHBORS...
MAINLY IN EXCHANGE FOR RIDES, SINCE I NO LONGER DRIVE.
BUT YOU ALSO MUST TRADE FOR FOOD YOU CAN'T GROW, YES?
LIKE FLOUR, OR SUGAR—
NEVER!
THAT WOULD MEAN ACCEPTING RATIONED ITEMS, WHICH WOULD DEFEAT MY PURPOSE...
I'M TAKING A PRINCIPLED STAND!
BESIDES, WHO NEEDS SUGAR WHEN YOU HAVE HONEY BEES?
WOW!
THAT EVENING...
ROSE, THIS PORK IS DELICIOUS!
AND YOU BUTCHERED THE PIG YOURSELF!
I JUST WISH I HAD POTATOES TO GO WITH IT...
THOUGH THE LACK OF CARBS IS HELPING ME TO LOSE WEIGHT!
HERE'S TO YOUR "NO-RATIONS DIET"! HA HA!

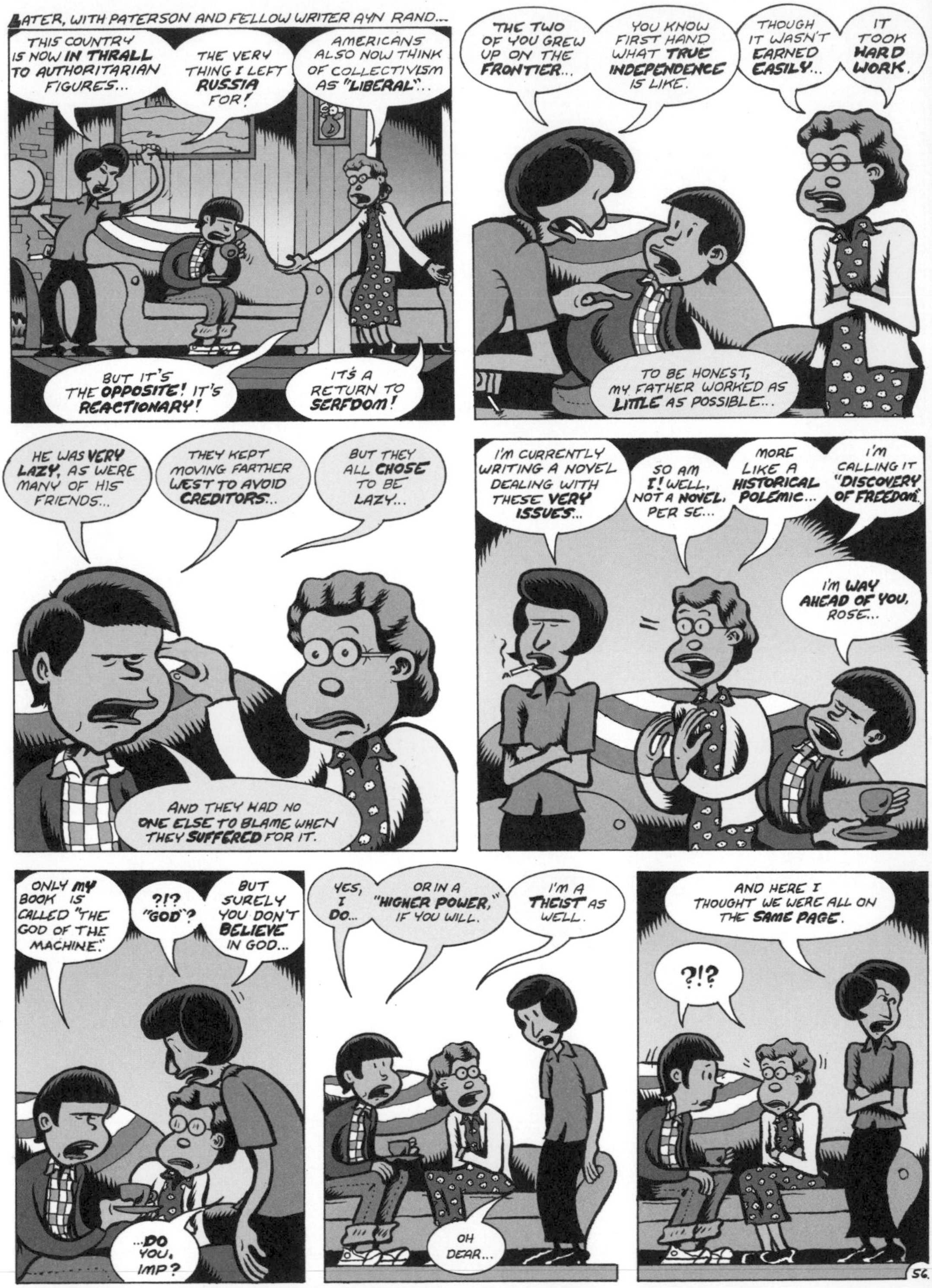
LATER, WITH PATERSON AND FELLOW WRITER AYN RAND...
THIS COUNTRY IS NOW IN THRALL TO AUTHORITARIAN FIGURES...
THE VERY THING I LEFT RUSSIA FOR!
AMERICANS ALSO NOW THINK OF COLLECTIVISM AS "LIBERAL"...
BUT IT'S THE OPPOSITE! IT'S REACTIONARY!
IT'S A RETURN TO SERFDOM!
THE TWO OF YOU GREW UP ON THE FRONTIER...
YOU KNOW FIRST HAND WHAT TRUE INDEPENDENCE IS LIKE.
THOUGH IT WASN'T EARNED EASILY...
IT TOOK HARD WORK.
TO BE HONEST, MY FATHER WORKED AS LITTLE AS POSSIBLE...
HE WAS VERY LAZY, AS WERE MANY OF HIS FRIENDS...
THEY KEPT MOVING FARTHER WEST TO AVOID CREDITORS...
BUT THEY ALL CHOSE TO BE LAZY...
AND THEY HAD NO ONE ELSE TO BLAME WHEN THEY SUFFERED FOR IT.
I'M CURRENTLY WRITING A NOVEL DEALING WITH THESE VERY ISSUES...
SO AM I! WELL, NOT A NOVEL, PER SE...
MORE LIKE A HISTORICAL POLEMIC...
I'M CALLING IT "DISCOVERY OF FREEDOM".
I'M WAY AHEAD OF YOU, ROSE...
ONLY MY BOOK IS CALLED "THE GOD OF THE MACHINE."
?!? "GOD"?
BUT SURELY YOU DON'T BELIEVE IN GOD...
...DO YOU, IMP?
YES, I DO...
OR IN A "HIGHER POWER," IF YOU WILL.
I'M A THEIST AS WELL.
OH DEAR...
AND HERE I THOUGHT WE WERE ALL ON THE SAME PAGE.
?!?

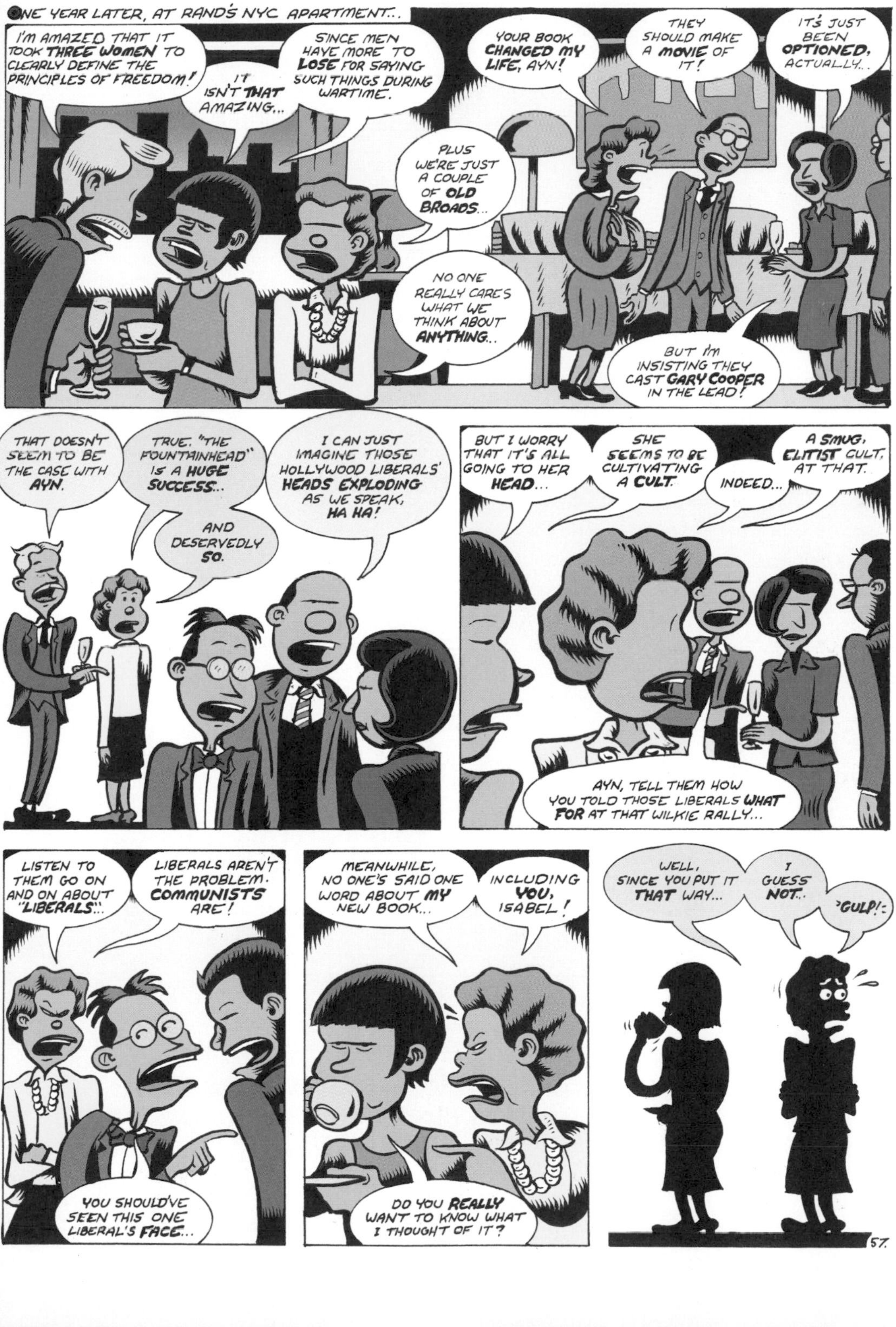
ONE YEAR LATER, AT RAND'S NYC APARTMENT...
I'M AMAZED THAT IT TOOK THREE WOMEN TO CLEARLY DEFINE THE PRINCIPLES OF FREEDOM!
IT ISN'T THAT AMAZING...
SINCE MEN HAVE MORE TO LOSE FOR SAYING SUCH THINGS DURING WARTIME.
PLUS WE'RE JUST A COUPLE OF OLD BROADS...
NO ONE REALLY CARES WHAT WE THINK ABOUT ANYTHING...
YOUR BOOK CHANGED MY LIFE, AYN!
THEY SHOULD MAKE A MOVIE OF IT!
IT'S JUST BEEN OPTIONED, ACTUALLY...
BUT I'M INSISTING THEY CAST GARY COOPER IN THE LEAD!
THAT DOESN'T SEEM TO BE THE CASE WITH AYN.
TRUE. "THE FOUNTAINHEAD" IS A HUGE SUCCESS...
AND DESERVEDLY SO.
I CAN JUST IMAGINE THOSE HOLLYWOOD LIBERALS' HEADS EXPLODING AS WE SPEAK, HA HA!
BUT I WORRY THAT IT'S ALL GOING TO HER HEAD...
SHE SEEMS TO BE CULTIVATING A CULT.
INDEED...
A SMUG, ELITIST CULT, AT THAT.
AYN, TELL THEM HOW YOU TOLD THOSE LIBERALS WHAT FOR AT THAT WILKIE RALLY...
LISTEN TO THEM GO ON AND ON ABOUT "LIBERALS"...
LIBERALS AREN'T THE PROBLEM. COMMUNISTS ARE!
YOU SHOULD'VE SEEN THIS ONE LIBERAL'S FACE...
MEANWHILE, NO ONE'S SAID ONE WORD ABOUT MY NEW BOOK...
INCLUDING YOU, ISABEL!
DO YOU REALLY WANT TO KNOW WHAT I THOUGHT OF IT?
WELL, SINCE YOU PUT IT THAT WAY...
I GUESS NOT...
GULP!

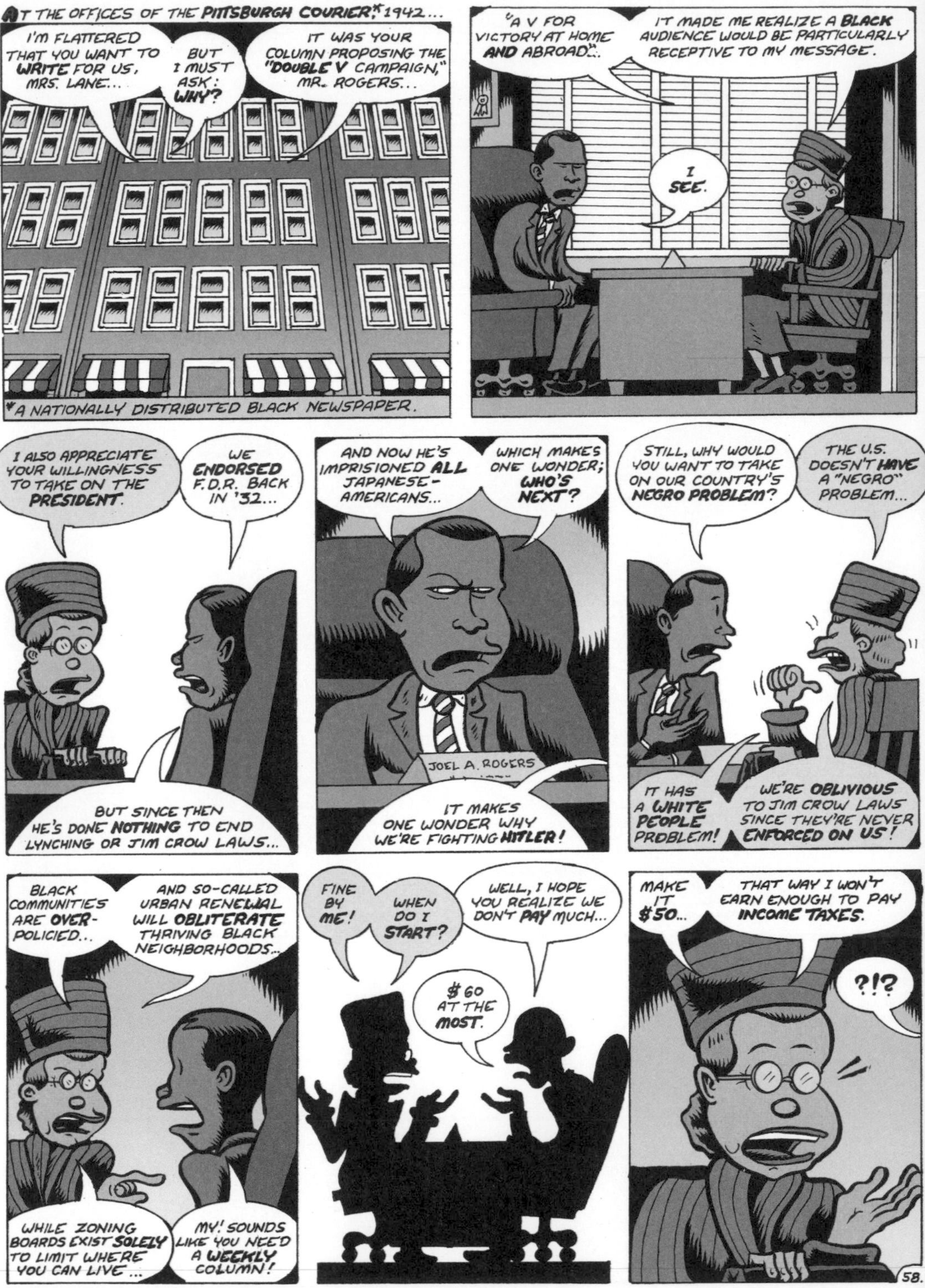
AT THE OFFICES OF THE PITTSBURGH COURIER,* 1942...
I'M FLATTERED THAT YOU WANT TO WRITE FOR US, MRS. LANE...
BUT I MUST ASK: WHY?
IT WAS YOUR COLUMN PROPOSING THE "DOUBLE V CAMPAIGN," MR. ROGERS...
*A NATIONALLY DISTRIBUTED BLACK NEWSPAPER.
"A V FOR VICTORY AT HOME AND ABROAD"...
IT MADE ME REALIZE A BLACK AUDIENCE WOULD BE PARTICULARLY RECEPTIVE TO MY MESSAGE.
I SEE.
I ALSO APPRECIATE YOUR WILLINGNESS TO TAKE ON THE PRESIDENT.
WE ENDORSED F.D.R. BACK IN '32...
BUT SINCE THEN HE'S DONE NOTHING TO END LYNCHING OR JIM CROW LAWS...
AND NOW HE'S IMPRISIONED ALL JAPANESE-AMERICANS...
WHICH MAKES ONE WONDER; WHO'S NEXT?
JOEL A. ROGERS
IT MAKES ONE WONDER WHY WE'RE FIGHTING HITLER!
STILL, WHY WOULD YOU WANT TO TAKE ON OUR COUNTRY'S NEGRO PROBLEM?
THE U.S. DOESN'T HAVE A "NEGRO" PROBLEM...
IT HAS A WHITE PEOPLE PROBLEM!
WE'RE OBLIVIOUS TO JIM CROW LAWS SINCE THEY'RE NEVER ENFORCED ON US!
BLACK COMMUNITIES ARE OVER-POLICIED...
AND SO-CALLED URBAN RENEWAL WILL OBLITERATE THRIVING BLACK NEIGHBORHOODS...
WHILE ZONING BOARDS EXIST SOLELY TO LIMIT WHERE YOU CAN LIVE...
MY! SOUNDS LIKE YOU NEED A WEEKLY COLUMN!
FINE BY ME!
WHEN DO I START?
WELL, I HOPE YOU REALIZE WE DON'T PAY MUCH...
$60 AT THE MOST.
MAKE IT $50...
THAT WAY I WON'T EARN ENOUGH TO PAY INCOME TAXES.
?!?

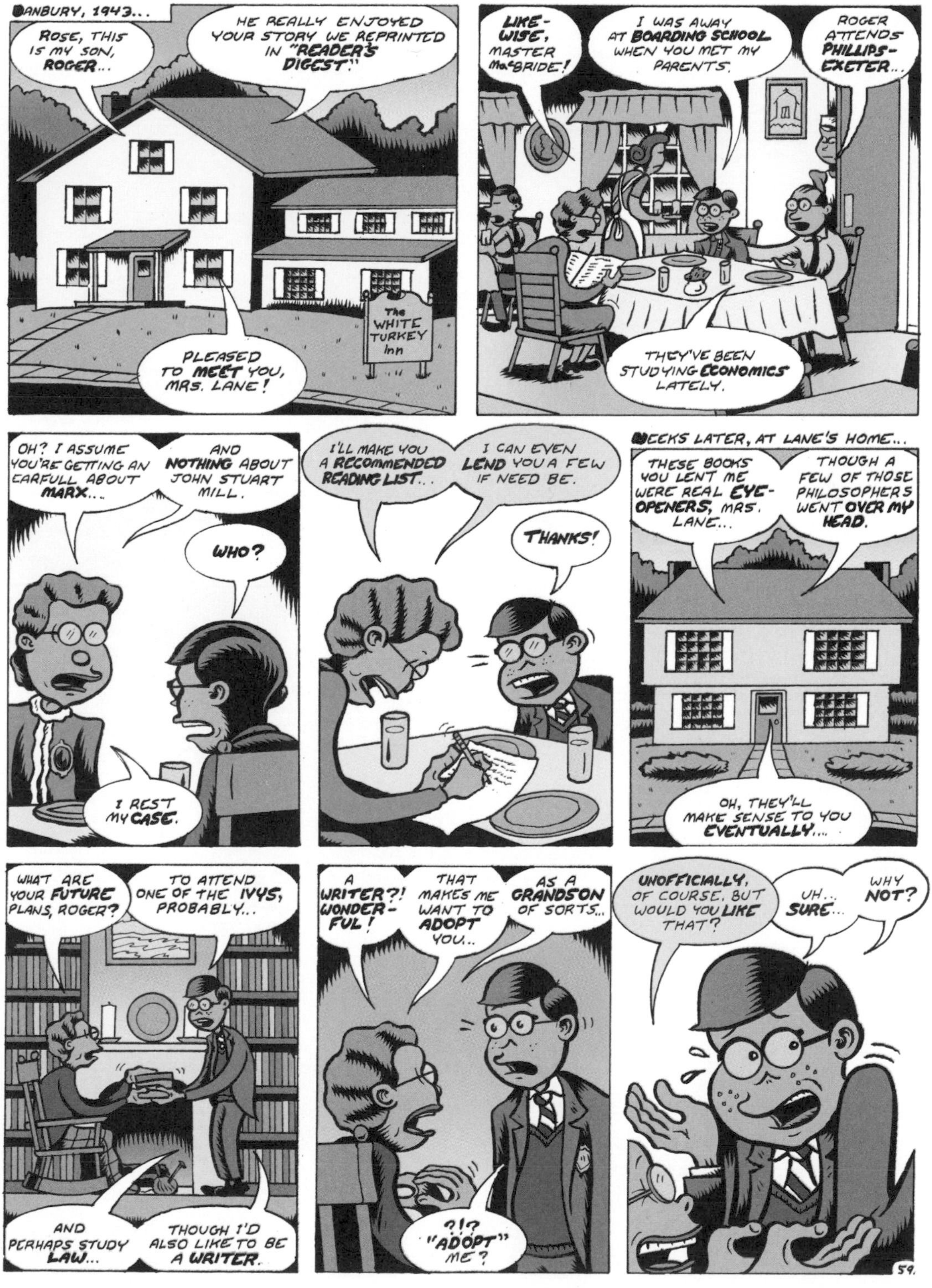
DANBURY, 1943...
ROSE, THIS IS MY SON, ROGER...
HE REALLY ENJOYED YOUR STORY WE REPRINTED IN "READER'S DIGEST."
PLEASED TO MEET YOU, MRS. LANE!
The WHITE TURKEY Inn
LIKE-WISE, MASTER MacBRIDE!
I WAS AWAY AT BOARDING SCHOOL WHEN YOU MET MY PARENTS.
ROGER ATTENDS PHILLIPS-EXETER...
THEY'VE BEEN STUDYING ECONOMICS LATELY.
OH? I ASSUME YOU'RE GETTING AN EARFULL ABOUT MARX...
AND NOTHING ABOUT JOHN STUART MILL.
WHO?
I REST MY CASE.
I'LL MAKE YOU A RECOMMENDED READING LIST...
I CAN EVEN LEND YOU A FEW IF NEED BE.
THANKS!
WEEKS LATER, AT LANE'S HOME...
THESE BOOKS YOU LENT ME WERE REAL EYE-OPENERS, MRS. LANE...
THOUGH A FEW OF THOSE PHILOSOPHERS WENT OVER MY HEAD.
OH, THEY'LL MAKE SENSE TO YOU EVENTUALLY....
WHAT ARE YOUR FUTURE PLANS, ROGER?
TO ATTEND ONE OF THE IVYS, PROBABLY...
AND PERHAPS STUDY LAW...
THOUGH I'D ALSO LIKE TO BE A WRITER.
A WRITER?! WONDER-FUL!
THAT MAKES ME WANT TO ADOPT YOU...
AS A GRANDSON OF SORTS...
?!? "ADOPT" ME?
UNOFFICIALLY, OF COURSE. BUT WOULD YOU LIKE THAT?
UH... SURE...
WHY NOT?

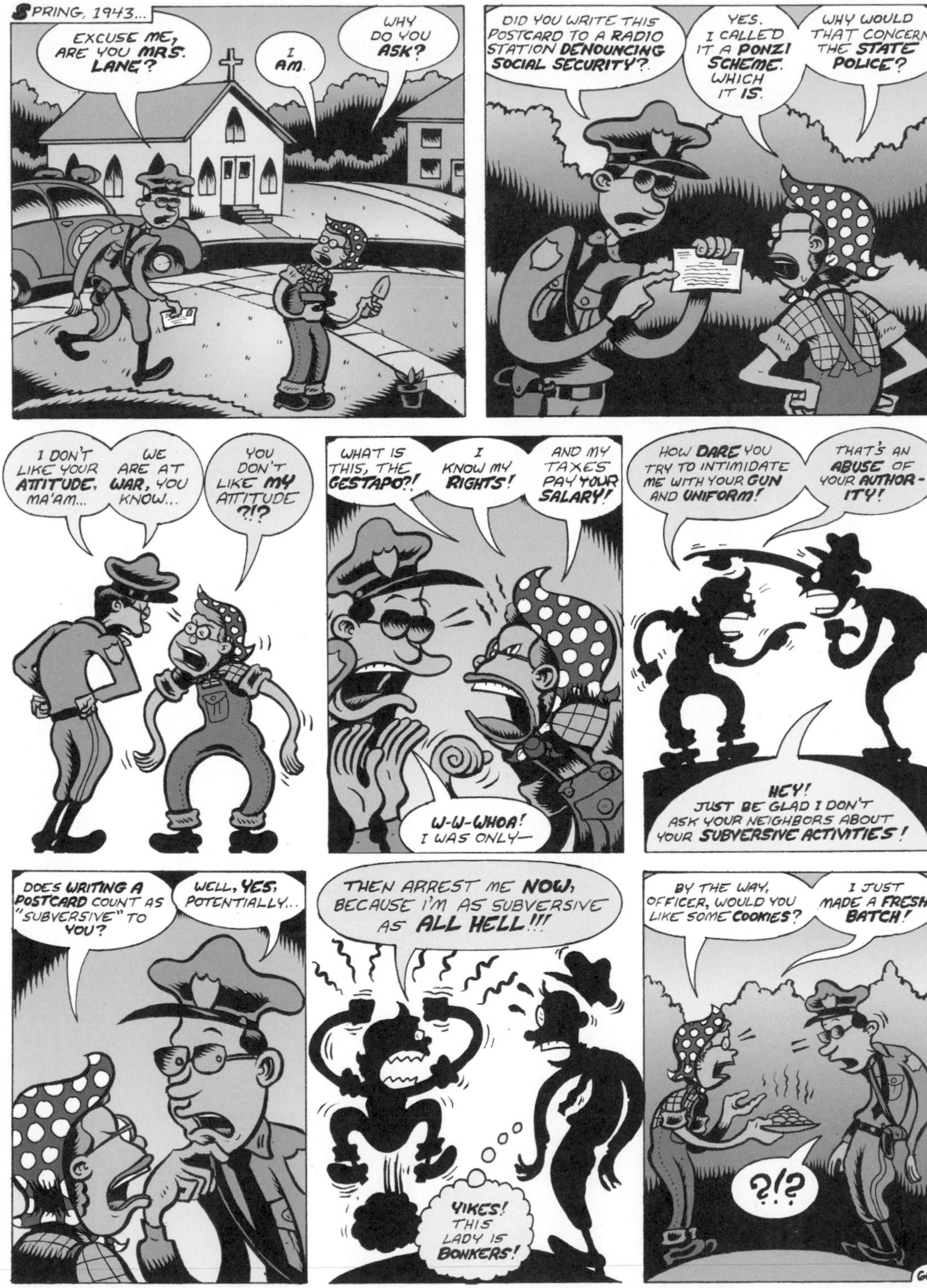
SPRING, 1943...
EXCUSE ME, ARE YOU MRS. LANE?
I AM.
WHY DO YOU ASK?
DID YOU WRITE THIS POSTCARD TO A RADIO STATION DENOUNCING SOCIAL SECURITY?
YES. I CALLED IT A PONZI SCHEME. WHICH IT IS.
WHY WOULD THAT CONCERN THE STATE POLICE?
I DON'T LIKE YOUR ATTITUDE, MA'AM...
WE ARE AT WAR, YOU KNOW...
YOU DON'T LIKE MY ATTITUDE ?!?
WHAT IS THIS, THE GESTAPO?!
I KNOW MY RIGHTS!
AND MY TAXES PAY YOUR SALARY!
W-W-WHOA! I WAS ONLY—
HOW DARE YOU TRY TO INTIMIDATE ME WITH YOUR GUN AND UNIFORM!
THAT'S AN ABUSE OF YOUR AUTHOR-ITY!
HEY! JUST BE GLAD I DON'T ASK YOUR NEIGHBORS ABOUT YOUR SUBVERSIVE ACTIVITIES!
DOES WRITING A POSTCARD COUNT AS "SUBVERSIVE" TO YOU?
WELL, YES, POTENTIALLY...
THEN ARREST ME NOW, BECAUSE I'M AS SUBVERSIVE AS ALL HELL!!!
YIKES! THIS LADY IS BONKERS!
BY THE WAY, OFFICER, WOULD YOU LIKE SOME COOKIES?
I JUST MADE A FRESH BATCH!
?!?
60.

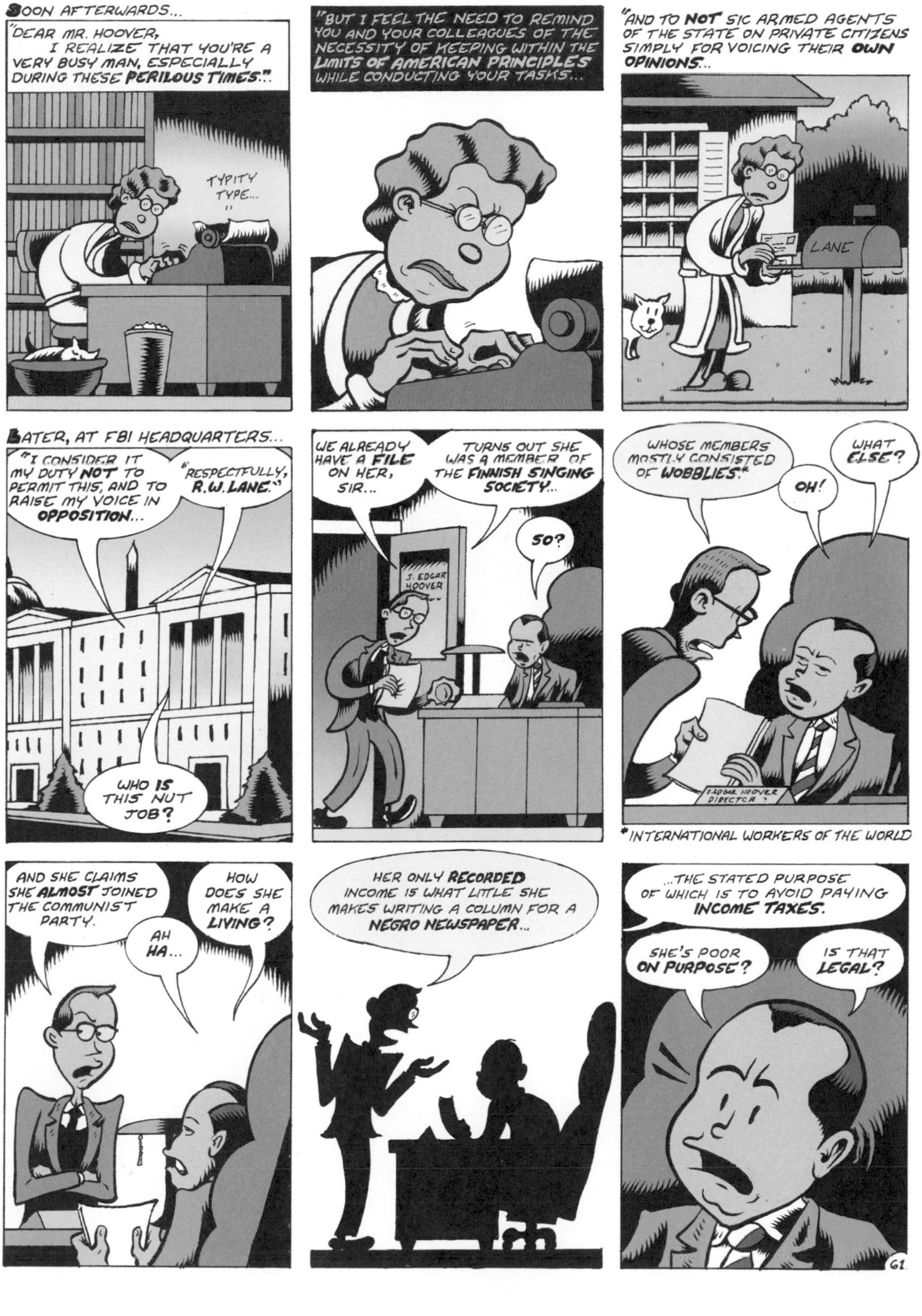
SOON AFTERWARDS...
"DEAR MR. HOOVER,
I REALIZE THAT YOU'RE A VERY BUSY MAN, ESPECIALLY DURING THESE PERILOUS TIMES..."
TYPITY TYPE...
"BUT I FEEL THE NEED TO REMIND YOU AND YOUR COLLEAGUES OF THE NECESSITY OF KEEPING WITHIN THE LIMITS OF AMERICAN PRINCIPLES WHILE CONDUCTING YOUR TASKS...
"AND TO NOT SIC ARMED AGENTS OF THE STATE ON PRIVATE CITIZENS SIMPLY FOR VOICING THEIR OWN OPINIONS...
LANE
LATER, AT FBI HEADQUARTERS...
"I CONSIDER IT MY DUTY NOT TO PERMIT THIS, AND TO RAISE MY VOICE IN OPPOSITION...
"RESPECTFULLY, R.W. LANE."
WHO IS THIS NUT JOB?
WE ALREADY HAVE A FILE ON HER, SIR...
TURNS OUT SHE WAS A MEMBER OF THE FINNISH SINGING SOCIETY...
J. EDGAR HOOVER
SO?
WHOSE MEMBERS MOSTLY CONSISTED OF WOBBLIES.*
OH!
WHAT ELSE?
J. EDGAR HOOVER DIRECTOR
*INTERNATIONAL WORKERS OF THE WORLD
AND SHE CLAIMS SHE ALMOST JOINED THE COMMUNIST PARTY.
AH HA...
HOW DOES SHE MAKE A LIVING?
HER ONLY RECORDED INCOME IS WHAT LITTLE SHE MAKES WRITING A COLUMN FOR A NEGRO NEWSPAPER...
...THE STATED PURPOSE OF WHICH IS TO AVOID PAYING INCOME TAXES.
SHE'S POOR ON PURPOSE?
IS THAT LEGAL?

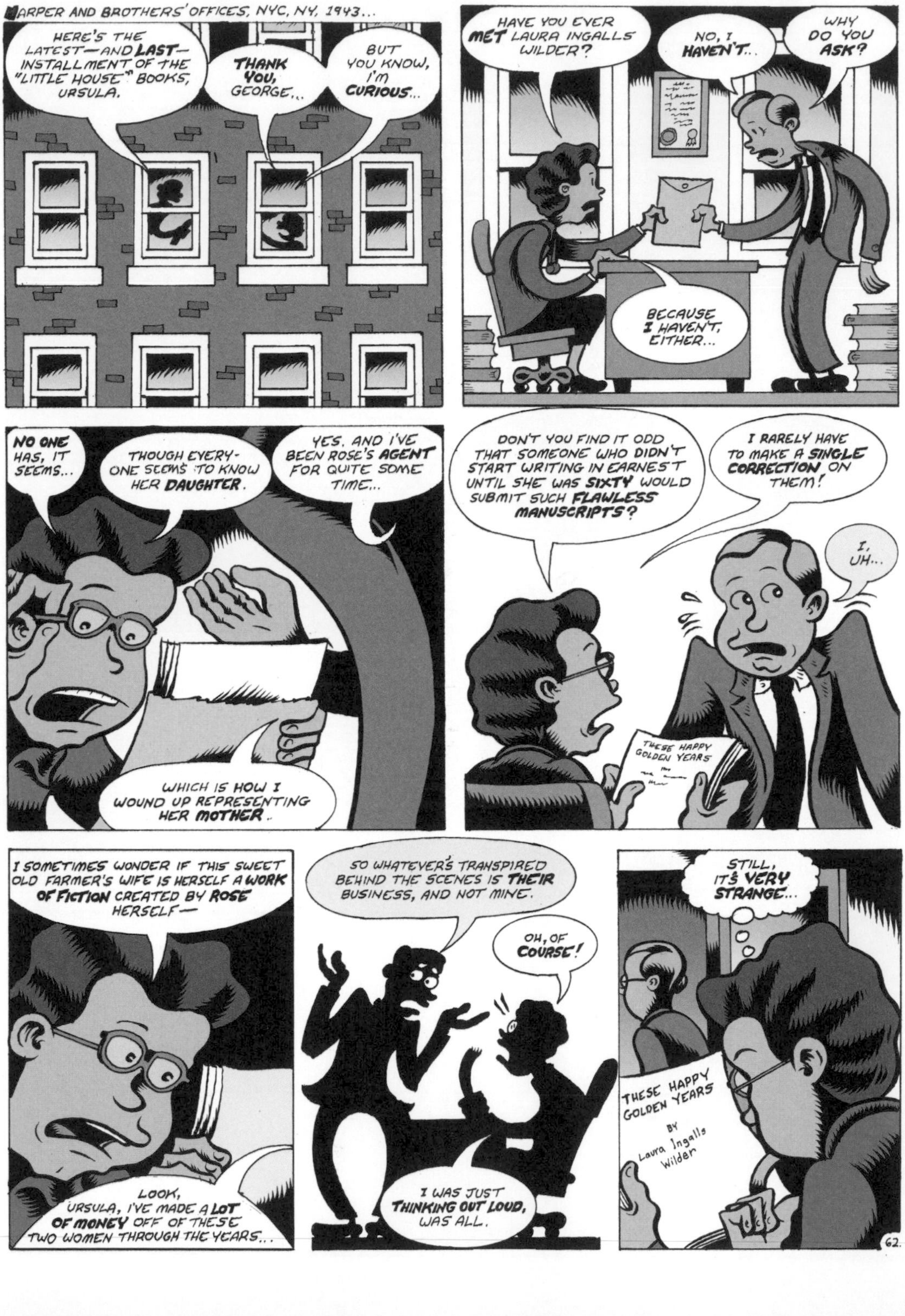
HARPER AND BROTHERS' OFFICES, NYC, NY, 1943...
HERE'S THE LATEST—AND LAST—INSTALLMENT OF THE "LITTLE HOUSE" BOOKS, URSULA.
THANK YOU, GEORGE...
BUT YOU KNOW, I'M CURIOUS...
HAVE YOU EVER MET LAURA INGALLS WILDER?
NO, I HAVEN'T...
WHY DO YOU ASK?
BECAUSE I HAVEN'T, EITHER...
NO ONE HAS, IT SEEMS...
THOUGH EVERY-ONE SEEMS TO KNOW HER DAUGHTER.
YES. AND I'VE BEEN ROSE'S AGENT FOR QUITE SOME TIME...
WHICH IS HOW I WOUND UP REPRESENTING HER MOTHER..
DON'T YOU FIND IT ODD THAT SOMEONE WHO DIDN'T START WRITING IN EARNEST UNTIL SHE WAS SIXTY WOULD SUBMIT SUCH FLAWLESS MANUSCRIPTS?
I RARELY HAVE TO MAKE A SINGLE CORRECTION ON THEM!
I, UH...
THESE HAPPY GOLDEN YEARS
I SOMETIMES WONDER IF THIS SWEET OLD FARMER'S WIFE IS HERSELF A WORK OF FICTION CREATED BY ROSE HERSELF—
LOOK, URSULA, I'VE MADE A LOT OF MONEY OFF OF THESE TWO WOMEN THROUGH THE YEARS...
SO WHATEVER'S TRANSPIRED BEHIND THE SCENES IS THEIR BUSINESS, AND NOT MINE.
OH, OF COURSE!
I WAS JUST THINKING OUT LOUD, WAS ALL.
STILL, IT'S VERY STRANGE...
THESE HAPPY GOLDEN YEARS
BY
Laura Ingalls Wilder

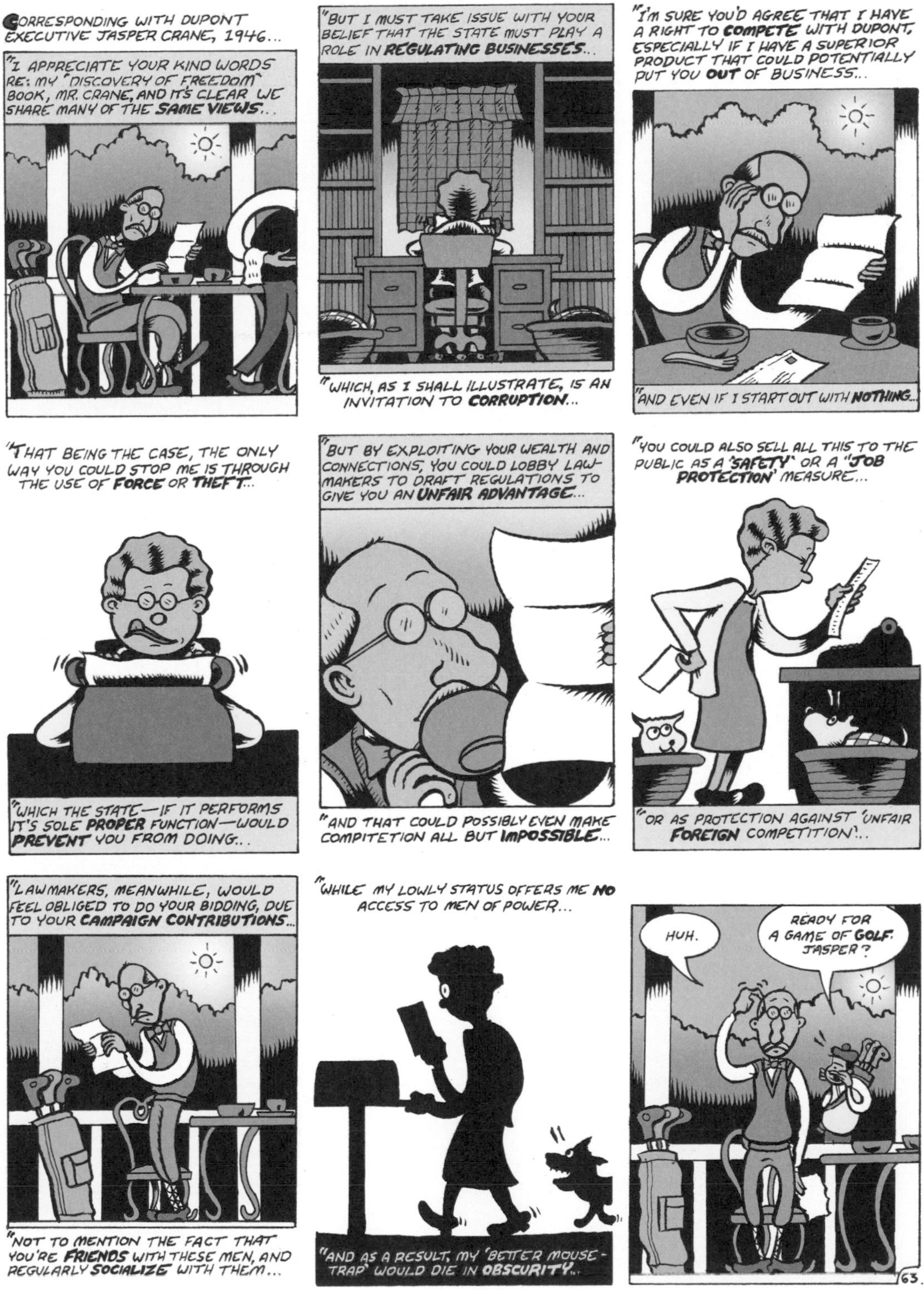
CORRESPONDING WITH DUPONT EXECUTIVE JASPER CRANE, 1946...
"I APPRECIATE YOUR KIND WORDS RE: MY "DISCOVERY OF FREEDOM" BOOK, MR. CRANE, AND IT'S CLEAR WE SHARE MANY OF THE SAME VIEWS...
"BUT I MUST TAKE ISSUE WITH YOUR BELIEF THAT THE STATE MUST PLAY A ROLE IN REGULATING BUSINESSES...
"WHICH, AS I SHALL ILLUSTRATE, IS AN INVITATION TO CORRUPTION...
"I'M SURE YOU'D AGREE THAT I HAVE A RIGHT TO COMPETE WITH DUPONT, ESPECIALLY IF I HAVE A SUPERIOR PRODUCT THAT COULD POTENTIALLY PUT YOU OUT OF BUSINESS...
"AND EVEN IF I START OUT WITH NOTHING...
"THAT BEING THE CASE, THE ONLY WAY YOU COULD STOP ME IS THROUGH THE USE OF FORCE OR THEFT...
"WHICH THE STATE—IF IT PERFORMS IT'S SOLE PROPER FUNCTION—WOULD PREVENT YOU FROM DOING...
"BUT BY EXPLOITING YOUR WEALTH AND CONNECTIONS, YOU COULD LOBBY LAWMAKERS TO DRAFT REGULATIONS TO GIVE YOU AN UNFAIR ADVANTAGE...
"AND THAT COULD POSSIBLY EVEN MAKE COMPITETION ALL BUT IMPOSSIBLE...
"YOU COULD ALSO SELL ALL THIS TO THE PUBLIC AS A "SAFETY" OR A "JOB PROTECTION" MEASURE...
"OR AS PROTECTION AGAINST 'UNFAIR FOREIGN COMPETITION'...
"LAWMAKERS, MEANWHILE, WOULD FEEL OBLIGED TO DO YOUR BIDDING, DUE TO YOUR CAMPAIGN CONTRIBUTIONS...
"NOT TO MENTION THE FACT THAT YOU'RE FRIENDS WITH THESE MEN, AND REGULARLY SOCIALIZE WITH THEM...
"WHILE MY LOWLY STATUS OFFERS ME NO ACCESS TO MEN OF POWER...
"AND AS A RESULT, MY 'BETTER MOUSE-TRAP' WOULD DIE IN OBSCURITY...
HUH.
READY FOR A GAME OF GOLF, JASPER?

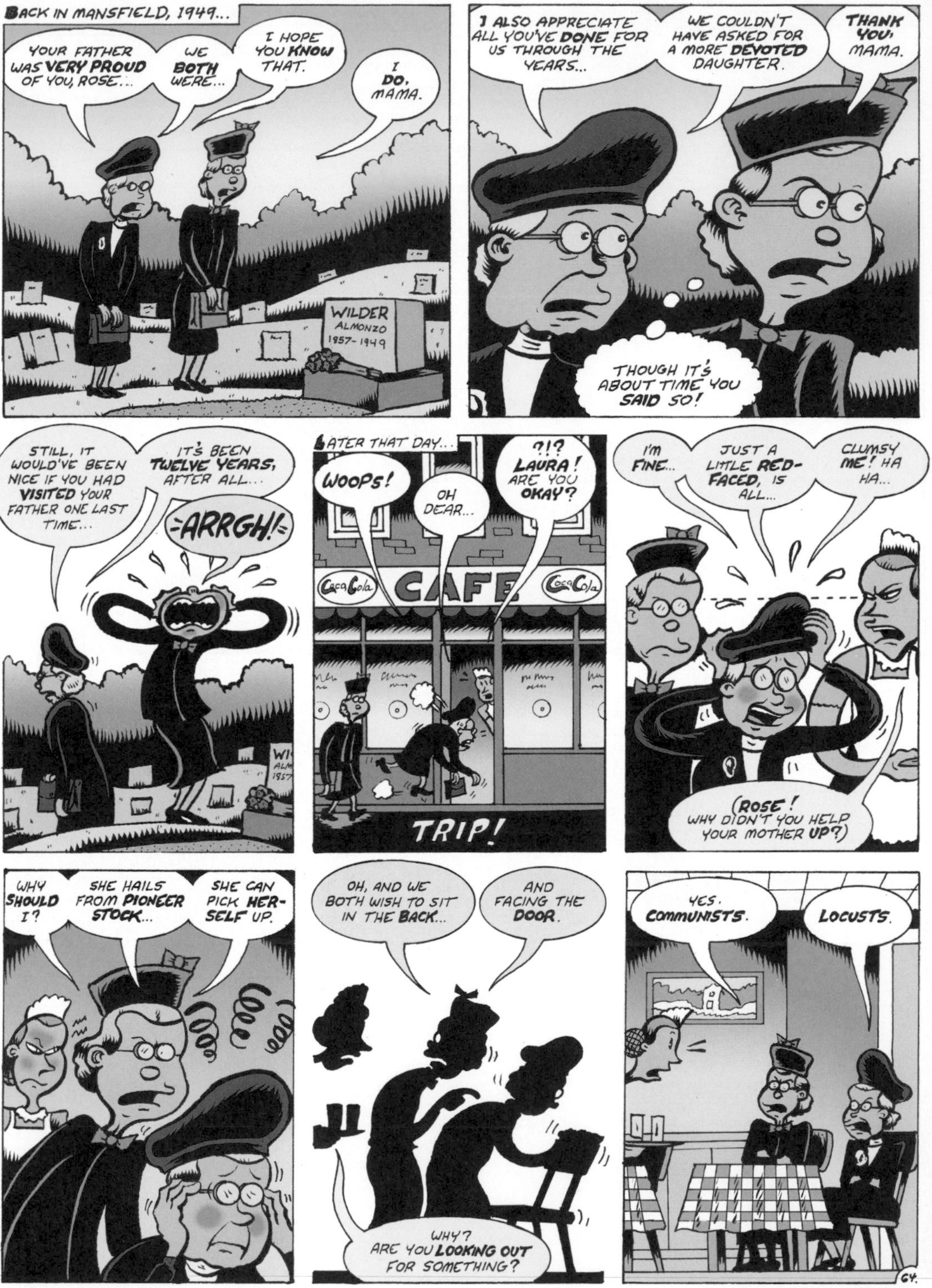
BACK IN MANSFIELD, 1949...
YOUR FATHER WAS VERY PROUD OF YOU, ROSE...
WE BOTH WERE...
I HOPE YOU KNOW THAT.
I DO, MAMA.
WILDER
ALMONZO
1857-1949
I ALSO APPRECIATE ALL YOU'VE DONE FOR US THROUGH THE YEARS...
WE COULDN'T HAVE ASKED FOR A MORE DEVOTED DAUGHTER.
THANK YOU, MAMA.
THOUGH IT'S ABOUT TIME YOU SAID SO!
STILL, IT WOULD'VE BEEN NICE IF YOU HAD VISITED YOUR FATHER ONE LAST TIME...
IT'S BEEN TWELVE YEARS, AFTER ALL...
ARRGH!
LATER THAT DAY...
WOOPS!
OH DEAR...
?!? LAURA! ARE YOU OKAY?
Coca Cola
CAFE
Coca Cola
TRIP!
I'M FINE...
JUST A LITTLE RED-FACED, IS ALL...
CLUMSY ME! HA HA...
(ROSE! WHY DIDN'T YOU HELP YOUR MOTHER UP?)
WHY SHOULD I?
SHE HAILS FROM PIONEER STOCK...
SHE CAN PICK HER-SELF UP.
OH, AND WE BOTH WISH TO SIT IN THE BACK...
AND FACING THE DOOR.
WHY? ARE YOU LOOKING OUT FOR SOMETHING?
YES. COMMUNISTS.
LOCUSTS.

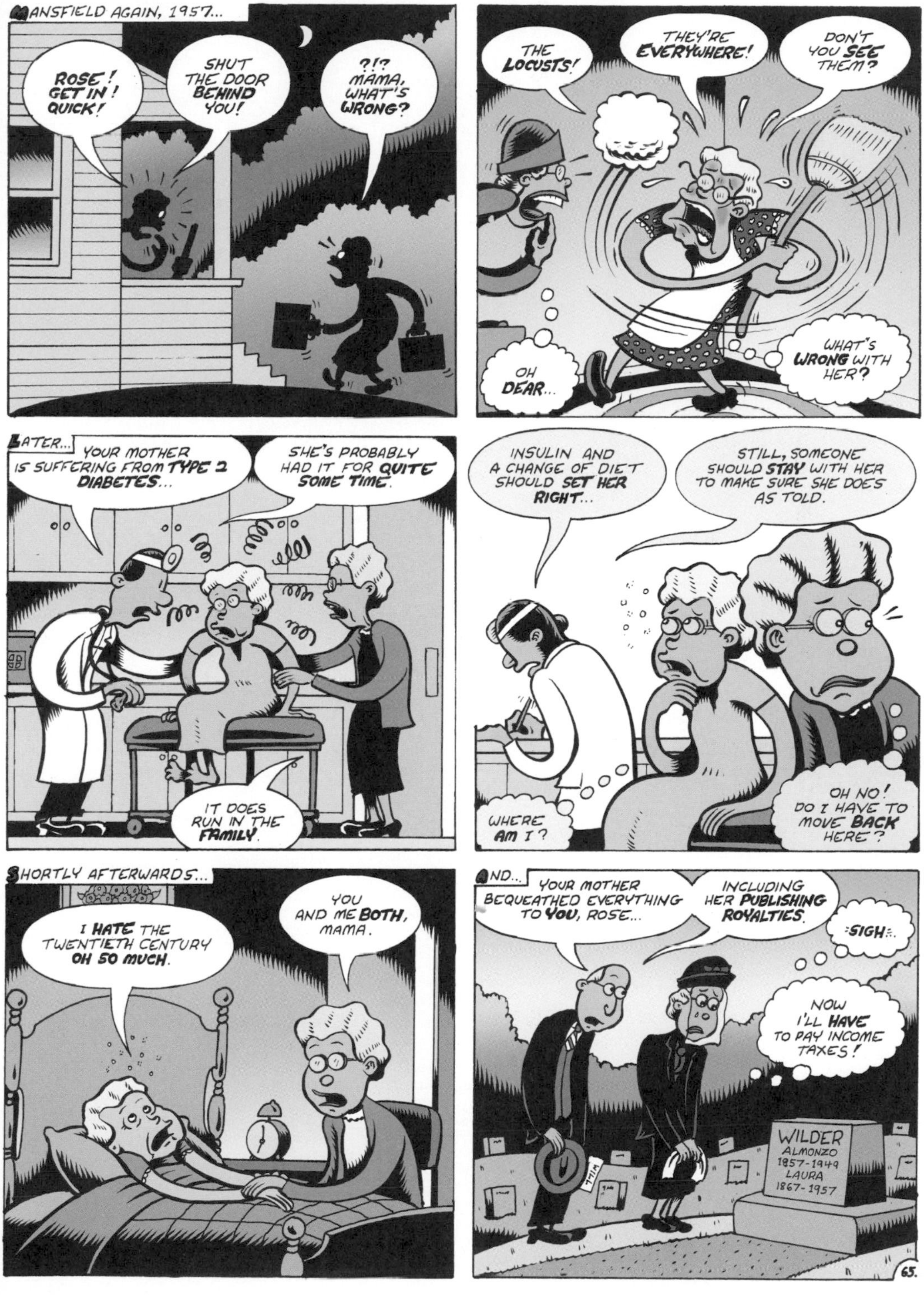
MANSFIELD AGAIN, 1957...
ROSE! GET IN! QUICK!
SHUT THE DOOR BEHIND YOU!
?!? MAMA, WHAT'S WRONG?
THE LOCUSTS!
THEY'RE EVERYWHERE!
DON'T YOU SEE THEM?
OH DEAR...
WHAT'S WRONG WITH HER?
LATER...
YOUR MOTHER IS SUFFERING FROM TYPE 2 DIABETES...
SHE'S PROBABLY HAD IT FOR QUITE SOME TIME.
IT DOES RUN IN THE FAMILY.
INSULIN AND A CHANGE OF DIET SHOULD SET HER RIGHT...
STILL, SOMEONE SHOULD STAY WITH HER TO MAKE SURE SHE DOES AS TOLD.
WHERE AM I?
OH NO! DO I HAVE TO MOVE BACK HERE?
SHORTLY AFTERWARDS...
I HATE THE TWENTIETH CENTURY OH SO MUCH.
YOU AND ME BOTH, MAMA.
AND...
YOUR MOTHER BEQUEATHED EVERYTHING TO YOU, ROSE...
INCLUDING HER PUBLISHING ROYALTIES.
SIGH
NOW I'LL HAVE TO PAY INCOME TAXES!
WILL
WILDER
ALMONZO
1857-1949
LAURA
1867-1957

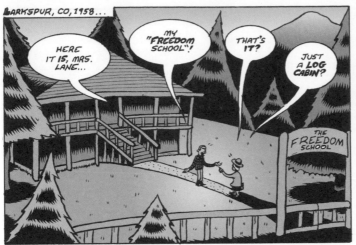

LARKSPUR, CO, 1958...
HERE IT IS, MRS. LANE...
MY "FREEDOM SCHOOL"!
THAT'S IT?
JUST A LOG CABIN?
THE FREEDOM SCHOOL
IT'S NOT MUCH TO LOOK AT, I KNOW, BUT—
DON'T BE SILLY, MR. LEFEVRE...
I LOVE IT!
SO FAR I ONLY HAVE A HANDFUL OF STUDENTS...
AND WE ONLY GATHER FOR BRIEF SUMMER SEMINARS...
TO DISCUSS WHAT THEY NO LONGER TEACH AT "REAL" COLLEGES...
THAT SOUNDS PERFECT.
YOUR BOOK IS WHAT INSPIRED ME TO START THIS SCHOOL...
SO WE'RE ALL VERY HONORED TO HAVE YOU HERE.
APPLAUSE
TRUST ME, THE HONOR IS ALL MINE... *CHOKE*
(SADLY, THIS MAY BE OUR LAST YEAR)...
(THE MORTGAGE IS DUE, AND I'VE COME UP SHORT.)
OH?
HOW SHORT?
ABOUT $1,500. BUT, I—
I CURRENLY HAVE $1,600 IN MY BANK ACCOUNT...
SO I'LL CUT YOU A CHECK FOR $1,500 RIGHT NOW.
?!? BUT THAT ONLY LEAVES YOU WITH $100!
YES. JUST ENOUGH TO GET ME BACK HOME!
ROSE WILDER LANE
$ 1,500.00
ROBERT LEFEVRE
MEMO: FREEDOM SCHOOL
$

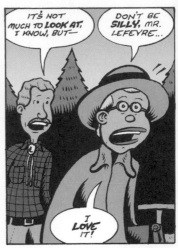

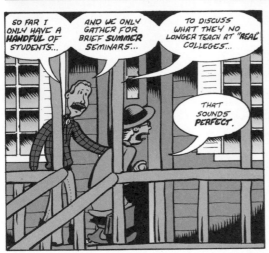

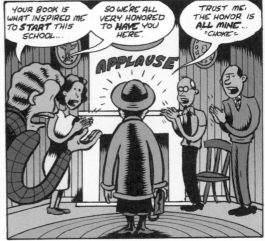

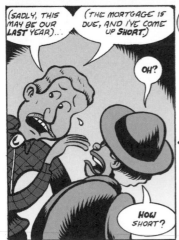

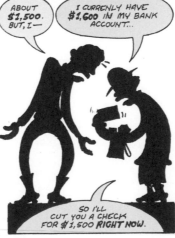

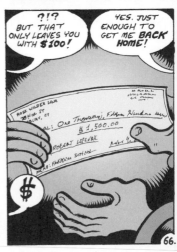

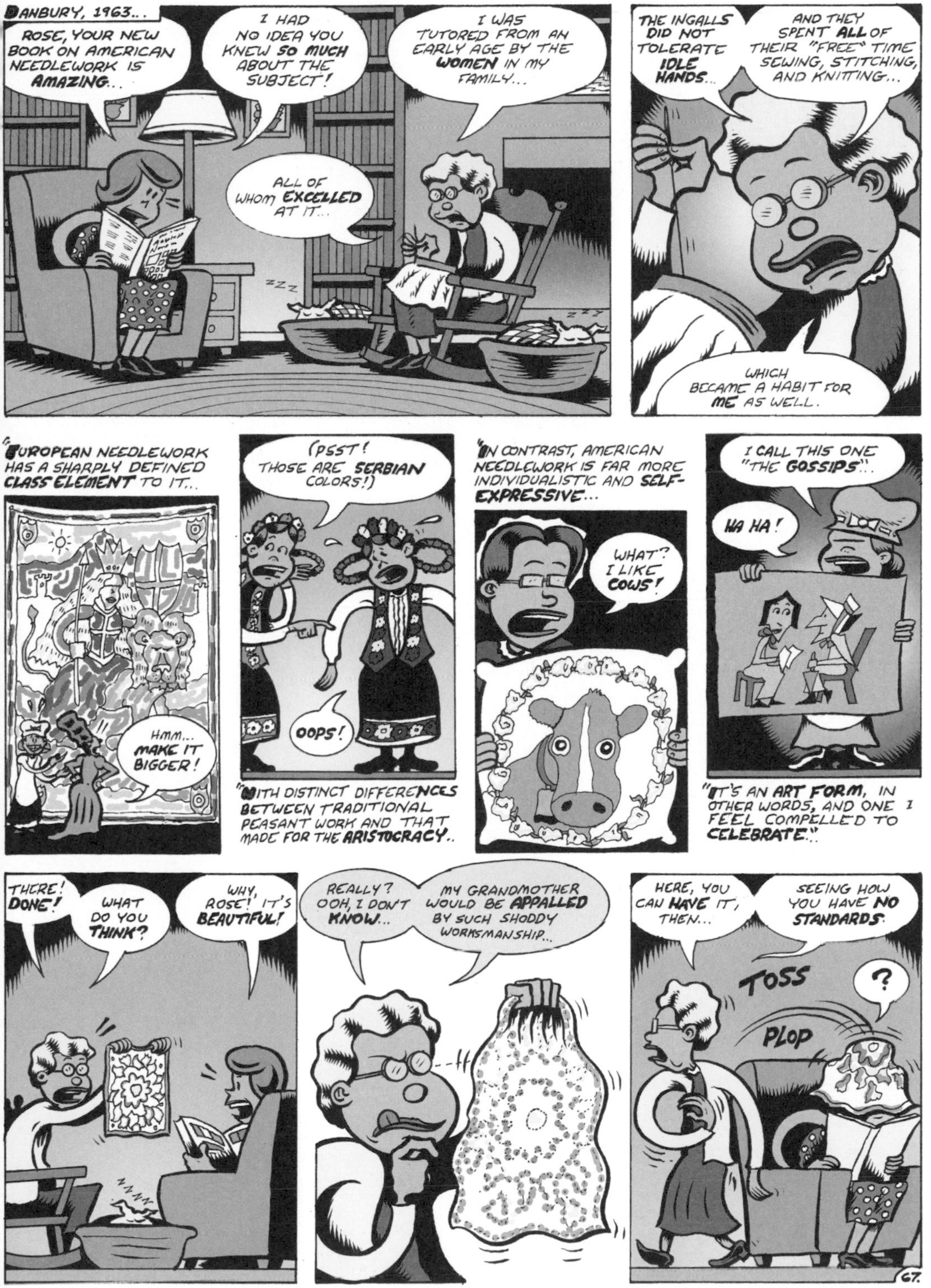
DANBURY, 1963...
ROSE, YOUR NEW BOOK ON AMERICAN NEEDLEWORK IS AMAZING...
I HAD NO IDEA YOU KNEW SO MUCH ABOUT THE SUBJECT!
I WAS TUTORED FROM AN EARLY AGE BY THE WOMEN IN MY FAMILY...
ALL OF WHOM EXCELLED AT IT...
ZZZ
ZZZ
THE INGALLS DID NOT TOLERATE IDLE HANDS...
AND THEY SPENT ALL OF THEIR "FREE" TIME SEWING, STITCHING, AND KNITTING...
WHICH BECAME A HABIT FOR ME AS WELL.
"EUROPEAN NEEDLEWORK HAS A SHARPLY DEFINED CLASS ELEMENT TO IT...
HMM... MAKE IT BIGGER!
(PSST! THOSE ARE SERBIAN COLORS!)
OOPS!
"WITH DISTINCT DIFFERENCES BETWEEN TRADITIONAL PEASANT WORK AND THAT MADE FOR THE ARISTOCRACY..
"IN CONTRAST, AMERICAN NEEDLEWORK IS FAR MORE INDIVIDUALISTIC AND SELF-EXPRESSIVE...
WHAT? I LIKE COWS!
I CALL THIS ONE "THE GOSSIPS"...
HA HA!
"IT'S AN ART FORM, IN OTHER WORDS, AND ONE I FEEL COMPELLED TO CELEBRATE."
THERE! DONE!
WHAT DO YOU THINK?
WHY, ROSE! IT'S BEAUTIFUL!
ZZZZ
REALLY? OOH, I DON'T KNOW...
MY GRANDMOTHER WOULD BE APPALLED BY SUCH SHODDY WORKSMANSHIP...
HERE, YOU CAN HAVE IT, THEN...
SEEING HOW YOU HAVE NO STANDARDS.
TOSS
?
PLOP

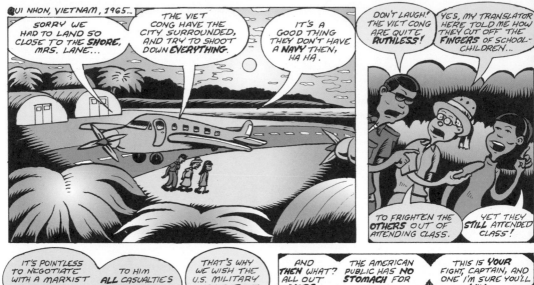

QUI NHON, VIETNAM, 1965...

SORRY WE HAD TO LAND SO CLOSE TO THE **SHORE**, MRS. LANE...

THE VIET CONG HAVE THE CITY SURROUNDED, AND TRY TO SHOOT DOWN **EVERYTHING**.

IT'S A GOOD THING THEY DON'T HAVE A **NAVY** THEN, HA HA.

DON'T LAUGH! THE VIET CONG ARE QUITE **RUTHLESS**!

YES, MY TRANSLATOR HERE TOLD ME HOW THEY CUT OFF THE **FINGERS** OF SCHOOL-CHILDREN...

TO FRIGHTEN THE **OTHERS** OUT OF ATTENDING CLASS.

YET THEY **STILL** ATTENDED CLASS!

IT'S POINTLESS TO NEGOTIATE WITH A MARXIST LIKE **HO CHI MINH**...

TO HIM **ALL CASUALTIES** ARE MERE **STATISTICS**.

THAT'S WHY WE WISH THE U.S. MILITARY WOULD **TAKE HIM OUT**!

AND **THEN** WHAT? ALL OUT **WAR**?

THE AMERICAN PUBLIC HAS **NO STOMACH** FOR THAT...

THIS IS **YOUR** FIGHT, CAPTAIN, AND ONE I'M SURE YOU'LL **WIN**.

THIS IS **AMERICA'S** FIGHT, TOO!

TRUE, ONLY I DON'T WANT TO SEE ANOTHER **KOREA**...

BUT I HAVE FAITH IN THE **RESILIENCE** OF THE VIETNAMESE PEOPLE...

BAH!

(I AGREE WITH **YOU**, MRS. LANE.)

AND **YOU** ARE VERY BRIGHT, **PHAN**!

I'M TOLD YOU PLAN TO **ATTEND COLLEGE** IN THE U.S., TOO. IS THAT TRUE?

YES, THOUGH I **CAN'T AFFORD** IT RIGHT NOW.

I'LL PAY FOR IT!

YOU'LL BE MY ADOPTED **GRAND-DAUGHTER**!

WOULD YOU **LIKE** THAT?

WHY, **OF COURSE**!

68.

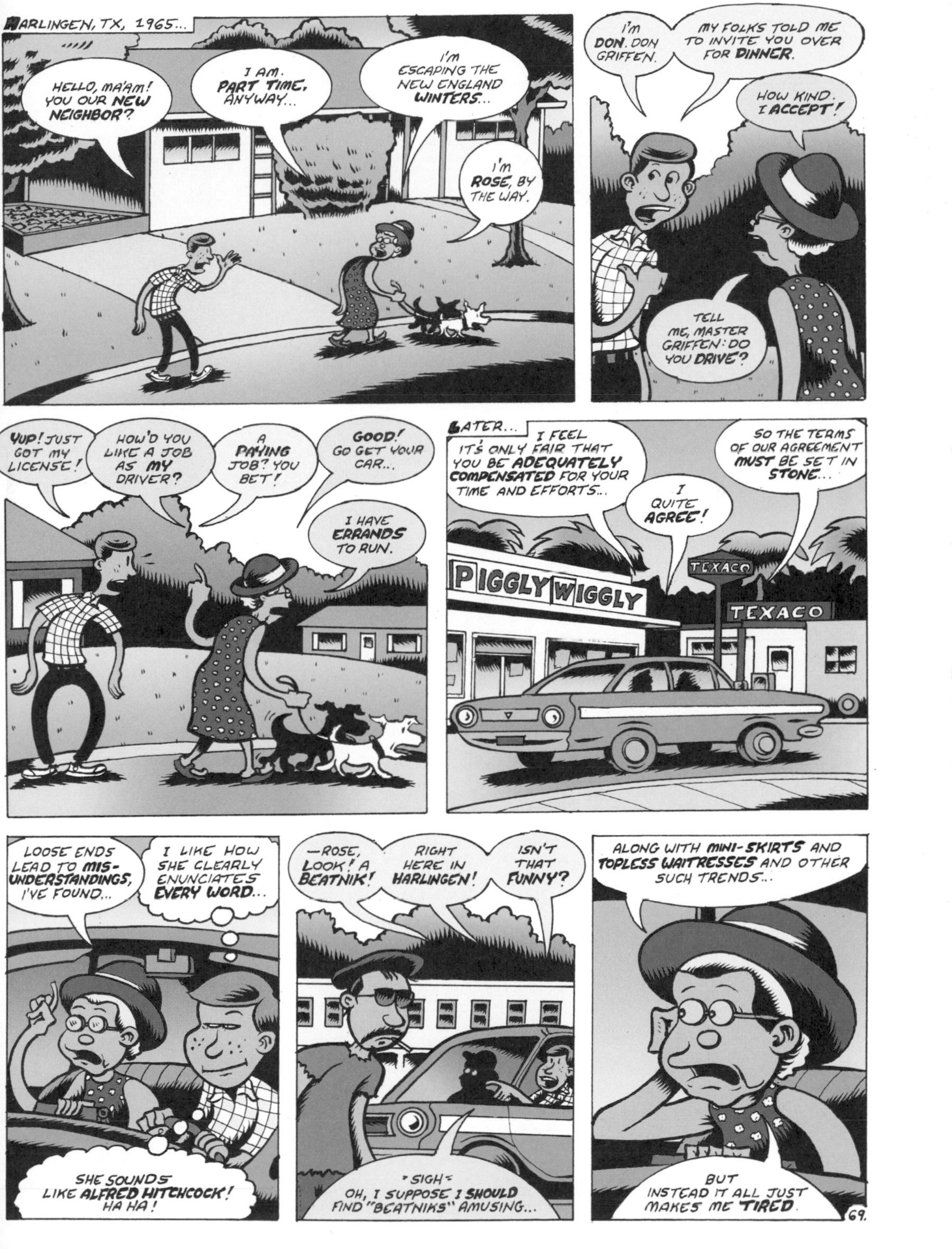
HARLINGEN, TX, 1965...
HELLO, MA'AM! YOU OUR NEW NEIGHBOR?
I AM. PART TIME, ANYWAY...
I'M ESCAPING THE NEW ENGLAND WINTERS...
I'M ROSE, BY THE WAY.
I'M DON. DON GRIFFEN.
MY FOLKS TOLD ME TO INVITE YOU OVER FOR DINNER.
HOW KIND. I ACCEPT!
TELL ME, MASTER GRIFFEN: DO YOU DRIVE?
YUP! JUST GOT MY LICENSE!
HOW'D YOU LIKE A JOB AS MY DRIVER?
A PAYING JOB? YOU BET!
GOOD! GO GET YOUR CAR...
I HAVE ERRANDS TO RUN.
LATER...
I FEEL IT'S ONLY FAIR THAT YOU BE ADEQUATELY COMPENSATED FOR YOUR TIME AND EFFORTS...
I QUITE AGREE!
SO THE TERMS OF OUR AGREEMENT MUST BE SET IN STONE...
PIGGLY WIGGLY
TEXACO
TEXACO
LOOSE ENDS LEAD TO MIS-UNDERSTANDINGS, I'VE FOUND...
I LIKE HOW SHE CLEARLY ENUNCIATES EVERY WORD...
SHE SOUNDS LIKE ALFRED HITCHCOCK! HA HA!
—ROSE, LOOK! A BEATNIK!
RIGHT HERE IN HARLINGEN!
ISN'T THAT FUNNY?
=SIGH= OH, I SUPPOSE I SHOULD FIND "BEATNIKS" AMUSING...
ALONG WITH MINI-SKIRTS AND TOPLESS WAITRESSES AND OTHER SUCH TRENDS...
BUT INSTEAD IT ALL JUST MAKES ME TIRED.

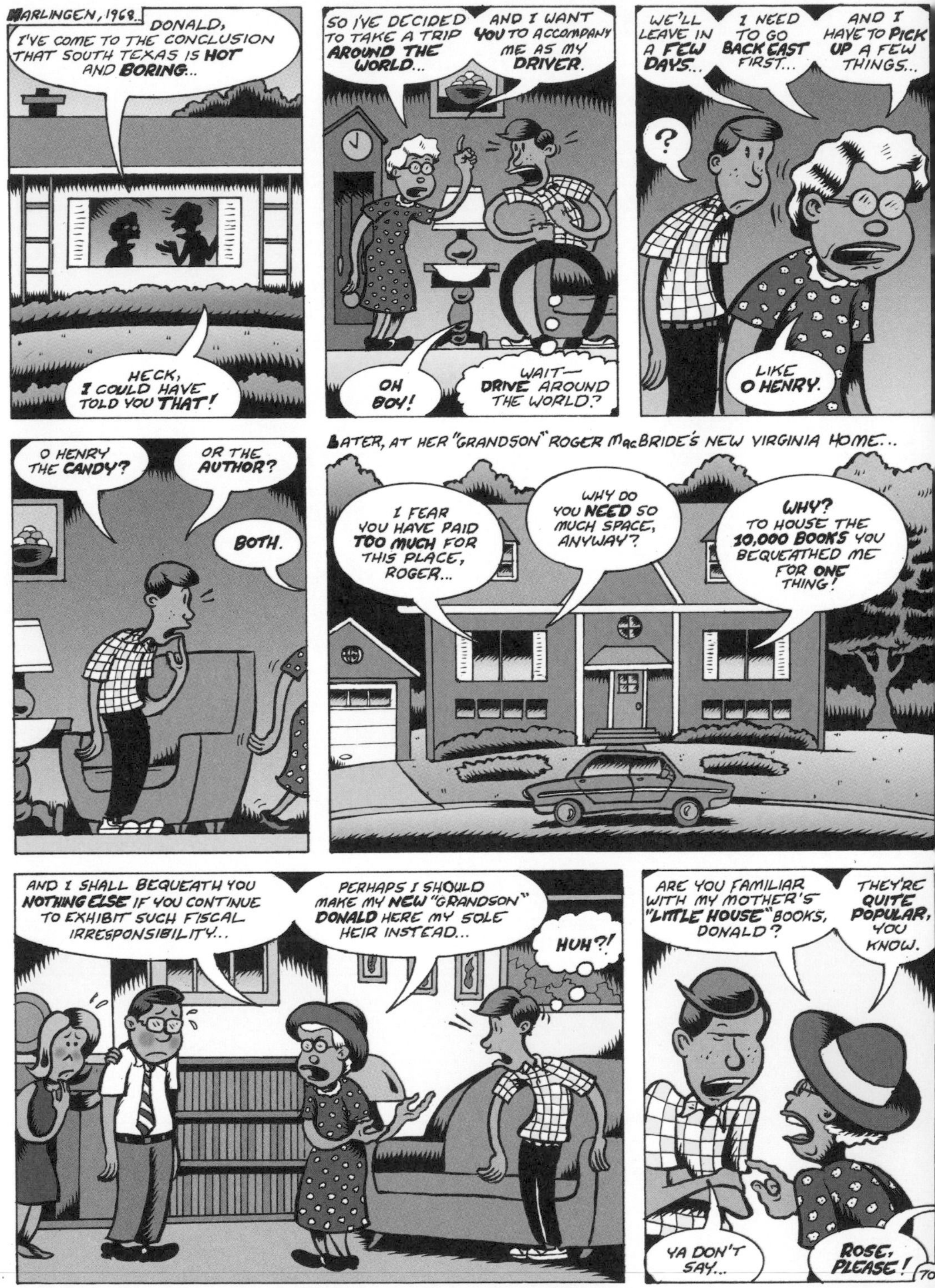

HARLINGEN, 1968...
DONALD, I'VE COME TO THE CONCLUSION THAT SOUTH TEXAS IS HOT AND BORING...
HECK, I COULD HAVE TOLD YOU THAT!
SO I'VE DECIDED TO TAKE A TRIP AROUND THE WORLD...
AND I WANT YOU TO ACCOMPANY ME AS MY DRIVER.
OH BOY!
WAIT— DRIVE AROUND THE WORLD?
WE'LL LEAVE IN A FEW DAYS...
I NEED TO GO BACK EAST FIRST...
AND I HAVE TO PICK UP A FEW THINGS...
?
LIKE O HENRY.
O HENRY THE CANDY?
OR THE AUTHOR?
BOTH.
LATER, AT HER "GRANDSON" ROGER MacBRIDE'S NEW VIRGINIA HOME...
I FEAR YOU HAVE PAID TOO MUCH FOR THIS PLACE, ROGER...
WHY DO YOU NEED SO MUCH SPACE, ANYWAY?
WHY? TO HOUSE THE 10,000 BOOKS YOU BEQUEATHED ME FOR ONE THING!
AND I SHALL BEQUEATH YOU NOTHING ELSE IF YOU CONTINUE TO EXHIBIT SUCH FISCAL IRRESPONSIBILITY...
PERHAPS I SHOULD MAKE MY NEW "GRANDSON" DONALD HERE MY SOLE HEIR INSTEAD...
HUH?!
ARE YOU FAMILIAR WITH MY MOTHER'S "LITTLE HOUSE" BOOKS, DONALD?
THEY'RE QUITE POPULAR, YOU KNOW.
YA DON'T SAY...
ROSE, PLEASE!

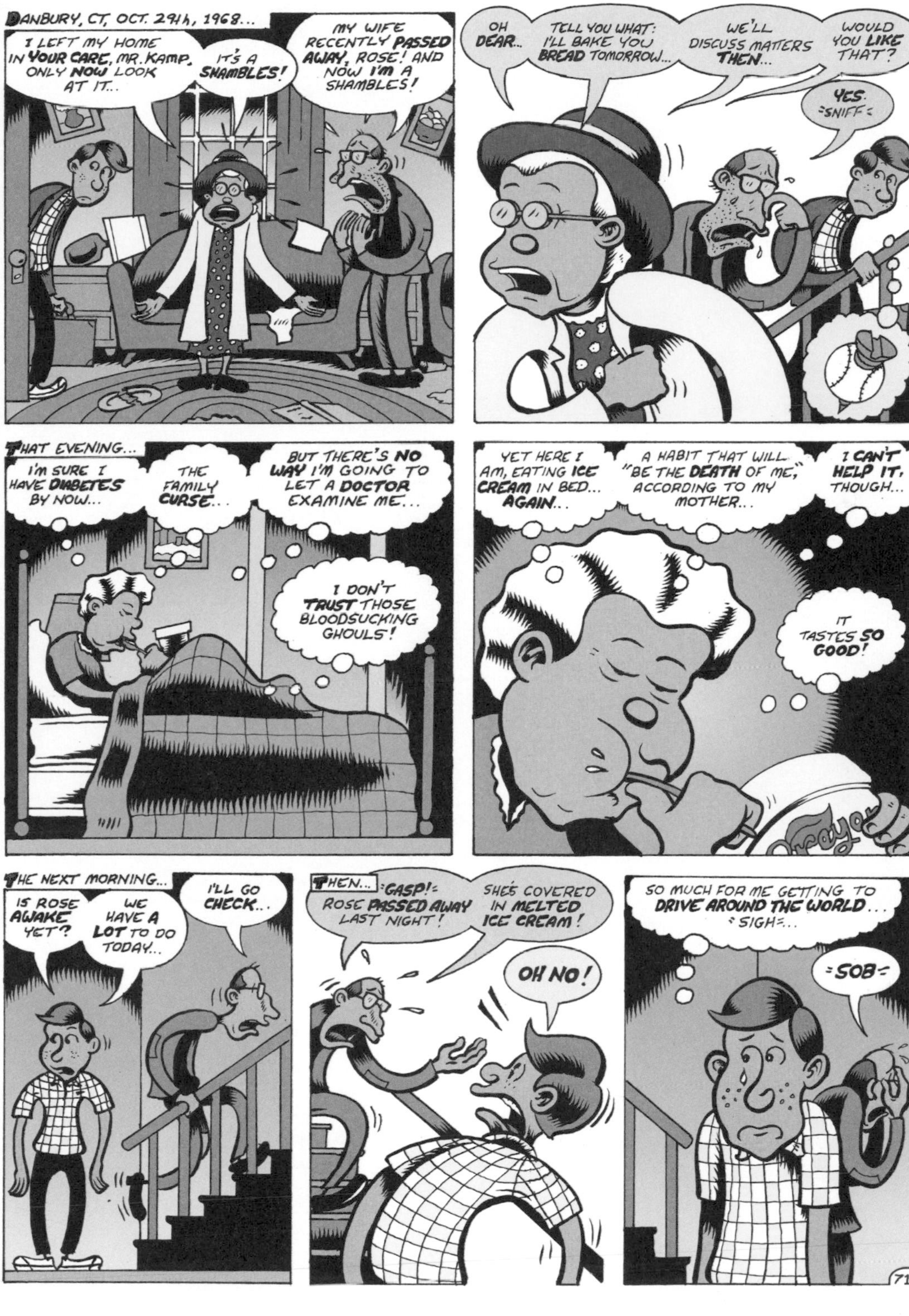
DANBURY, CT, OCT. 29th, 1968...
I LEFT MY HOME IN YOUR CARE, MR. KAMP. ONLY NOW LOOK AT IT...
IT'S A SHAMBLES!
MY WIFE RECENTLY PASSED AWAY, ROSE! AND NOW I'M A SHAMBLES!
OH DEAR...
TELL YOU WHAT: I'LL BAKE YOU BREAD TOMORROW...
WE'LL DISCUSS MATTERS THEN...
WOULD YOU LIKE THAT?
YES. =SNIFF=
THAT EVENING...
I'M SURE I HAVE DIABETES BY NOW...
THE FAMILY CURSE...
BUT THERE'S NO WAY I'M GOING TO LET A DOCTOR EXAMINE ME...
I DON'T TRUST THOSE BLOODSUCKING GHOULS!
YET HERE I AM, EATING ICE CREAM IN BED... AGAIN...
A HABIT THAT WILL "BE THE DEATH OF ME," ACCORDING TO MY MOTHER...
I CAN'T HELP IT, THOUGH...
IT TASTES SO GOOD!
THE NEXT MORNING...
IS ROSE AWAKE YET?
WE HAVE A LOT TO DO TODAY...
I'LL GO CHECK...
THEN... =GASP!=
ROSE PASSED AWAY LAST NIGHT!
SHE'S COVERED IN MELTED ICE CREAM!
OH NO!
SO MUCH FOR ME GETTING TO DRIVE AROUND THE WORLD... =SIGH=...
=SOB=

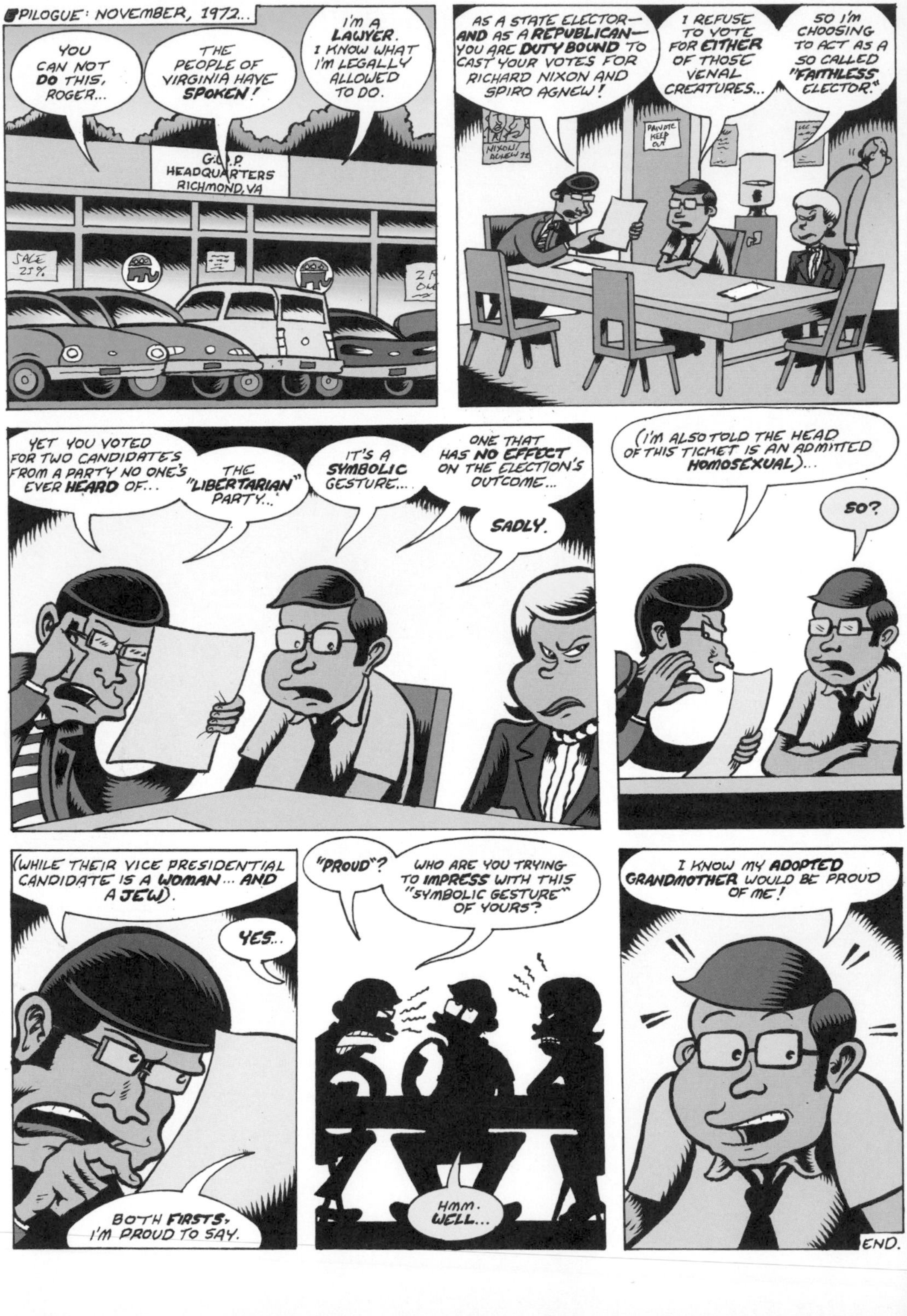
EPILOGUE: NOVEMBER, 1972...
YOU CAN NOT DO THIS, ROGER...
THE PEOPLE OF VIRGINIA HAVE SPOKEN!
I'M A LAWYER. I KNOW WHAT I'M LEGALLY ALLOWED TO DO.
G.O.P. HEADQUARTERS RICHMOND, VA
AS A STATE ELECTOR— AND AS A REPUBLICAN— YOU ARE DUTY BOUND TO CAST YOUR VOTES FOR RICHARD NIXON AND SPIRO AGNEW!
I REFUSE TO VOTE FOR EITHER OF THOSE VENAL CREATURES...
SO I'M CHOOSING TO ACT AS A SO CALLED "FAITHLESS ELECTOR."
YET YOU VOTED FOR TWO CANDIDATES FROM A PARTY NO ONE'S EVER HEARD OF...
THE "LIBERTARIAN" PARTY...
IT'S A SYMBOLIC GESTURE...
ONE THAT HAS NO EFFECT ON THE ELECTION'S OUTCOME...
SADLY.
(I'M ALSO TOLD THE HEAD OF THIS TICKET IS AN ADMITTED HOMOSEXUAL)...
SO?
(WHILE THEIR VICE PRESIDENTIAL CANDIDATE IS A WOMAN... AND A JEW).
YES...
BOTH FIRSTS, I'M PROUD TO SAY.
"PROUD"?
WHO ARE YOU TRYING TO IMPRESS WITH THIS "SYMBOLIC GESTURE" OF YOURS?
HMM. WELL...
I KNOW MY ADOPTED GRANDMOTHER WOULD BE PROUD OF ME!
END.

WHO, WHAT, WHERE, WHEN AND WHY

ABOVE
Rose Wilder Lane posing for a publicity photo, NYC, NY, c.1929. Though she was an avid conversationalist (writer Floyd Dell said she was the greatest storyteller he'd ever met), Lane also had a shy demeanor—which, combined with her cherubic face, kept most people in the dark as to the storm of ideas and emotions that were constantly raging inside her head.

PAGES 1 AND 2
Rose Wilder Lane was born in DeSmet, Dakota Territory (now South Dakota), on December 5, 1886. Her mother, LAURA INGALLS WILDER (1867–1957) was born in Wisconsin, but moved frequently throughout her childhood as her father made several attempts at homestead farming (only the last attempt proved successful), before settling down for good in the town of DeSmet. Wilder worked as both a teacher and a dressmaker from the age of fifteen before marrying at age nineteen. Her nickname, "Mama Bess," came about when Almanzo's sister, also named Laura, lived with them briefly. To differentiate between the

two, Almanzo took to calling his wife "Bess" (short for Elizabeth, her middle name). Daughter Rose then started calling her Mama Bess, and the name stuck—particularly among Lane's own friends.

ABOVE
The Ingalls, c. late-1880s. Left–right: Caroline ("Ma"), Carrie, Laura, Charles ("Pa"), Grace, and Mary.

Lane's Father, ALMANZO WILDER (1857–1949) was born in upstate New York. His family moved to Spring Valley, MN, where they prospered both as farmers and horse breeders. Almanzo moved to the DeSmet area at the age of twenty-two to try his hand at "batchin' it" (i.e.: a bachelor homesteader).

ABOVE
The Wilder Family, c. late-1860s. Almanzo is standing, second from the left. Lane's Aunt Eliza Jane is standing, second from the right.

The "Homestead Acts," the first of which was enacted in 1862, offered free land to anyone willing to move west and cultivate the land. Stipulations varied, but in the Midwest, farmers were expected to "prove up" the land by planting a set amount of grain and timber within five years. Abandoning your claim, even for a short time, could leave your land vulnerable to squatters (aka "claim jumpers"). Homesteaders also had to pay for their own supplies, which left many in debt. The climate of the Great Plains was particularly unsuitable for traditional farming methods, where savage winters and extended droughts wiped out entire communities. Farmers were also at the mercy of price-gouging railroad companies, upon whom they depended to get their grain to Eastern markets. Unsurprisingly, successful claims were the exception. Such were the conditions that Lane's parents—and a young Lane herself—grew up in.

Recent critics of Wilder and Lane's anti-government views repeatedly point out that their families were themselves the recipients of government largess by accepting free land via the Homestead Acts. Yet the only investment the US Government made on that land was when they purchased the Louisiana territory in 1803 at the cost of three cents per acre. Other than that, the land was simply stolen from Native Americans, whom the federal government had a vested interest in suppressing and displacing. To help further that goal, the federal and state governments actively encouraged settlers like the Ingalls and Wilders to move to the front lines of that *literal* culture clash—and once their farms were up and running, they could then be added to the tax rolls. So yeah, "free land" indeed.

Pictured on pages 1 and 2 is Wilder's younger sister, CARRIE INGALLS (1870–1946), who lived with the Wilders at the time. Lane herself was particularly close to her mother's youngest sister, GRACE INGALLS (1877–1941), to whom she was closer in age to than her mother was.

The Wilders assumed Almanzo suffered a stroke, but historians now believe he had a "mild" case of polio that permanently weakened both of his feet and one of his knees.

Lane's brother died at two weeks old, before he'd been named. Some sources claim Lane didn't remember having a brother, and didn't learn of his existence until her old age. I find this a bit hard to believe, especially since Lane vividly remembered her father's illness and the subsequent fire, but I can't confirm it either way.

PAGE 3
PETER INGALLS (1866–?) was Wilder's "double cousin," in that his father was Wilder's father's brother, and his mother was Wilder's mother's sister. He lived with the Wilders during the previous hard times in DeSmet. He married and remained in Westville, FL (and made good on his claim), much to the dismay of Wilder, who hated her cousin's wife—along with the entire state of Florida and all of its inhabitants!

PAGE 4
Originating as a minor player in the New Testament, the legend of the Wandering Jew took on a life of its own in the Middle Ages when a proliferation of pamphlets describing his exploits and travails spread throughout Europe. Lane never outgrew a serious case of wanderlust, and routinely referred to herself as a "Wandering Jew."

ABOVE
Lane's role model, the Wandering Jew.

In spite of her own conservative, traditionalist nature, Wilder was never as devout as her own mother, in that the Wilders seemed to have rarely attended church. She and Almanzo also regarded themselves as relatively progressive parents, in that they rarely spanked their daughter, and generally tolerated (or ignored?) her blasphemous musings.

PAGE 5
Wilder stumbled upon a brochure extoling the virtues of Missouri's Ozark Mountains, though the pictures of

hills, trees, and *water* alone were enough to make her want to move there.

The Wilder's purchased a large tract of land that they happened to pass outside of Mansfield, MO. Wilder named their new home "Rocky Ridge," and she and her husband lived there for the rest of their lives.

PAGE 6 AND 7

The Wilders were dirt poor when they first arrived in Mansfield, and Lane never got over the shame associated with it. "There's no dignity in poverty!" she would exclaim, whenever someone would attempt to romanticize the poor. Wilder, meanwhile, used reverse snobbery as a coping mechanism, before becoming just a regular, run-of-the-mill snob once they became financially stable.

"Fiskoopo" allegedly had its own set of grammatical rules and tenses. Lane eventually taught it to the chickens.

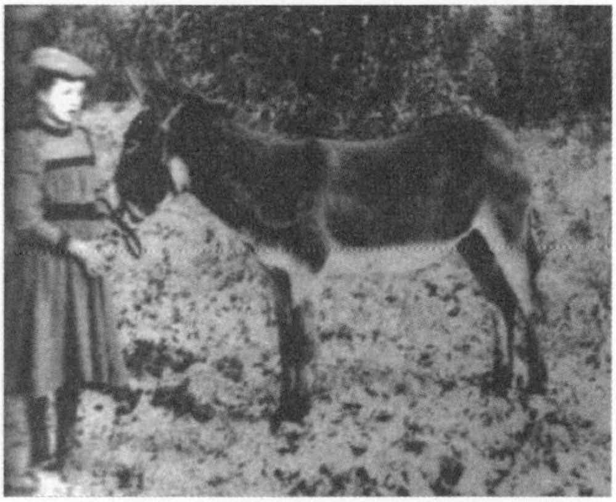

ABOVE

Lane with her beloved jackass, Spookendyke, c. 1895.

PAGE 8

Finances forced the Wilders to move into town, where Almanzo worked as a teamster, while his wife cooked prepared meals for railroad workers. Lane generally hated small town life, where she always felt like an outcast. Outwardly she was shy and awkward (a former classmate, in describing Lane's grooming habits, told biographer William Holtz that she simply "didn't know *how*"), but she also possessed an IQ that was through the roof, and read everything she could get her hands on. This in a sense made her more worldly than her classmates—*and* her instructors, it seems, in that she routinely stormed out of class, informing her parents that she was *smarter* than her teachers. And her parents were inclined to agree.

Though Lane's parents always identified as farmers, they more often than not had to do non-farm-related work to get by, ultimately (and most lucratively) culminating in Laura's writing career.

PAGE 9

ELIZA JANE WILDER THAYER GORDON (1850–1939), aka Auntie E.J., was Almanzo's older sister, and she figures prominently in both Lane's and Wilder's fiction. Originally a schoolteacher (Wilder was one of her students), she later worked as a reporter and government employee in Washington, D.C., before getting married. She also was a rare bachelorette homesteader, and allegedly made good on her claim. Lane recalls her Aunt living comfortably when she stayed with her in Louisiana, but other sources say her rich husband was dead by this time, leaving her disinherited, and she was (briefly) married to someone else.

Wilder was never too fond of her sister-in-law, so it's surprising she allowed her daughter to stay with her—especially since Lane was growing up to be so much like her fiercely independent Auntie.

Lane self-identified as a socialist from this time forward, believing that socialism (and possibly communism) was the natural solution to the societal ills brought on by the industrial revolution. She didn't begin to question this view until after she traveled through Europe in the early 1920s.

PAGE 10

Lane made it clear that she was sexually experienced by this time, though exactly *what kind* of experience that entailed is hard to say, since she was always quite vague when it came to such details.

Paul Cooley and his family moved from the Dakotas to Mansfield at the same time the Wilders did. Lane and Cooley were "childhood sweethearts" in a sense, and fictionalized versions of him often appeared in her work. Cooley later became a lawyer and local politician, and he and Lane corresponded with each other for the rest of their lives.

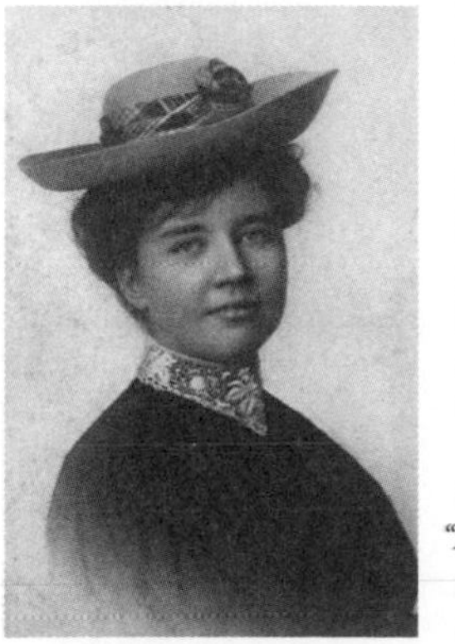

LEFT

"Bachelor Girl" Lane, Kansas City, MO, c. 1906.

PAGE 11
Lane worked as a telegraph operator in at least a half dozen different cities throughout the Midwest, which helped to satisfy her wanderlust.

It's unknown exactly where or how Lane met her future husband, though he most certainly was one of the many "traveling men" (the very type of man her mother warned her to stay away from!) to approach her telegraph desk.

PAGE 12
Lane married CLAIRE GILLETTE LANE (1887–1950) on March 24, 1909, in San Francisco. Though the same age as Lane, Gillette (he most often went by his middle name, though Lane usually called him Claire) was considerably more well-traveled than her, and was already an experienced salesman, ad writer, and newspaper reporter—all of which Lane herself was interested in, and was eager to learn from him.

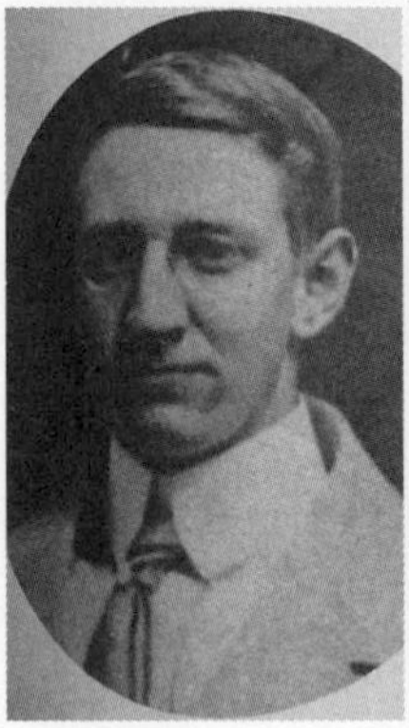
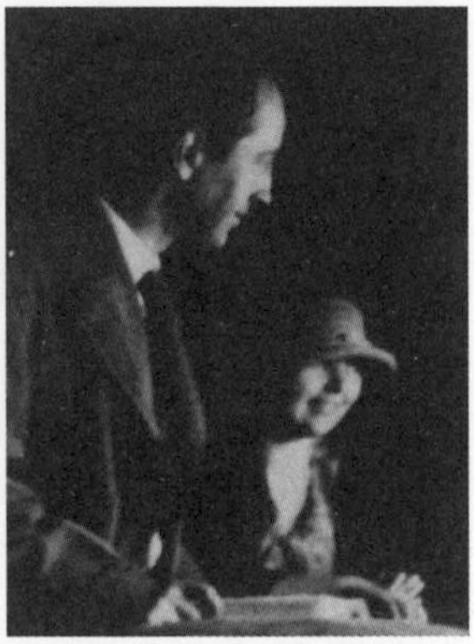

ABOVE
(L) Claire Gillette Lane and (R) The Lane's wedding, 1909.

From the moment she became a confirmed (if short lived) "bachelor girl," Lane self-identified as a feminist—a concept that she almost totally associated with self-reliance and independence. "Parasite" was a derogatory term she and her feminist friends used to describe any childless woman who refused to get a job, and simply lived off of her husband.

It's unclear when Lane began to experience severe mood swings like the one depicted here, but it was around this time that she began to recount them in her writings.

PAGE 13
Lane had cut out newspaper articles advocating the use of painkillers during childbirth and pinned them on her bedroom wall—apparently as a message to her mother, who had a different opinion on the matter.

Though Lane spoke as if she had to endure the death of her son alone, Gillette was definitely with her, since he signed the death certificate.

PAGES 14 AND 15
Lane and Gillette wound up traveling through all forty-eight states over the next four years, getting involved with all kinds of get-rich quick schemes, some of which may have even been legal. When times were good they spent lavishly on fur coats and luxury automobiles; at other times they'd be climbing out of hotel windows to avoid paying the bill. Though initially enthralled by this high stakes lifestyle, Lane soon wearied of it, and eventually the two settled into successful careers as farmland sales agents in central California.

To maximize their income, the Lanes usually worked independently, which made Lane reliant on not only knowing how to drive an automobile, but how to maintain and repair one. She loved the freedom that a car offered, and later owned what was allegedly one of the only two automobiles in all of Albania. She also purchased her parents' first car in 1924 and taught them both how to drive—not an easy task at first for her teamster father, who once drove into a tree while trying to "pull in the reins" instead of stepping on the break, which sent his daughter's face through the windshield (she was fine, other than describing her nose as a "basketful of groans"). But it was a near-accident several years later while driving through the Rocky Mountains that shook Lane so badly she never drove again, and instead "bartered" for rides from others in exchange for money or favors.

Lane once speculated that her husband might be "slightly mad," what with all of his hair-brained schemes, but I suspect that he continued to concoct them in a vain attempt to keep her engaged, since she no longer had any need for him. I say this because after they did split up, Gillette remained a realtor in California, while Lane was the one who wound up traveling the world, and trying her hand at countless different career opportunities. One might even suspect she was doing a bit of projecting with him in this regard.

Gillette comes off even worse in the way he was fictionalized in Lane's first novel, *Diverging Roads*, where he's presented as a self-centered, irresponsible bully. And then there's an early newspaper column of hers entitled "Why Men?" in which she lists her biggest pet peeves regarding the opposite sex—most of which deal with cigars, and all of which are about her ex-husband. Yet Gillette was always in favor of Lane having her own career, and never pressured her into taking on a traditional wifely role. So once again, I sense a lot of projection here, with Lane using her ex to represent all that was wrong with what she had come to regard as the oppressively sexist nature of the institution of marriage.

Gillette remarried two more times after their split, though his widow would later state that Rose was his "greatest love." Conversely, when Lane learned of her ex-husband's death in 1950, she wrote to a friend that she couldn't even remember what he looked like. The poor guy!

"Can't you, just once, *be human*?" Gillette was probably just venting when he said this, but the phrase stuck in Lane's craw forever. Not that she took it to mean that she's *inhuman*, but rather that her emotional responses differ considerably from most people's. That she's *off*, somehow.

Lane was the first licensed female realtor in the state of California.

ABOVE
Gillette Lane with his mother-in-law in Sequoia National Park, 1915, when the Lane's were still pretending to be a happy couple.

PAGES 16 AND 17
By this time Lane was suffering from not just severe mood swings but countless physical maladies—

which may or may not have been a by-product of her depression, but she was in pain regardless. That she was given free samples of the patent medicines she sold—most of which were either opium- or cocaine-based—made it far too easy for her to become dependent on them, though she soon weaned herself off of them. Lane wrote about this suicide attempt for *Cosmopolitan* in 1926, and in a quite honest and forthright manner (though others found the piece too sensationalistic). Sadly, she continued to suffer from suicidal tendencies throughout most of her life.

PAGE 18
Lane worked as both a staffer and freelancer for the *San Francisco Bulletin* from 1915 to 1921, where she performed many different roles: reporter, columnist, serialized fiction writer, and eventually feature writer, which included several serialized biographies of contemporary public figures.

The *Bulletin*'s managing editor, FREMONT OLDER (1856–1935), was the epitome of the crusading journalist: championing the little man and fighting corruption at every turn. Lane adored Older, and spoke of him not merely as her greatest mentor, but as the *only* mentor she ever needed. She also never stopped using him as a sounding board, and the two of them corresponded with each other until his death.

ABOVE
(L) Fremont Older and (R) Bessie Beatty

Journalist and future radio host BESSIE BEATTY (1886–1947) was briefly roommates with Lane, and helped the latter secure a job at the *Bulletin*. The two women also frequently collaborated, most notably when they interviewed hundreds of sex workers for the paper in an attempt to humanize them, as a response to a ginned-up moral panic designed to gentrify the Tenderloin District.

When Older eventually chose the more experienced Beatty for the coveted position of European war correspondent, Lane had to settle for the role of Hollywood correspondent as a consolation prize. (For what it's worth, the handful of film industry stories she filed make for fantastic reads.)

"A Jitney Romance." Sigh. Hey, we all gotta start somewhere! In her youth, Lane was in fact a voracious reader of what we would now think of as romance novels, which she envisioned authoring herself one day. As a result, hints of purple prose infected her earliest writing, including *Diverging Roads*, though she eventually worked such tendencies out of her system.

PAGE 19

Illustrator BERTA HOERNER HADER (1890–1976), together with her future husband, Elmer, became successful children's books authors. Roommates Lane, Hader, and Beatty marked the beginning of a professional women's networking/support system that helped Lane (and vice versa) for decades to come. In fact, a few of these women (including Hader) had a hand in the development of Wilder's *Little House* series.

Lane was very much a part of San Francisco's radical bohemian scene during her years there, and her politics took on a hard left bent as well—though she never expressed her views in the same strident manner that would characterize her later political evolution. Besides, her passions during her young adulthood were not politics but philosophy and modernist literature—both of which she read voraciously and wrote about and discussed relentlessly.

Beatty used to advocate celibacy for single women, to avoid the distractions associated with a sex life. So not only was Lane surprised when her friend married in 1926, she also took it as a betrayal, feeling that the two of them had some sort of a pact between them to never wed.

BELOW

(L) Berta Hader (in costume?) with her husband Elmer and (R) Lane the proto-hippie (in costume?), San Francisco, c. 1917

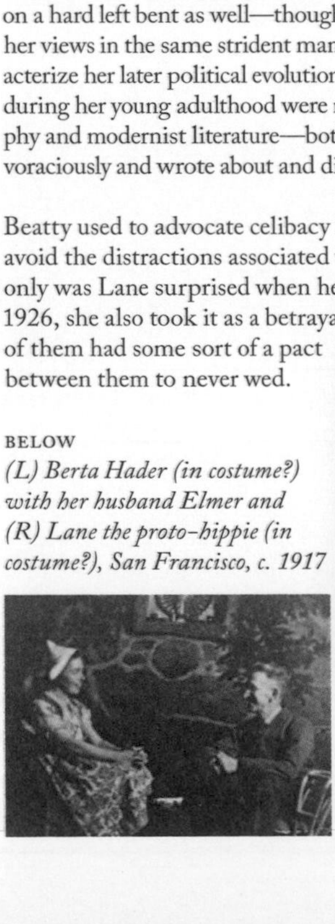

PAGE 20

Between 1915 and 1920 Lane wrote five celebrity biographies for the *Bulletin*, all of which were later published in book form. Her subjects, in order, were: stunt pilot Art Smith, filmmaker Charlie Chaplin, auto manufacturer Henry Ford, author (and Lane acquaintance) Jack London, and future President Herbert Hoover, though at the time he was widely hailed as the engineer/efficiency expert who organized and ran a food distribution system that helped prevent mass starvation in Europe during and after World War I. What all of these men have in common are their rags-to-riches stories, which Lane both wanted to celebrate and emulate.

With the exception of the Art Smith book (who most likely only cared about having his name spelled correctly), there were controversies surrounding all of these biographies, which were entirely due to the "you are there" or "as told to" styles they were written in. One could almost call what she did ghost-writing, only without the approval of the presumed "author."

This literally means putting words in people's mouths as a way to move the story along and keep the reader riveted, though for the people being written about this also came off as looney toons. Hoover, for example, allegedly wondered how "this woman" (Lane) could pretend to know what was being discussed in his mother's kitchen when he was three (he denied having any objections to Lane years later, however—when he was an *ex*-president, and the two of them became pen pals). Ford also allegedly *hated* Lane's bio, though he took no legal action over it.

HE WAS A MAN
ROSE WILDER LANE
HARPERS
HE WAS A MAN
ROSE WILDER LANE
E
S

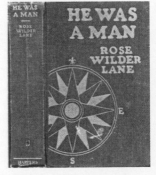

Meanwhile, Jack London had recently died, but his widow, Charmian, threatened to sue Lane for defamation in his name, and succeeded in suppressing the publication of the book. (Lane avoided personal liability by using the old "I'm just a poor farm girl trying to earn a living" routine on Mrs. London, which worked.) In defense of Lane, it needs to be pointed out that Charmian had her own self-serving, facts-be-damned biography of her late husband to publish, while London himself has a mixed legacy, which includes stories ghost-written *for* him by a then-unknown Sinclair Lewis (and not to let her own labor be wasted, Lane repackaged her bio of London as a work of fiction and published it under the title *He Was a Man* in 1925).

As for Chaplin: Lane briefly interviewed him and ran the elaborated results in serialized form in the *Bulletin* with no comments from her subject. It wasn't until a book of it was published that Charlie blew a gasket. The combination of it being sold as an *auto-*biography, along with Lane possibly getting too close (even if she was guessing) to the actual truth of his family's sordid past may have led to him filing a successful "cease and desist" lawsuit. What's oddest of all is that that book is *still* in print, and still marketed as an "as told to" autobiography, under the title *Charlie Chaplin's Own Story!*

PAGE 21
As "poor" as they claimed to be, Lane and Hader rented the entire house at 31 Jones St. in Greenwich Village and then subleted the extra space. Elmer Hader briefly lived with them after being discharged from the service and before he and Berta relocated upstate and began building their famous storybook castle on a cliff overlooking the Hudson River.

By the time Lane moved to New York she was already contributing articles and short stories to various widely read national magazines, all of which paid far better than newspapers like the *Bulletin*. Indeed, the $750 she made here off of *Ladies' Home Journal* is the equivalent of $15,000–$20,000 in today's money, so Lane was now well on her way to a very lucrative career as a freelance writer.

PAGES 22 AND 23
Working in some capacity for the Red Cross proved to be a big boon for many ambitious women after World War I, especially since it afforded an opportunity to travel overseas—even if it was to war-torn hellholes. But then that was part of the appeal: to prove that they can put up with any living conditions that men can.

Joining Lane on page 22 is author and editor FLOYD DELL (1887–1969) and his second wife, Bertha Marie Gage. Dell, along with Max Eastman, managed the socialist newspaper *The Masses*, whose antiwar stance led to him and others being tried twice for sedition during World War I (both trials ended in hung juries). Though he's rarely read today, Dell was quite well-known and widely read in the early twentieth century. Dell was very close to Lane, and remained life-long friends with her, even after their politics sharply diverged, and Lane frequently visited him at his home in Croton-on-Hudson, NY.

ABOVE
(L) Floyd Dell and (R) John Reed.

Journalist and Communist activist JOHN REED (1887–1920) was very involved with many socialist causes before getting thoroughly caught up in the excitement surrounding the Bolshevik Revolution in Russia, where he wound up dying of typhus shortly after this scene. Some historians question whether Reed was in New York precisely at this time Lane described, but the two of them had many mutual friends, and surely met often somewhere. Plus, Lane's descriptions of him strongly imply that "Jack" made quite an impression on her.

Lane was frequently teased by her Bohemian friends for being a bit more fussy and uptight than the rest of them. This took its cruelest form when author Sherwood Anderson depicted her in his novel *Dark Laughter* as "Rose Frank," a midwestern ex-pat in Paris who posed as a sexual sophisticate, but who needed a fainting couch when a party got a little *too* bacchanalian for her. This portrayal outraged Lane for two reasons: one, that fellow midwestern square Anderson was one to talk; and two, that being discussed sexually *at all* by men, let alone publicly, brought up the worst fears instilled in her by her small town upbringing.

Lane was even more outraged when Dorothy Thompson's ex-husband, Josef Bard, portrayed both Lane and his ex-wife as "women of easy virtue" in his novel *Shipwreck in Europe* (though Thompson herself was amused by their portrayal). Biographer Holtz theorizes that Lane's (over?) reaction to these portrayals was due in part to her subconsciously conflating the prostituting of herself to the "prostituting" of her writing skills. Who knows. Maybe?

PAGE 24
DOROTHY THOMPSON (1893–1961) eventually became a household name as a war correspondent and radio broadcaster during World War II, and even before

then her *New York Herald-Tribune* column was so widely read that *Time* dubbed her "the second most influential woman in America" (after Eleanor Roosevelt). At the time Thompson met Lane, she already had several journalistic "scoops" under her belt, but their early correspondences suggest a teacher/pupil relationship between the two, with Lane in the role of tutor.

Lane used to fuss over Thompson in a way that bordered on a romantic obsession, by constantly praising her beauty and talent. She also could be quite possessive of her, and at first refused to even meet Thompson's second husband, author Sinclair Lewis, by "joking" that he "stole" her from him. (Lane did eventually meet Lewis, however, and the two became very good friends.)

ABOVE
Dorothy Thompson, c. 1920s.

PAGE 25
Lane was initially attracted to the ex-pat journalist ARTHUR GRIGGS for reasons similar to those that drew her to her ex-husband: He knew Paris like the back of his hand, along with the many ways that multilingual American scribes like the two of them could make a buck. He also served as a guide to that city's all-night social whirl, though those all-night revelries—as well as the younger Griggs's excessive drinking—soon exhausted her, and she successfully swore off drinking (save for an occasional toast) for good. Lane's one lifelong vice, however, was cigarettes, which she took up during her San Francisco days primarily as a form

of protest, since women were discouraged from smoking in public back then, though she soon become addicted to her feminist "statement."

One of the first signs of what was to become a powerful maternal instinct in Lane was that she seemed to *enjoy* nursing Griggs during his frequent hangovers, which left him in a helpless, almost childlike state.

Lane was quite prone to misandrist outbursts during this time of her life, though it had little to do with males in general (in fact, her most enduring friendships were almost entirely with men), but rather within the context of sex and romance, which was the one aspect of her emotional life she struggled with more than any other. On the surface, the conflict was largely about maintaining such relationships while also holding on to her cherished independence, but the built-in insecurities that go hand-in-hand with such relationships seemed to be more than she could contend with.

Indeed, Lane often sounded like a needy adolescent in her private writings, with frantic "why hasn't he written or called?" pleadings mixed with unfounded accusations of attempts at domination when her latest beau *did* write or call. The men in her life literally *could not win* with her. The oddest thing about this behavior was how it contrasted with the relative fearlessness Lane exhibited in all other facets of her life— a fact that wasn't lost on her either, yet she was never able to successfully tackle it, and she eventually gave up on men as love interests altogether.

RIGHT
Lane during the walking tour depicted on Page 25.

PAGE 26
GUY MOYSTON was, like Griggs, another Europe-based American journalist, albeit one with considerably less baggage than his predecessor (by the way: I can find very little biographical information on either man, including birth and death dates). Since both Moyston and Lane's professions entailed constant travel, they agreed to a very casual, no-strings-attached type of relationship, which suited both of them during their time overseas.

The short story being discussed here, entitled "Innocence," is indeed award-worthy, and is one of Lane's finest works. Written from the point of view of a five-year-old, it recounts the Wilders' brief stay in Florida in 1891, and of her mother's hostility toward the locals (which Lane amplified into justifiable paranoia for dramatic purposes).

Lane's self-consciousness at appearing alongside writers she admired served as a rationale for doing "hack work" for better paying publications—most notably the *Saturday Evening Post*, for whom she wrote numerous serialized novels. The book versions of the first of these, *Hill-Billy* (1925) and *Cindy* (1928), were actually published by Harpers, and Lane loudly objected to the "trashy" way that the company marketed those books—which is curious, seeing how she had such low regard for those two titles herself.

PAGE 27
Countless experiences like the one portrayed on this page marked the beginning of Lane's questioning what role governments should or shouldn't play when it comes to solving society's ills. More often than not she concluded that the state's "cures" were worse than the supposed problems they were addressing, and would be stunned when some of her fellow Americans (or in this case, an Englishman) could witness the same scenes yet conclude that these autocratic regimes were "on to something." Still, Lane wasn't the only former socialist who was reaching the same conclusions, as her contemporary Max Eastman was witnessing similar events and reacting much like she did.

ABOVE
Passport photos, c. 1920s.

PAGE 28 AND 29
REXH (pronounced "Redge") META (1906–1985), who most likely was older than twelve at this time, learned to speak English from Red Cross volunteers, who also gave him the donated American pajamas he was wearing when Lane met him. Besides keeping himself clothed and fed, Meta also fended for the younger children who survived his village's massacre, which clearly touched Lane's heart.

RIGHT
Meta in his Cambridge uniform, c. 1932.

Though she never officially adopted him, Lane always referred to Meta as her "son," and continued to provide for him financially after she moved back to the United States for good in 1928. Meta eventually did attend and graduate from Cambridge (where he not only was the sole Albanian on campus, but most likely the only one in all of Britain at the time), before returning to Albania, where he married and had a daughter (whom he named after Lane). He was working as a mid-level government bureaucrat when the Italian fascist regime invaded Albania in 1939, after which Meta and his family spent the duration of Italy's control in a concentration camp. They returned after the war, only to suddenly find themselves out of favor with Enver Hoxha's newly installed communist regime, during which Meta was either imprisoned or living under house arrest for the rest of his life.

Lane was unable to contact Meta during and after the war, and all attempts to get him and his family relocated proved futile. Intermediaries were at least able to confirm that he was still alive, but the entire situation left Lane frantic. Once the Cold War ended in 1989, Lane's heir, Roger MacBride, was able to relocate Meta's daughter to the US, but Meta and his wife were long dead by then.

Meta was the first in a long line of wards and protégés whom Lane insisted on referring to as her "children" and "grandchildren." By this time, Lane was exhibiting a powerful maternal streak that also extended to friends and animals, and contributed to some awkward boundary-line blurring in her future relationships.

PAGE 30
At this point I should mention that Lane bounced around Europe and the Mideast between 1920–24 at such a frantic pace—and with a constantly alternating cast of characters accompanying her—that I had no choice but to drastically simplify

the people and places involved, or risk having no semblance of a clear narrative thread to keep the reader engaged.

One important player I chose to leave out, since her role in Lane's life so closely resembled other players, was fellow San Franciscan divorcee ANNETTE ("PEGGY") MARQUIS, who accompanied Lane to many of the most desolate, dangerous places in her travels (including her harrowing trip to the Caucuses pictured on this page). Together, these two women suffered from theft, dehydration, and malnutrition, as well as near-fatal and recurring bouts of malaria. Lane grew increasingly annoyed with Marquis, however, once the latter had run out of money, and frequently referred to her as a "mooch." Marquis returned to the US shortly afterwards, while Lane continued her dangerous travels on her own.

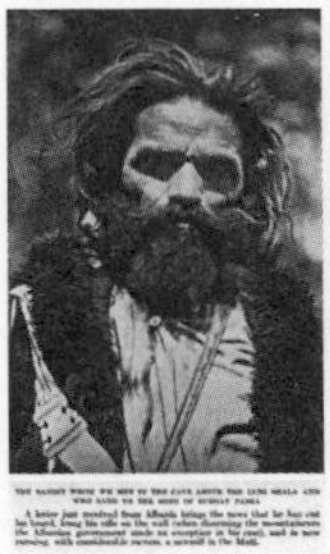

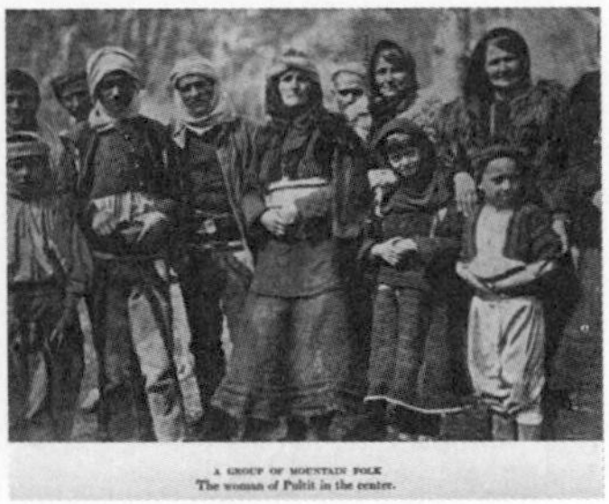
A GROUP OF MOUNTAIN FOLK
The woman of Pultit in the center.

ABOVE
Photos and captions are from Lane's best-selling 1923 Albanian travelogue, Peaks of Shala, *with photos by her then-traveling companion Peggy Marquis.*

Lane's plan was to travel around the world and arrive in San Francisco via the Far East, but by the time she reached Baghdad, homesickness and desert sand flies got the best of her, and she returned to Europe, followed by a trip home to Mansfield, before returning once again back to Europe. Like I said, you need a scorecard to keep up with her!

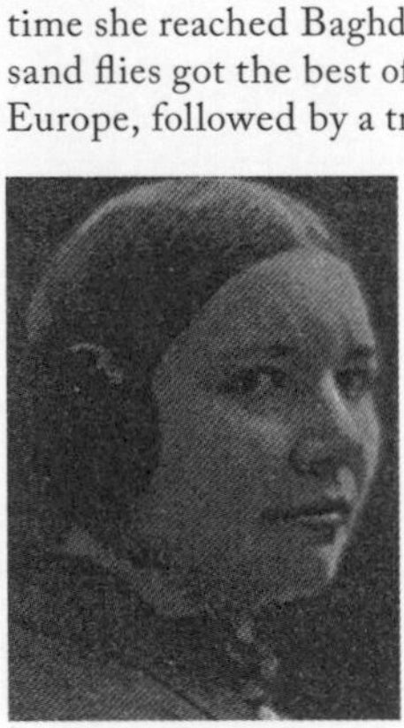

LEFT
Lane sports a Princess Leia look while in Albania.

PAGE 31
New England native HELEN DORE BOYLSTON (1995–1984) served on the frontlines as a nurse anesthetist during World War I (she later recounted her experiences in her first book, *Sister: The War Diary of a Nurse*, in 1927). She continued to work as a nurse after the war, but a trust fund set up by a friend of her dentist father also made it possible for her to live a more carefree existence, which she wound up doing, and with Lane as a companion.

PAGE 32
Lane and Boylston crossed paths only occasionally in Europe before meeting again in the US in 1924, after which they became inseparable. They returned to Europe together in 1925 or '26, which is when they concocted this hair-brained plan. (William Holtz later collected letters from these two women recounting their move to Albania into an engaging book called *Travels with Zenobia*).

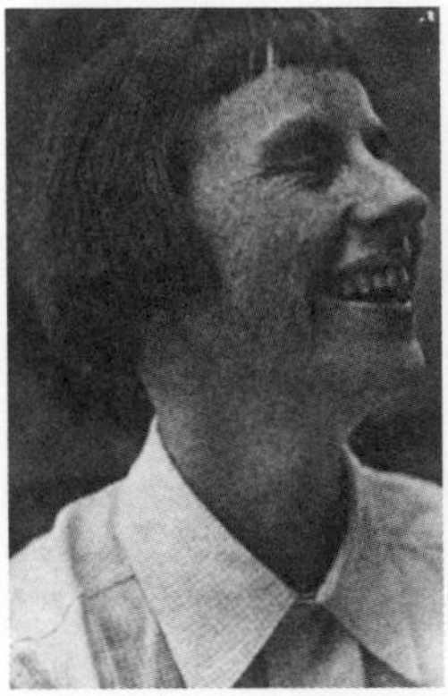

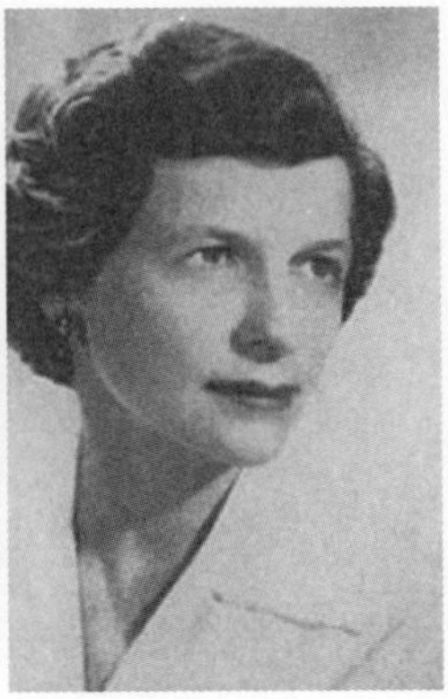

ABOVE
Boylston was quite the tomboy during her time with Lane, but her latter dust jacket photos show her sporting a far more conventional look.

PAGE 33
Lane adored the then *very* tribal, not-yet Westernized country of Albania—in large part *because* it was so disconnected from modern society, but also because she claimed to have witnessed the purest acts of human kindness there, even in the midst of their never-ending blood feuds. She also became fascinated with the history of Islam while there, and devoted an entire chapter in her 1943 polemic, *The Discovery of Freedom*, to that culture's heyday. (In typical fashion, Lane overgeneralizes quite a bit in that chapter, though Islamic scholars appreciated her acknowledging the role the pre-Ottoman Caliphates played in advancing not just technological progress, but the advancement of freer, more pluralistic societies in general.)

AHMET ZOGU (1895–1961) was prime minister, then president, and eventually the self-declared King of Albania (taking on the name King Zog) in 1928. When Lane and Boylston first met Zogu, he was such an unimposing figure that Boylston thought he was a porter (and tried to tip him), but they all soon became close friends. Yet as he took on loftier titles he also assumed increasingly dictatorial powers—something that Lane normally would be highly critical of, but Albania was such an unstable place at the time (with Zogu surviving at least fifty-five assassination attempts) that she took something of a forgiving stance toward his governing policies.

If Zogu's alleged proposal was sincere, and if she had accepted, Lane would have wound up becoming an actual *queen*—albeit one living in exile after 1939.

RIGHT
King Zogu and his eventual wife, Queen Geraldine, in 1938.

PAGE 34
Lane's motives for moving back to Rocky Ridge Farm has always been vague—a false-alarm cancer scare with her father was one story, as was the dangerous living conditions in Albania (though they always *were* dangerous, she still often spoke of moving back there), but plain old guilt over having "abandoned" her parents was also a factor, and quite possibly the *only* one.

After reading her palm, a soothsaying neighbor of the Wilders once informed a gloating Laura that she was "a woman who always gets her way," to which Lane later wrote: "she had to *read her palm* to figure that out?" This anecdote certainly describes Lane's parents' relationship, which was marked by frequent arguments that Laura *always* won—and she wasn't above throwing full-on *temper tantrums* to get her way, either. A man of few words to begin with (Laura's nickname for her husband was "the Oyster"), and with no patience for gossip (the phrase "It's none of our business!" should have been etched on his tombstone), it's no wonder that Almanzo preferred to hide in the cornfield than land in his wife's crosshairs.

Seeing how these were the people who raised her, it's curious that Lane viewed marriage as not only a form of slavery, but that *women* were the slaves. When biographer Holtz interviewed a frail Boylston toward the end of her life, she still vividly recalled the way Laura controlled and manipulated her husband and daughter, and still resented her for it.

PAGE 35
As is made plain here, Guy Moyston was no longer content with his and Lane's "casual" arrangement, and desperately wanted to settle down with her. He eventually married someone else, and they raised two kids in Croton-on-Hudson.

I had recently learned that Moyston had helped write Margaret Sanger's first autobiography, 1931's *My Fight for Birth Control* (which I had formally assumed Sanger wrote by herself). This pairing was far from random too, since Moyston had long been a supporter in Sanger's cause, and even helped found the Holland-Rantos pharmaceutical company for the sole purpose of manufacturing contraceptives. (The company still exists today, only as a manufacturer of lubricating jelly, after selling off their condom-making division to the Trojan company decades ago.) It probably didn't hurt Moyston that the company also made a lot of money.

PAGE 36
Justamere clubs ("just a mere," get it?) were usually ad hoc women's clubs formed for a single purpose, such as to raise money for, say, a library, or a dog pound. Wilder was more often than not the chairwoman of such clubs, as well as the gavel-wielder of the local Ladies' Aid societies. The general effectiveness of these mutual aid organizations was a major factor in Wilder and Lane's later criticism of federal government welfare programs, which they regarded as a less-efficient usurpation of their homegrown efforts.

Lane clearly inherited her mother's attention to detail. They both were always making lists!

Dorothy Thompson is the visitor on this page, though Lane played host to countless writer friends as they made their way between New York and Hollywood.

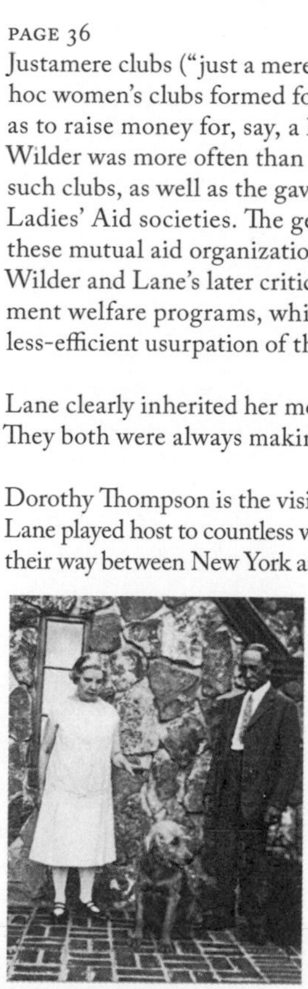

LEFT
Laura and Almanzo Wilder (and "Nero") stand outside the stone house Lane had built for them in 1928.

PAGE 37
Lane's new all-women posse pictured here includes writer CATHARINE BRODY, a Mid-

west newspaper reporter (as they *all* were) with literary aspirations. She eventually had some sort of a career going in Hollywood writing treatments, and while crashing off and on at Rocky Ridge, she wrote her first (and only?) novel, 1932's *Nobody Starves*. Regrettably, biographical background on her is slim, though what we know for certain is that she was Wilder's worst nightmare, what with her cigarette holders and pencil skirts and saying hello to men. Weirdest of all was that Brody considered Wilder a friend, and always stopped off in Mansfield during her travels to visit "Mama Bess" even *after* Lane had moved away, while Wilder would always pretend to not be at home.

LEFT
Catharine Brody, c.1933

MARY MARGARET MCBRIDE (1899–1976) was yet another Missourian newspaper reporter who soon was writing for the same high-end magazines as Lane. McBride was folksy, oversized, and vulnerable, which stood in stark contrast to her partner (in every sense of the word) Stella Karn, who always had the big goofball's back. The two of them eventually became the Oprah Winfrey and Gayle King of the radio era, when every housewife *loved* "MMM," while every husband would roll his eyes at the aw-shucks naiveté of her celebrity interviews, as well as the unbridled enthusiasm she employed when hawking her sponsors' products.

It's alarming how forgotten McBride is now compared to her former notoriety, but such is the fate of most former radio stars.

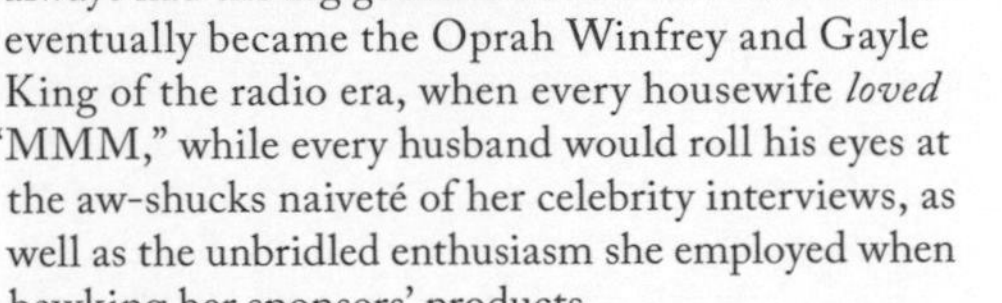

ABOVE
Left–right: McBride, Beatty, and Thompson: the Queens of the Airwaves c. 1940s.

It did not escape Lane's attention how, by the 1940s, three of her former best friends: McBride, Beatty,

and Thompson (whom Lane dubbed "The Irish Mafia"), were ruling radio's airwaves, and their success made her briefly consider following in their footsteps. But that consideration was short lived, and thankfully so, since not only did Lane have a slow, deliberate delivery, but her mind was not at all in the same place as the typical radio listener, who didn't want to listen to *anyone* talk about Thomas Paine for five hours.

Regarding Lane's own sexuality: the current consensus among people who closely follow her work is that she was bisexual, and that she and Boylston in particular were lovers, but no one is willing to say as much in print—largely because there's no hard evidence that that was the case, which would make any such talk pure speculation (though I also sense that there's some vague fear of litigation involved, as if anyone would regard such speculation as "libelous" in 2019). As to why no evidence exists: great question, since Lane bared her soul in her diaries about *everything*, so why would she exempt that? This has fueled rumors that the estate's gatekeepers had withheld such evidence to "protect the brand," though people who know (or have known) said gatekeepers assured me that that would be unthinkable.

Meanwhile, another Lane biographer told me to consider where rural midwestern women like Lane's minds were at the time: when there was no modern concept of "sexual identity," and how some combination of loneliness, shame, and intimacy could lead female friendships to waver to and from the platonic to the physical without comment. That would make sense when considering what a boundary-line blurrer Lane was, if one ignores the fact that she'd also lived in San Francisco, New York, Paris, and Weimar-era Berlin. In other words, Lane was no naïve Ozark hillbilly, wallowing in denial of what she may or may not have been doing.

Turning to Boylston's estate is no help either, since her heirs destroyed all of her personal effects (*whoops!*), so there's no evidence that poor ol' spinster Troub ever had a lover of either gender in her entire life. But what the hell was she doing in stupid Mansfield when she could've afforded to live anywhere? She didn't even like Lane's mother! And consider the massive nervous breakdown Lane experienced when she and Boylston split for good (see Page 41), which suggests that they were lovers without qualification. And this is the first time you'll ever read such talk in print—though even I felt it would be presumptuous to present her alleged bisexuality as fact in the comic itself.

Curiously, in spite of this sapphic circus taking place on her own property, Wilder and her neighbors reserved their real indignation for when any *male* visitor happened to spend the night at Rocky Ridge. Once, during a sewing circle (of all places), a neighbor snarkily noted that Lane always seemed to have extra sheets hanging out to dry after a man paid a visit ("because, you know, *sex*," Lane later noted). In the height of irony, Boylston then threatened to *beat up* the offending neighbor unless she took back her words, while Lane took delight in Boylston's chivalry—yet *still* none of the women present managed to put two and two together. You can't make this stuff up!

Lane regularly received front cover credit on the many large circulation magazines she contributed to throughout the 1920s and '30s (most notably the Post, *as pictured to the right), which literally made her a household name at the time.*

THE SATURDAY EVENING POST
ROSE WILDER LANE · F. BRITTEN AUSTIN · JACK DEMPSEY
THE CAT'S-PAW
ROSE WILDER LANE · FRANK P. STOCKBRIDGE
ROSE WILDER LANE · THOMAS WOLFE
ROSE WILDER LANE · OWEN JOHNSON
BEGINNING FREE LAND By ROSE WILDER LANE

PAGE 38
Prior to the stock market crash, Lane was making roughly $20,000 a year off of her writing (almost $500,000 in today's money), and was one of the highest paid feature writers in the country. Lane's first agent, Carl Brandt, represented a long list of literary heavyweights, and must have had the cushiest job in the world prior to the crash. Lane eventually felt she had no choice but to look for a hungrier, more resourceful agent (though Boylston herself stuck with Brandt, and was well served by him years later).

The hard times also meant the public no longer had much interest in reading about "jazz babies," or lost souls looking for themselves in Paris. What people *did* want to read about instead was anyone's guess, though Lane (and Wilder) soon settled on the answer, i.e.: stories about *true grit*, as well as reminders that Americans had survived even tougher times in the past.

"All we have to do is remain invincible" did indeed become Lane's motto, though she would always say it with tongue firmly planted in cheek.

PAGE 39
By 1931 the value of Boylston, Lane, and the Wilders stock portfolios had virtually evaporated due to the prolonged depression. Lane felt particularly guilty about her parents' losses, since she was the one who set up their portfolio for them. As a result, she became more determined than ever to get her mother's memoirs published, as a form of penance as well as to set up a new income stream for her. Originally titled *Pioneer Girl*, this memoir passed through several editors' desks and underwent several permutations before finally seeing the light of day as *Little House in the Big Woods* in 1932.

Lane's own career had also yet to recover, and she was now doing more ghost-writing than ever to make ends meet, most notably for the broadcaster and travel writer Lowell Thomas.

PAGE 40
Wilder/Lane Biographer Christine Woodside suggests that Wilder's emotionally detached parenting style may have done permanent damage to Lane as a child, and would explain the awkward, desperate cravings for love that marked Lane's later relationships. While I generally agree, I also can easily imagine a child raised by Wilder, yet who wasn't as physiologically complex as Lane, turning out just fine. These two were simply an odd match, temperamentally speaking.

PAGE 41
Mr. Bunting sounded like a real pain in the ass—always getting sick, always running away, always picking fights with the Wilders' much larger dog, Nero—and poorer neighbors were soon routinely kidnapping Mr. Bunting and later returning him to Lane, knowing she would fork over the reward money with no questions asked. But the dog's flaws were probably a big part of *why* she adored him so. *Who else* would care for him? And he fits into a lifelong pattern of her "adopting" broken and/or desperate animals *and* people, going all the way back to Spookendyke.

Mr. Bunting was a Maltese Terrier, a breed that Lane usually owned a pair of for the rest of her life (some she named after her favorite political philosophers, though her last pair were lazily dubbed "Pepe" and "Pepe's Brother"). She also could never reconcile herself with these animals' inevitable demises, and would find herself bedridden with grief for weeks after each one's passing.

SUE BARTON
Student Nurse
By Helen Dore Boylston
Sue Barton,
STUDENT NURSE
SUE BARTON
STUDENT
NURSE
HELEN DORE BOYLSTON
Sue Barton:
STUDENT NURSE
Helen Dore Boylston
Sue Barton
STUDENT NURSE

RIGHT
Just some of the countless editions of Boylston's Sue Barton, Student Nurse, *which I'm guessing must have sold about a hundred billion copies by now.*

While Boylston certainly learned a lot about writing from Lane, she didn't blossom as a writer until she was out of Lane's shadow. Her own seven volume young adult series, *Sue Barton, Student Nurse*, premiered in 1936, along with the four volume series *Carol Goes Backstage*, about a fictional actress named Carol Page. Both series were hugely successful, and both are still in print. Boylston also wrote a biography of Red Cross founder, Clara Barton (whom the fictional Sue Barton was named for).

Boylston and Lane rarely wrote to each other after their split, and eventually became estranged. Lane had a sad tendency of quietly souring on her female friends. Perhaps she simply expected too much from them, but she also couldn't bring herself to express any lingering hurt feelings or resentments to them, and chose to avoid them instead.

PAGE 42
Though Lane had sworn off drugs and alcohol, she tended to self-medicate with comfort food during her depressions, which resulted in wild weight fluctuations. (Amusingly, Lane's Aunt Grace recalled that two of the first words Lane learned to say as a child were "butter" and "crackers.")

PAGES 43 AND 44
Thus begins a well-documented, twelve-year-long creative tug of war between mother and daughter, during which a specific set of differences kept resurfacing. Most common was Wilder's obsession with factual accuracy, while Lane had to keep reminding her mother of one of the most basic tenants of writing: the "use it or lose it" rule, i.e.: if your Aunt Docia isn't going to do or say anything to move the story along, then write her out of the scene altogether. That said aunt was actually there is just useless information.

That Lane was still reminding her mother of these writing basics *four volumes into the series* not only shows incredible obstinance on Wilder's part, but also would explain why Lane was sounding increasingly impatient with her mother in their correspondences, and even a bit condescending (though toward the end of the series' run Wilder was exhibiting far less resistance to her daughter's input). This dynamic also contributed to a gradual role-reversal of sorts between them, with Wilder becoming the "rich and famous" one, while Lane became the more dominant and "bossier" (yet lesser known) of the two.

ABOVE/LEFT
Though illustrator Garth Williams has long been associated with the Little House *series, the earliest editions were charmingly illustrated by the artist Helen Sewell.*

PAGE 45
Let the Hurricane Roar (1933) was the first of Lane's three family memoir novels, and, along with *Free Land* (1938), covers very similar ground as Wilder's *Little House* books, particularly 1935's *Little House on the Prairie* and 1937's *On the Banks of Plum Creek*. Though Lane's novels were best sellers at the time (and all are still in print), they're now quite obscure in relation to the iconic status Wilder's "juveniles" soon took on. So a natural reaction to Lane's novels by a modern reader is that she "ripped off" her mother, even though they were all written at the

same time, and were inspired by the same material both women were actively gathering at the time. That said, it *is* weird that Lane would blend the contents of her and her mother's books in such a casual manner. My guess is it was her own subconscious way of getting "credit" for the work she was doing on her mother's books, though I have no way of confirming that theory.

While Wilder did read at least some of her daughter's work, she had very little to say about it, and was allegedly scandalized by Lane's first novel, *Diverging Roads*, mainly because it had *kissing scenes* in it (as well as an acknowledgement of the existence of brothels), though the fact that Lane was her own daughter no doubt made Wilder even more self-conscious of such transgressions.

The combination of Wilder's prudishness, along with the lack of physical affection exhibited by her parents (who slept in separate single beds), led Lane to conclude that her mother "hated sex."

LET THE HURRICANE ROAR
Rose Wilder Lane

Hurricane first ran as a serial in the *Saturday Evening Post* in 1932, and it recounts the story of newlyweds "Caroline" and "Charles" (yes, her grandparents' names, though the story's plot is pure fiction) during their first year on their homestead, when circumstances forced Caroline to endure a brutal winter alone with her infant son.

This tale is quite gripping, and practically begs to be adapted for the stage or screen—and in fact was, twice: once as a radio play starring Helen Hayes in 1943; and later as a TV movie in 1976, redubbed *Young Pioneers*, which, unfortunately, has the same saccharine quality as the *Little House* TV series. (Lane's heir, Roger MacBride, then rereleased Lane's novel under that title, and changed the protagonists' names to "Molly" and "David" to avoid confusing TV viewers).

1935's *Old Home Town* (I couldn't find an image of its original dust jacket) is a collection of short stories recounting Lane's formative years in a fictionalized version of Mansfield (that ran in both *Ladies' Home Journal* and *Saturday Evening Post*), that she later effectively cobbled together into a cohesive format that closely resembles her nemesis Sherwood Anderson's classic, *Winesburg, Ohio.*

OLD HOME TOWN
Rose Wilder Lane

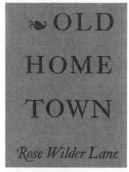

Old Home Town is, in my opinion, Lane's finest work. Like her peer (and ideological twin) Zora Neale Hurston's masterpiece *Their Eyes Were Watching God*, *Old Home Town* has an unmistakable feminist theme that simultaneously avoids any hint of stridency, as she recounts the suffocating gender roles that people had to endure in turn-of-the-century small town America (particularly the women), as well as the often cruel ways these social mores were enforced (particularly by the women). This book also illustrates the generational conflicts between Lane and her mother, and how they evolved (though Lane's overall portrayal of her parents are quite sympathetic and affectionate in this book).

Though fictionalized, Mansfield residents had no trouble recognizing themselves and others in the *Old Home Town* stories, and would rush to the newsstands with each installment, ready to be scandalized. Lane later divided the town's populous into two groups: those who were upset over appearing in her stories, and those who were upset that they *hadn't*.

Rose Wilder Lane
FREE LAND

1938's *Free Land* was Lane's most ambitious and successful novel, as well as her last (she later claimed the book "exhausted" her, and never again attempted another work of fiction). Like *Hurricane*, this book uses family history as a starting point—this time about her own father Almanzo's earliest attempts at homesteading—though, as always, many of the events are pure fiction. This is a much grittier, "adult" version of what occurs in the *Little House* books (the way Wilder herself originally wanted to tell her family's stories), with the title itself being deliberately ironic, i.e.: yes, the land was technically given away for free, but other costs (not just financial, but mental and physical) could be astronomical.

To research this book, Lane naturally turned to her father for information, and based on the questionnaires he filled out for her, one could see why his wife dubbed him "the Oyster." When asked: "Did you get lonely living on your own?" "Did you ever get sick?" "What did a bushel of wheat go for?" He'd reply: "Yes." "No." "$1." Even when asked to elaborate he'd come up short (Q: "What were the early saloons like?" A: "Saloons."). One theory as to why Wilder wanted her daughter to move back to Rocky Ridge was simply so she'd have someone to talk to. Sounds plausible!

PAGES 46 AND 47
John and Al Turner's parents died in a car accident, and they wound up living with their uncle, the sheriff of a nearby town. The sheriff's wife didn't want them around, however, which is why they wound up accepting Lane's hospitality. (John Turner initially didn't want his brother moving in with Lane, fearing that Al might blow the whole sweet deal he had going.)

Lane assumed full responsibility for the Turner boys, and always referred to them as her "sons," yet as with Rexh Meta, she never formally adopted them. Though in the case of John Turner, Lane found herself a handful. While often charming and good-natured, John was also moody, rebellious, and far more interested in cars, sports, and girls than in his studies. Still, like a heartsick teenager determined to rehabilitate her delinquent boyfriend, Lane obsessed over John (Al didn't "need" her as much), and even kept a record of their good times and quarrels. (In yet another example of Lane's boundary blurring, her relationship with Turner occasionally sounded more like that of *lovers* than of a mother and son, though there's nothing to suggest she ever crossed that line in a physical sense.)

PAGE 48
The Dust Bowl (1934–1940) was the worst ecological disaster in US history; the result of a prolonged drought combined with shortsighted farming methods. Clouds of dirt, as high as five thousand feet, engulfed huge swaths of the Great Plains, with the dust carrying as far as the Atlantic coast. Lane traveled into the heart of the devastation primarily to learn about the economic impact it was having on wheat farmers, though she likely had her ears open for human-interest stories as well.

The woman accompanying Lane here is CORINNE MURRAY, a Mansfield neighbor who worked for (and later lived with) Lane as a housekeeper, while Murray's husband was employed by Lane and her parents as a handyman. The Murrays' marriage was an unhappy one, though Lane did her best to stay out of their marital woes. (Lane once was *stabbed in the arm* by a female friend back in her San Francisco days after trying to help the woman leave an abusive marriage, and the scar she still carried from it served as a reminder not to intervene in such matters.)

Murray was more intelligent than the average Mansfield native, and provided Lane with good company. She and Lane may have also been lovers, though, as is always the case, there is no hard evidence of this. Wilder, meanwhile, resented Murray's presence at Rocky Ridge, and had the woman evicted several years later while Lane was out of town—and had one of Lane's dogs shot at the same time. Wilder may have had good reasons for all of this—the details are fuzzy—but it all marked a nadir in Wilder and Lane's relationship, and contributed to Lane moving away from Mansfield for good.

LEFT
Garet Garrett

PAGES 49 AND 50
GARET GARRETT (born Peter Edward Garrett, 1878–1954) was a journalist, editor, and author specializing in economics, and used his position as the financial editor of the *Post* to loudly criticize President Roosevelt's New Deal policies. He is now remembered (depending on who is doing the remembering) as a member of the "Old Right," a classical liberal, or a proto-libertarian. (Yet like so many other libertarian-ish thinkers of his era, Garrett harbored a few inexplicable pet theories, the most notable of which was a Malthusian-like fear that the world can only support a finite number of *machines*, and that once we pass that threshold, well…*look out!*)

Garrett was eating lunch at a diner when a would-be hold-up man misfired his gun into his neck.

While Garrett wasn't Lane's editor at the *Post*, he encouraged that magazine's real boss, George Horace Lorimer, to run what was to be Lane's first overtly political treatise, "Credo" (which was later published as a pamphlet entitled *Give Me Liberty*—and the theme of which was eventually expanded into her 1943 polemic *The Discovery of Freedom*).

Lane's brief romance with Garrett was, as far as anyone knows, her last affair. And though she was the one who nipped it in the bud (over Garrett's objections), she maintained a correspondence with him in which she often sounded like a pouty schoolgirl, culminating in her dramatically informing him that, should he write back to her, she would *not* respond. So naturally he didn't write back, and she spent the next two weeks frantically wondering why he *didn't* write back!

Lane spent much of 1936 in Columbia, MO, while doing research for an ambitious history of Missouri project that wound up being scuttled by its would-be publisher.

PAGE 51
While the majority of the American public generally supported FDR and his New Deal policies, those opposed to it were numerous (and passionate) enough to constitute a ready audience for critics of his policies. That all changed after World War II, however, when such criticisms were deemed "unpatriotic."

THE SATURDAY EVENING POST

CREDO

By ROSE WILDER LANE

Give Me Liberty · LANE

ABOVE
(L) "Credo," as it originally appeared in the Post *in 1936 and (R) the expanded, renamed hardcover "pamphlet" version of the same, released shortly afterwards as the result of popular demand.*

LEFT
Literary critic Isabel Mary Bowler Paterson. Paterson saved her harshest critiques for her own work, describing herself as a "third rate Virginia Woolf imitator."

PAGE 52
Canadian-born ISABEL PATERSON (1886–1961) was best known during her lifetime as the much admired (and feared) literary critic of the *New York Herald-Tribune* from 1924 to 1949, though she also authored eight (mostly) successful novels between 1917 and 1940. Paterson's life paralleled Lane's in almost every way imaginable: born into a restless, westward-moving pioneer family (who regularly crisscrossed the US/Canadian border, back when it was just a line on a map), she was a voracious reader with little formal education. She was briefly married (but kept her husband's name), and avoided matrimony like the plague thereafter. And just like Lane, she started her writing career at a west coast newspaper, before becoming a successful novelist.

Also like Lane, Paterson's own self-made, independent life and career shaped her politics and worldview, and she regularly used her weekly *Turns With a Bookworm* column to take digs at the Roosevelt administration and his collectivist-minded supporters. This included most of Paterson's readers and colleagues, whom she soon was alienating, though like-minded authors such as Lane were drawn to her for this very reason.

"IMP," Paterson's initials, was how she signed her work, and some people called her by that nickname, though others called her "Pat." No one referred to her as "Isabel."

Lane often attended the little church across the street from her new home, but solely for social reasons. She liked bake sales.

Pictures of Lane's long-time Danbury home at 23 King St. can be viewed online (including real estate sites like Zillow), where one can see that most of the obsessive remodeling she did on the place remains intact. Regardless of her income at any given time, Lane spared little expense when it came to home improvements, which she described as her "one vice."

Lane's New York City apartment at 550 E. 16th St. was in a poor neighborhood formerly known as the Gas House District. The entire area was razed during World War II to make way for the Stuyvesant Town and Cooper Village apartment complexes, while Lane's apartment was replaced by a Con Edison facility.

Woman's Day started out as an A&P-based coupon and recipe-laden giveaway before becoming a newsstand magazine in 1937. It was the last of what became known as the "Seven Sisters," the homemaker-targeted magazines that also included *Better Homes and Gardens, Family Circle, Good Housekeeping, Redbook, McCall's* and *Ladies' Home Journal,* which by the 1960s had a combined circulation of almost fifty million.

Lane wrote for all of these magazines at one time or another, though her longest relationship was with *Woman's Day,* particularly under the editorship of Eileen Tighe, who gave Lane a lot of freedom (some would argue *too much* freedom) to write about whatever struck her fancy. And along with the photo feature they ran about Lane's tenement apartment, they later did the same with her Danbury home, all of which made *Woman's Day* seem like the unofficial home of the Rose Wilder Lane Fan Club.

PAGE 53

As did his brother Al, John Turner did quite well for himself, winding up with a successful career as an engineer. While later crediting Lane for much of his success, he also confessed that he had to completely break free from her to keep from hating her.

The young woman on this page and the bottom of the previous page is NORMA LEE BROWNING (1914–2001), whom Lane met in Columbia, MO, where Browning was a journalism student at the University of Missouri. Were she not already an adult, Lane most likely would have "adopted" Browning as well, as the two of them developed a devoted and long-lasting mother/daughter relationship. Browning wound up having an award-winning career as a reporter for the *Chicago Tribune,* often working in tandem with her photojournalist husband, Russell Ogg.

ABOVE

(L) *Norma Lee Browning (on the right) with Erle Stanley Gardner (playing a judge) on the set of* Perry Mason, *1966 and (R) Lane photographed by Browning's husband, Russell Ogg, in her NYC apartment, c. 1940. Browning and Ogg lived in that same tenement building prior to Lane moving in.*

PAGE 54

Lane wrote many articles (mainly for *Woman's Day*) strenuously urging her countrymen to resist calls

for war prior to the attack on Pearl Harbor, which rendered such efforts moot.

There has long been an effort to brand all pre-World War II anti-war activists such as Lane as somehow sympathetic to the Axis powers (as if it's impossible *not* to take sides), and Wilder biographer Caroline Fraser recently used every dirty trick in the book to paint Lane as some kind of a closet Hitler groupie. Yet how anyone can read Lane's work and honestly come to such a conclusion is unfathomable, since everything she ever believed in is the *exact opposite* of fascism. Lane also had long denounced nationalism— along with the demonization of "unwelcome" races, religions, and ethnic groups that goes with it—as a form of collectivism, as well as a divide-and-conquer strategy employed by authoritarians of all kinds.

PAGE 55

Virginia Manor spent almost a year with Lane, during which I assume she did a lot of digging. Biographer Woodside noted the irony of how, decades earlier, a young Lane urged her mother to give up farming and take up writing, yet now that Wilder was a successful full-time writer, Lane was suddenly spending most of her time farming!

LEFT

Ayn Rand, c. 1940s.

PAGE 56

Russian-born AYN RAND (born Alisa Zinov'yevna Rosenbaum, 1905–1982) immigrated to the US in 1926, where she soon found work as a screenwriter in Hollywood. Rand was still a struggling novelist at the time she befriended Isabel Paterson, who then introduced her to Lane. To say these three women shared a similar political and philosophical outlook would be putting it mildly, and as a group they emboldened each other to speak their minds at a time when what was on their minds *was* close to being regarded as treasonous.

Rand's 1943 novel *The Fountainhead* was a huge success, and, along with her 1957 novel *Atlas Shrugged,* probably inspired more people to embrace libertarian philosophy than any other written work. Ironically, Rand herself always rejected the "libertarian" label, a movement that to her mind was too heavily populated with libertines, who lacked moral or aesthetic standards. (Rand once even declared libertarians to be her "enemy," though she's declared almost everyone and everything to be her enemy at one time or another.)

Instead, Rand promoted her own self-styled philosophy—one that she dubbed "Objectivism"—which, though at its roots is very free-minds-and-free-markets based, also promoted a lot of aesthetic assumptions that just happened to reflect Rand's own personal tastes. That, combined with Rand's domineering personality, lead to the creation of what can only be described—as Lane did—as a cult. (Lane also was a bit envious of Rand's sudden meteoric success, which may have fueled her distaste for Rand's followers.)

In her own book, *The Discovery of Freedom,* Lane rapidly covers the history of Western Civilization, while highlighting the moments and events that lead to the evolution of a free society that (as of 1943) was best exemplified by the United States. She also repeatedly points out that submission to tyranny is humanity's natural inclination; that individual freedom is hard earned, and even harder to maintain. Thus, Lane's urging of her fellow Americans—and of people everywhere—to be ever vigilant in the fight for freedom became a common theme not just in this book, but also in all of her political writings.

Paterson's *The God in the Machine* covers very similar ground—so much so that some wonder if one had copied the other. (The Lane-hating biographer Fraser naturally presents Lane as the culprit of this alleged crime, while also reluctantly acknowledging that Lane's book came out first. She also ignores the fact that *Freedom*'s themes started with 1938's "Credo.") Among the minor things that differentiate the two books is Paterson's interesting take on how the Christian church contributed to the rise of individual rights and freedoms, while Lane makes an equally interesting point of giving early Islam its due in the same regard. (The atheist Rand, meanwhile, was appalled by *all* of this talk of religion.) Other than that, the biggest difference between the two books is their authors' different personalities and writing styles.

Of these three women, Paterson was the most no-nonsense, and made a point of never getting carried away with emotion, or of flying off the handle. She was very "just the facts, ma'am," and the tightly written

Machine reflects that. Lane, of course, was quite the opposite, and in *Freedom* (as in all of her nonfiction), historical facts are just a snowy hill for her to ride her sled on. In fact, *Freedom* often comes off as a 262-page rant—which in some ways it was, since she wrote it at a feverish pace, fearing that if she paused to reflect she might chicken out of writing it altogether.

Lane herself was somewhat embarrassed by the results, and did nothing to promote the book—the first and only printing of which, during her lifetime, was only one thousand copies. (Lane did make some half-hearted efforts to correct and revise *Freedom* in the following years, but nothing ever came of it.) Yet the freewheeling nature of *Freedom* is also its best feature—at least for anyone who shares Lane's take on things, in which case reading it is like riding along *with* her on her metaphorical sled! So in that sense it's a good thing that she never did "fix" it.

Alas, Lane, Paterson, and Rand quickly became estranged from each other, and for vague, poorly defined reasons. For Lane and Paterson it allegedly was over a disagreement regarding Joseph Stalin. Like, *huh*? (When not debating semantics, Lane and Rand's correspondences mostly consist of the two of them excoriating *male* libertarian writers for "getting everything wrong.") Libertarians have long made self-deprecating jokes about how to them, *two* is a crowd, and that trying to organize them is like herding cats. Assuming that's accurate, the movement's three founding women certainly exemplified it.

LEFT
Albert J. Nock.

The man talking to Lane and Paterson on page 57 is the author and editor ALBERT JAY NOCK (1870–1945), who was the first to comment on the boldness of these three "Sirens of Liberty," and who made male liberty defenders (including himself) "look like Confederate money."

Nock had much in common with his peer H. L. Mencken in that both men's initial humorous and healthy skepticism increasingly gave way to pessimism, misanthropy, and age-old bigotries. Whatever credibility he has as a so-called "early libertarian thinker" is far outweighed by his inconsistencies and plain old nastiness.

Nock's last gig was as the editor of the National Economic Council's monthly *Review of Books*—a job that, upon his death in 1945, was handed over to Lane, who held the position until 1950 (at which point she concluded that American literature had devolved into nihilistic navel-gazing, and quit).

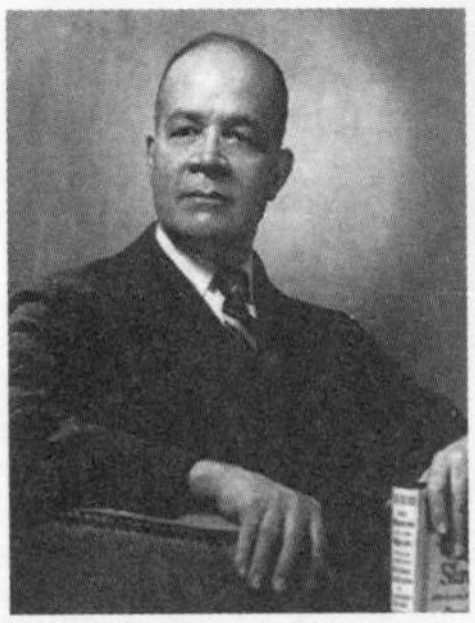

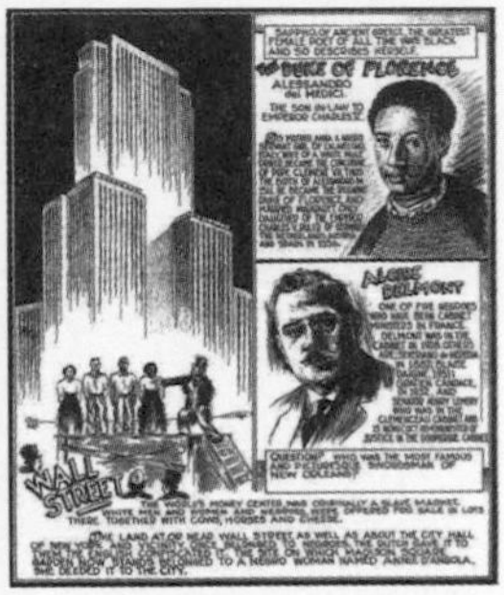

ABOVE
Joel Augustus Rogers. Rogers also authored a weekly comic for the Courier *called "Your History," an Afrocentric version of "Ripley's Believe it or Not."*

PAGE 58
The *Pittsburgh Courier* was the largest nationally distributed black newspaper in the US at the time. Author and historian JOEL AUGUSTUS ROGERS (1880–1966) was just a contributing editor to the *Courier* at the time. It was not at all unusual that the *Courier* published Lane, since the paper's staff was very diverse, both ethnically and ideologically.

As hinted at on this page, Lane raised many issues in her column (titled "Rose Wilder Lane Says") that are still with us, and suggests she would have been sympathetic to the recent Black Lives Matter movement. But by 1945 an increasingly partisan editorial board could no longer tolerate her FDR (and later, Truman) bashing, and let her go. (It was then that she took on the book review job at the National Economic Council for a similar barebones fee, though after she left *that* job—and until she inherited her mother's estate in 1957—she mainly lived off of her occasional *Woman's Day* features.)

In their excellent article "Selling Laissez-faire Anti-racism to the Black Masses," scholars Linda Royster Beito and David T. Beito point out that Lane's *Courier* column so closely echoed the opinions of Zora Neale Hurston that, in their words, "it is often impossible to tell them apart." Which makes one wonder if the two of them were even aware of each other (though both were such voracious readers that it's highly unlikely they never came across each other's work).

PAGE 59
ROGER LEA MACBRIDE (1929–1995) was the son of an editor for *Reader's Digest*, which had just published an abridged version of one of Lane's novels. Lane was eager to mentor the young man due mainly to his openness toward her own political philosophy, and eventually came to see him as her standard-bearer after she passed on.

Lane also eventually made MacBride the heir of her estate—and, by extension, her mother's estate, which has been the source of some controversy and contention ever since (more on that later). And true to form, MacBride did get an Ivy League education, followed by a brief career in law before turning his attentions toward politics—as well as the *Little House* empire (again, more on that later).

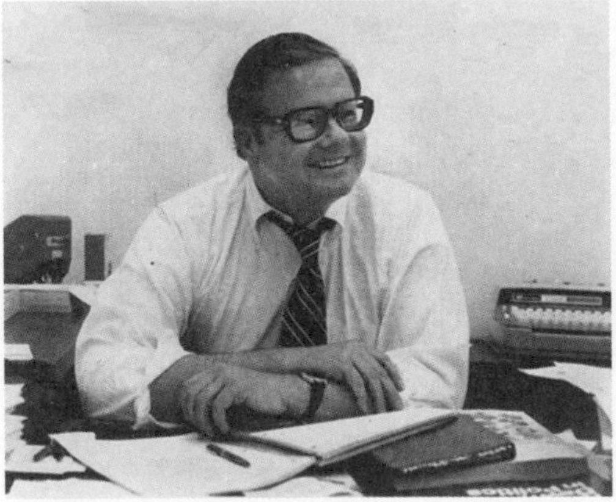

ABOVE
Roger MacBride, c. late 1960s.

PAGES 60 AND 61
A postmaster forwarded the postcard in question to the FBI, who in turn asked the Connecticut state police to "look into it." The whole incident was indeed an outrage, and Lane made sure everyone knew it by writing an article for a local paper, subtly entitled "What is This, The Gestapo?" The story then went national after it was picked up by the wire services.

In Lane's telling of the incident, she neglected to mention her cookie peace offering, though that little detail did make it into her copious FBI file, which wound up being over 100-pages long. This being decades before the enactment of Freedom of Information Act, Lane of course had no idea the Feds were keeping such close tabs on her. That fact alone would have enraged her, though it's pretty funny that, due solely to her past associations, this world champion commie hater was still suspected of being a Red!

PAGE 62
GEORGE T. BYE (1887–1957) was Lane's second literary agent, he being of the "hustling" type Lane was hoping to find when all hell broke lose after the crash of 1929. Bye was a Missouri newspaperman (Lane's favorite brand of human) who built his second career largely by exploiting celebrities' fleeting notoriety to package and sell a book (then known as "stunt books"), with a ghostwriter doing the heavy lifting.

ABOVE
(L) Ursula Nordstrom, c. late 1960s. (R) George T. Bye, standing, R, behind his friend and client Eleanor Roosevelt, c. 1930s.

The *Little House* editor pictured on this page is URSULA NORDSTROM (1910–1988), who took over Harpers's children's division in 1940, and thus inherited the *Little House* series at its halfway point. Nordstrom, I should note here, almost single-handedly reinvented and reinvigorated children's books in the mid-twentieth century, with almost every great writer and artist you could name in that genre (Crockett Johnson, Syd Hoff, Margaret Wise Brown, Maurice Sendak, etc.) thriving under her auspices. Nordstrom once noted that only E.B. White and Laura Ingalls Wilder's work required no copyediting, though she had no idea that the latter's flawlessly type-written manuscripts (Wilder never used a typewriter) were composed by Wilder's daughter.

Prior to Nordstrom, the series was edited by IDA LOUISE RAYMOND—though the first official editor of the *Little House* series was VIRGINIA KIRKUS (1893–1980), who left Harpers shortly afterwards to start her own book review publication, which still thrives to this day as *Kirkus Reviews*. Prior to all of these women, however, was the brief involvement of writer and editor ERNESTINE EVANS (1889–1967), and it was she who

once speculated that Wilder may have been a literary invention of Lane's.

PAGE 63
In spite of its tiny print run, Lane's *Discovery of Freedom* had a far-reaching influence, such as on people like chemist JASPER CRANE (1881–1969), who served on the board of the DuPont Corporation for seventeen years. Lane and Crane had a lively correspondence between 1946 and 1966 (much of which is collected in the Roger MacBride edited *The Lady and the Tycoon*), which perfectly exemplifies (as portrayed here) the still-persistent conflict between free market capitalism and crony corporatism.

ABOVE
Wilder's only known book signing took place in the Springfield, MO, in 1952 (pictured above). This complete lack of promotion and marketing on her part made her books' popularity even more remarkable.

PAGES 64 AND 65
Lane was only nineteen years younger than her mother, so by this time they *both* were crotchety, white-haired old ladies who both had their own personal paranoias—though in Wilder's case they could at least be chalked up to dementia. (I have no idea if her delusions were grasshopper-based, but based on her childhood experiences, it seemed as good a guess as any.)

As for Lane, she was thoroughly caught up in the Red Scare mania that was gripping the entire country at this point, and occasionally convinced herself that the KGB was out to get her personally (as they should have been)! Meanwhile, her desperation to connect with like-minded commie-haters lead to a few dubious, conspiratorial correspondents of the John Bircher mold (an organization that, once it started in 1958, she felt she had much in common with). That being said, Lane never was in favor of witch-hunts, or of the tactics of the House Un-

American Activities Committee, whose activities to her mind *were* un-American.

PAGE 66

ROBERT LEFEVRE (1911–1986) was a "businessman" with a bizarre, checkered past (particularly his involvement with the inexplicably weird "I AM" religious cult) before starting his Freedom School in 1956. Lane's *Discovery of Freedom* was a major inspiration for LeFevre (who, like Lane, was more of an anarchist than a libertarian, though he stubbornly rejected that label), and LeFevre even named the school's main lodge after her.

RIGHT
(L) Robert LeFevre, c. 1970s and (R) Freedom School attendees pose outside "Rose Wilder Lane Hall"—which still exists, only is now owned (ironically) by a public school district.

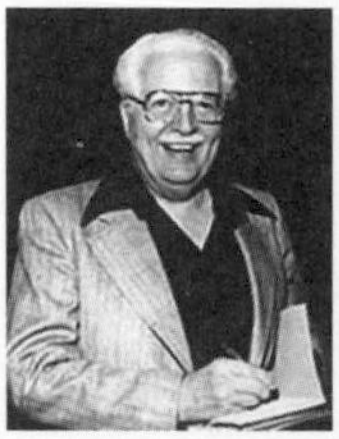

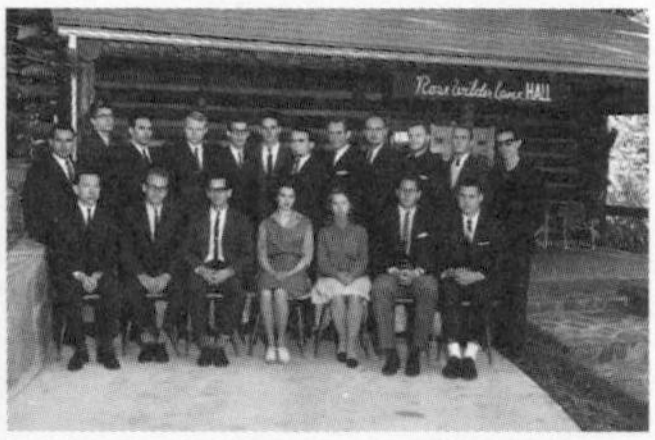
Rose Wilder Lane HALL

After a flood devastated the Colorado campus in 1965, LeFevre moved the Freedom School (along with its newly accredited counterpart, Rampart College) to Santa Ana, CA, before the entire enterprise went belly up in 1973.

David and Charles Koch (along with Roger MacBride) attended the Freedom School in the 1960s, which is where the tenuous link between Lane and the much-despised (if you're a registered Democrat) Koch Brothers stems from. This connection has also led the partisan journalist Mark Ames to not just suggest but flat-out *brand* LeFevre as a "fascist." LeFevre may have been many things, but he never advocated anything that was even remotely fascistic (a word that in its current usage has lost all meaning, other than as a stand-in for "jerk" or "doodyhead").

RIGHT
(L) Lane's all-time bestseller and (R) Eunice W. Cook's "The Gossips."

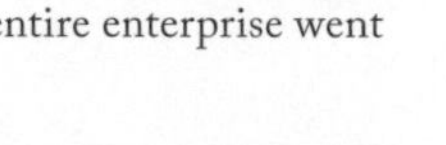
Woman's Day Book of
American Needlework
by Rose Wilder Lane

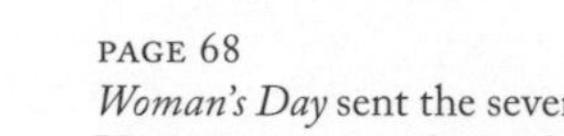

PAGE 67

The *Woman's Day Book of American Needlework* is roughly a decade's worth of articles Lane wrote on the subject for that magazine. It also is by far the best-selling book Lane ever wrote, simply for the instructions and massive amount of practical information it offers. It also reveals Lane to be incredibly knowledgeable on the subject, though as is her want, she goes a little overboard in her eagerness to explain not so much the aesthetic differences between Old and New World needlework, but the political philosophies *behind* those differences. As a result, many of the people who bought and loved this book also couldn't help but wonder: "what is this woman yammering on about?"

The other woman appearing on this page simply represents one of the many Danbury neighbors Lane had befriended.

"The Gossips," a silk appliqué dating from 1832 by a farmer's wife named Eunice W. Cook, long remained in her family's possession, but she must have lent the original sample she made of it (in 1813, when she was only ten) to somebody, because over the next one hundred years that image wound up appearing in countless advertisements on both sides of the Atlantic.

PAGE 68

Woman's Day sent the seventy-eight-year-old Lane to Vietnam to cover the civil war that was raging there (against the US military and other news agencies' wishes, since no one wanted to get stuck "babysitting somebody's grandma"). The US had not yet fully gotten involved until a year later, which surely must have disappointed Lane (especially with the draft that went along with it, which she accurately regarded as a form of slavery), since her article expressed tremendous confidence in the South Vietnamese winning that war on their own—*misplaced* confidence, it turns out, since her antipathy toward communism caused her to turn a blind eye toward the South Vietnamese government's rampant corruption. While Lane was correct in noting the Vietnamese people's long history of expelling foreign invaders, she never foresaw that it would be the Americans and their allies they'd wind up expelling.

PHAN NGYUEN THI HONG was actually the younger sister of Lane's interpreter, but she exhibited so much spunk that Lane couldn't resist unofficially "adopting" her. But her taking on the financial responsibilities for Phan's US education was more gradual than I portrayed it here, as was their grandmother/granddaughter relationship, though Lane would wind up spending her remaining Christmases with Phan.

PAGES 69 TO 71

Once while traveling cross-country with Browning and Ogg, the latter became seriously ill, forcing them to spend an extended period of time in south Texas. Lane fell in love with their area, and eventually bought a winter home there.

Lane's new neighbors, the Griffens, still own and operate a seed and nursery business that the family's owned since 1909. Soon both Donald and his sister were referring to Lane as "Grandma." Don Griffen's relationship with Lane was somewhat reminiscent of the one she had with Boylston, in that he seemed to be totally up for any hair-brained scheme she came up with, no questions asked. A trip around the world? Why the hell not! I also love the way young Griffen's perspective suddenly places this old women (who longed for the nineteenth century) in the context of a world full of television sets and go-go boots. It's so weird!

Lane's plans for a globe-circling trip (to be financed by the ever-indulgent *Woman's Day*) involved taking a cruise ship to Gothenburg, Sweden, where she intended to buy a Volvo (why not *rent* one? And did she think you had to *go* to Sweden to buy a Volvo? Who knows). After that, they were to make their way to Australia somehow, or perhaps Fiji —one of those places that people love to "drive" to. All in all a brilliant plan! But alas, it was not to be.

It Isnt Safe To Be an American
Kamp, Joseph P
BEHIND the LACE CURTAINS of the
YWCA
THE BIGOTS BEHIND THE SWASTIKA SPREE

ABOVE

Joseph Kamp was just tellin' it like it is, man.

The man minding Lane's house was JOSEPH KAMP (1900–1993), a conspiracy theorist and prolific author of pamphlets "proving" that just about everything you could think of was a communist plot, including the YWCA (because of course!) and the Goldwater campaign (like, duh)—hell, even *Nazi Germany* was a commie plot. (Except for when it wasn't, that is. Kamp had a hard time keeping track, seeing how he was just making it all up as he went along.) He even advocated abolishing the *United States*, just to *avoid* its inevitable takeover by the Russians. What a patriot!

After years of accusing politicians of being commie dupes, Kamp was dragged before Congress in 1950, where he was accused of "lobbying," and found in contempt for refusing to identify his donors (most likely because he didn't want to admit he didn't *have* any "donors"), and was sentenced to three months in prison. Lane considered him a martyr as a result, and took pity on him, which is how he wound up being her home's, uh, "caretaker."

When Wilder left the rights to her *Little House* books to her daughter, her will also stipulated that, upon *Lane*'s death, the rights should go to the Mansfield public library. How or why Lane ignored this stipulation is unknown. Perhaps she forgot? Or more likely she simply thought the estate would be in better hands with her "grandson" than with some librarian she'd never met. Either way, the Library took no action until MacBride himself died in 1995—and eventually won a sizable settlement, though the rights still remain with MacBride's heirs.

ABOVE

(L) Actor Michael Landon playing Charles Ingalls on the Little House *TV series and (R) the real Charles Ingalls. Oh, Hollywood, will you ever stop being ridiculous?*

MacBride's own contribution to the *Little House* legacy mainly involves the immensely popular 1970s TV series, *Little House on the Prairie*, though that show's unabashedly Hollywood-ized treatment of Wilder's work annoyed more devoted Wilder fans both then and now. MacBride then authored a *new* series of *Little House* books—ones that featured his "grandma," Rose herself, coming of age in the Ozark Mountains. This also, on the face of it, was a pretty ballsy move, though in both instances one could argue that MacBride was simply responding to an undeniable demand for more *Little House* related material (and the TV show wasn't even his idea, but came about after MacBride was approached by producer Ed Friendly, who was looking to emulate then-popular wholesome TV fare like *The Waltons*). There also is no doubt that that series greatly expanded the readership of Wilder's work, and no one questions that MacBride always had Wilder and Lane's best interests at heart. If he also happened to make a ton of money in the process of honoring them, well, so be it!

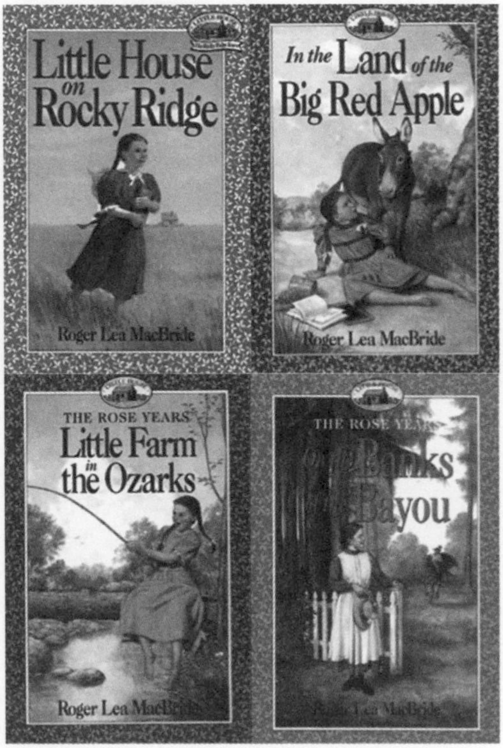
Little House on Rocky Ridge
Roger Lea MacBride
In the Land of the Big Red Apple
Roger Lea MacBride
THE ROSE YEARS
Little Farm in the Ozarks
Roger Lea MacBride

ABOVE
The saga continues, only now starring "Little Rose." Because who can ever get enough of Spookendyke?

As for what Wilder or Lane would have made of all of this, well, I don't know if either of them even *owned* a television, let alone pondered TV adaptations of their work. The whole thing is too alien to even contemplate. Bring back the nineteenth century! Though I can't imagine them not having a problem with MacBride authoring "new" *Little House* books (ones that quite liberally mined both women's own out-of-print and unpublished material, to boot), so there's that. (Yet since MacBride's own passing there now is a series of *Little House* books starring Wilder's *mother* as a child—and yet another series starring her *grandmother*. What's next, "Little CAVE on the Prairie"?)

Lane's will asked for her to be cremated and buried at sea. MacBride did the former, but couldn't bring himself to do the latter (oh, *come on*, Roger!), and instead sent her remains to Mansfield, to be buried alongside her parents.

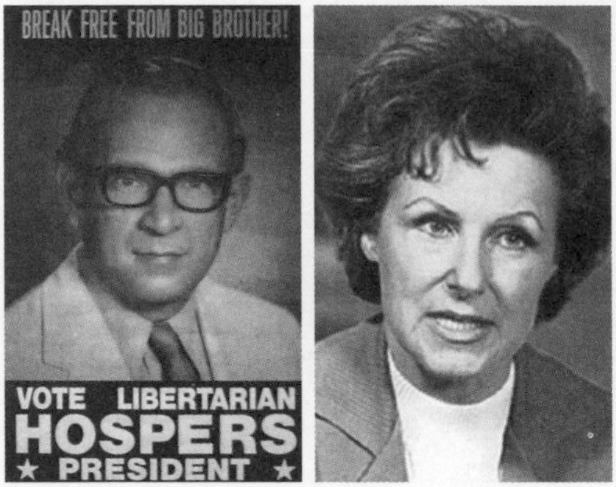
BREAK FREE FROM BIG BROTHER!
VOTE LIBERTARIAN
HOSPERS
PRESIDENT

ABOVE
(L) A 1972 John Hospers campaign poster and (R) Tonie Nathan.

PAGE 72 (EPILOGUE)
The Libertarian Party was created in 1971, and the man heading their first Presidential ticket was author and philosophy professor JOHN HOSPERS (1918–2011), who was a friend and follower of Ayn Rand (until she declared him her "enemy," that is). THEADORA "TONIE" NATHAN (1923–2014) was working as a TV and radio producer in Oregon when she was nominated to be Hospers's running mate. The two of them received 3,674 votes.

Roger MacBride was the treasurer of Virginia's Republican Party when he broke ranks and voted for Hospers and Nathan. This act of defiance made MacBride persona non grata within the GOP, but made him a folk hero within the Libertarian Party, who then rewarded him by nominating him to be their *next* presidential candidate in 1976. He and his running mate, future Libertarian Party presidential candidate David Bergland, received a much more impressive 172,553 votes, due in part to MacBride's much bigger media presence, including an interview on William F. Buckley's *Firing Line*, where he gave his "grandmother" Rose Wilder Lane a shout-out.

BIBLIOGRAPHY

Much has been written by and about Lane, though much of it is primarily about her mother. So I did a bit of picking and choosing below, in an attempt to limit it to material pertinent to interest in Lane. I also didn't list anything edited or ghostwritten by Lane.

BOOKS AUTHORED BY LANE

Art Smith's Story (1915) (biography)
Charlie Chaplin's Own Story (1916) (biography)
Henry Ford's Own Story (1917) (biography)
Diverging Roads (1919) (fiction)
The Making of Herbert Hoover (1920) (biography)
The Peaks of Shala (1923) (non-fiction travel)
He Was A Man (1925) (a fictionalized version of Lane's Jack London biography)
Hill-Billy (1925) (fiction)
Cindy (1928) (fiction)
Let the Hurricane Roar (1932) (fiction–later reprinted as *Young Pioneers*).
Old Home Town (1935) (fiction)
Give Me Liberty (1936) (nonfiction)
Free Land (1938) (fiction)
The Discovery of Freedom (1943) (nonfiction)
Woman's Day Book of American Needlework (1963)

ANTHOLOGIES, CORRESPONDENCES AND ANNOTATED WORK (WITH PUBLICATION DATES)

On the Way Home (1962) Diary entries by Wilder from 1894, with "settings" provided by Lane prior to publication.

The Lady and the Tycoon (1973) Correspondences between Lane and Jasper Crane from 1946–'66, edited by Roger MacBride.

Travels With Zenobia (1983) Letters and diary entries by Lane and Helen Dore Boylston from 1927, edited by William Holtz.

Dorothy Thompson & Rose Wilder Lane: Forty Years of Friendship (1991) Letters between Thompson & Lane between 1921 and 1960, edited by William Holtz.

A Little House Sampler (1995) A collection of writings by both Wilder and Lane, edited by William Anderson.

The Rediscovered Writings of Rose Wilder Lane: Literary Journalist (2007) A varied collection of newspaper and magazine articles by Lane, edited by Amy Mattson Lauters.

BIOGRAPHIES

Rose Wilder Lane: Her Story (1977) by Roger MacBride, though he gave the (by then long dead) Lane cowriter credit, presumably because he heavily relied on Lane's own writings (as he always did) to fill these pages, and reads more like fiction (which shouldn't be too surprising, consid-ering the source). I'm listing this book here simply because since it's Lane's first "biography," technically speaking.

Laura's Rose (1986) by William Anderson. Anderson was Laura Ingalls Wilder's first biographer, and remains the world's foremost scholar on all things relating to Wilder. This slight, forty-six page pamphlet is typical of the many books and pamphlets Anderson published on the Wilder family, though they usually are written with a YA readership in mind, and thus tend to avoid anything that could be construed as controversial. Still, his books are quite informative, and always worth reading.

The Ghost in the Little House (1993) by William Holtz. This is by far the most comprehensive biography yet writ-ten that focuses on Lane alone. As its (rather mislead-ing) title suggests, this book also marks the first public, open discussion of Lane's involvement with Wilder's *Little House* books, which was not at all well received at the time. Holtz has also been accused of being overly sympathetic to Lane (he does exhibit incredible patience and understanding when discussing some of her more histrionic behavior), while coming off as a bit conde-scending towards her mother (choosing to refer to Wilder as "Mama Bess" throughout the book sure didn't help). Still, this biography remains required reading for anyone interested in learning more about Lane.

A Wilder Rose (2013) by Susan Wittig Albert. Perhaps as homage to Lane's own early biographies, this book is written in a novel-like format, in which a late middle-aged Lane recalls past events to an attentive young Norma Lee Browning. A curious approach, but it's an engaging read, and very sympathetic to both mother and daughter.

Libertarians on the Prairie (2016) by Christine Woodside, is about Lane and Wilder equally, and specifically about their stormy relationship while working on the *Little House* series. In spite of the book's title, author Woodside doesn't share Wilder and Lane's (especially the latter's) political views, but she presents both women in a fair and sympathetic manner regardless.

Prairie Fires (2017) by Caroline Fraser. Though officially a biography of Wilder, this book is almost equally about Lane. Fraser conducted exhaustive research in compil-ing this book (and won a Pulitzer prize as a result), and though it's relatively sympathetic toward its main subject, it also is an unbridled demonization of her daughter. Fraser exhibits a near pathological hatred for Lane, as she spins, frames, and/or distorts almost every word the woman had ever written in the most negative light imag-inable, leaving the reader with the blatantly false impres-sion that Wilder's daughter was a greedy, selfish, bigoted monster. Fraser also attributes motives and attitudes to Lane that often are quite literally opposite of the truth. I thought I was hallucinating when I read this book. To call it a disappointment would be putting it mildly.

Alternative comic creator Peter Bagge is best known for the '90s comic series *Hate*, featuring the semi-autobiographical antihero Buddy Bradley, whose adventures have been collected in two volumes: *Buddy Does Seattle* and *Buddy Does Jersey*, both from Fantagraphics.

Bagge has also created three graphic novels: *Reset*, *Apocalypse Nerd* (both Dark Horse), and *Other Lives* (DC/Vertigo). The journalistic strips Bagge has done for *Reason* have also been collected into a book entitled *Everybody Is Stupid Except For Me* (Fantagraphics). More recently, Bagge has written and drawn full-length biographical comics, *Woman Rebel: The Margaret Sanger Story* (Drawn & Quarterly), *Fire!: The Zora Neale Hurston Story* (Drawn & Quarterly), and a collection of short biographical strips entitled *Founding Fathers Funnies* (Dark Horse) in early 2016.

Peter Bagge lives in Tacoma, WA, with his wife, Joanne.